HISTORICAL
ATLAS
OF
ANCIENT
AMERICA

HISTORICAL
ATLAS
OF

ANCIENT
AMERICA

Norman Bancroft Hunt

Checkmark Books™
An imprint of Facts On File, Inc.

Historical Atlas of Ancient America

Copyright © 2001 by Thalamus Publishing

Checkmark Books
An imprint of Facts On File, Inc.
132 West 31st Street
New York, NY 10001

Library of Congress Cataloging-in-Publication Data
Bancroft-Hunt, Norman
   Historical atlas of ancient America / Norman Bancroft Hunt.
         p. cm.
   Includes index.
   ISBN 0-8160-4783-9 (acid-free paper)
   1. America—Antiquities—Maps. 2. America—Historical geography—Maps
3. Indians of Mexico—Antiquities—Maps. 4. Mexico—Antiquities—Maps.
5. Central America—Antiquities—Maps.   I. Title
   G1101.E6 B3 2001
   912.7—dc21   2001018263

You can find Facts On File on the World Wide Web at:
http://www.factsonfile.com

For Thalamus Publishing
Project editor: Warren Lapworth
Maps and design: Roger Kean
Illustrations: Oliver Frey
Four-color separation: Michael Parkinson and Thalamus Studios
Jacket design: Roger Kean

Printed and bound in Spain by Graficromo S.A.

ISBN: 0-8160-4783-9

10 9 8 7 6 5 4 3 2 1
This book is printed on acid-free paper

PICTURE CREDITS
AKG London: 183, 189; Ann Ronan: 188; The British Museum: 81, 156, 160, 172, 177, 186; Corbis: 150; Corbis/Paul Almasy: 124, 125, 128–129, 129, 139; Corbis/Archivo Iconografico S.A.: 146 left, 171, 182, 184, 185, 187 bottom; Corbis/Yann Arthus-Bertrand: 136–137, 145; Corbis/Bettmann: 151, 154, 178; Corbis/Bowers Museum of Cultural Art: 34, 35, 120; Corbis/Burstein Collection: 121; Corbis/Richard A. Cooke: 16, 18–19, 82, 83 top, 108–109, 135, 149, 161 top; Corbis/Sergio Dorantes: 88, 89 right, 157 bottom; Corbis/Macduff Everton: 59 top, 87, 133 bottom, 134, 148; Corbis/Dave G. Houser: 63, 67; Corbis/Kimbell Art Museum: 44, 55 top, 166; Corbis/Danny Lehman: 7 top, 17, 20, 21 top, 21 bottom, 38–39, 50–51, 51, 71 top, 86, 94, 95, 140, 162, 165, 176; Corbis/Charles & Josette Lenars: 22 left, 24, 26, 27, 45, 56, 65, 74–75, 75, 89 left, 92, 97, 98, 101, 114, 116, 119 bottom, 131, 141 right, 187 top; Corbis/Craig Lovell: 64, 77, 83 bottom; Corbis/Francis G. Mayer: 22 right; Corbis/Buddy Mays: 78–79; Corbis/John Noble: 62–63; Corbis/Gianni Dagli Orti: 8, 11, 13, 23, 25, 31 top, 31 bottom, 42, 43, 52, 53 left, 53 right, 55 bottom, 57 top, 58 bottom, 69, 74, 78, 84, 85, 93, 96, 99, 108, 110, 113 top, 113 bottom, 118, 119 top, 120–121, 126, 127, 141 left, 144, 146 right, 147 top, 147 bottom, 150–151, 152, 153, 155, 157 top, 158, 159, 161 bottom, 164, 167 right, 170, 175, 180, 181; Corbis/The Purcell Team: 9, 168–169; Corbis/Fulvio Roiter: 57 bottom; Corbis/Bill Ross: 7 bottom, 58 top, 76–77; Corbis/Hans Georg Roth: 130; Corbis/Kevin Schafer: 73, 117; Corbis/Seattle Art Museum: 163; Corbis/Michael T. Sedam: 112; Corbis/Roman Soumar: 46–47, 86–87; Corbis/Vanni Archive: 90, 91, 133 top; Corbis/Nik Wheeler: 54, 138; Corbis/Michael S. Yamashita: 174; David Hixon: 32 top, 32 bottom, 33 top, 33 bottom; Naturalight Productions Ltd, Belize: 48, 49 top, 49 bottom; Thalamus Publishing: 1, 59 bottom, 104, 105 top, 105 bottom, 137; Thalamus Studios: 2–3, 5; Thalamus Studios/Oliver Frey: 30, 71 bottom, 122, 123, 173; Werner Forman Archive: 70, 115; Werner Forman Archive/Anthropology Museum, Veracruz: 10; Werner Forman Archive/Biblioteca Universitaria, Italy: 103; Werner Forman Archive/British Museum, London: 15; Werner Forman Archive/Dallas Museum of Art: 14; Werner Forman Archive/Hamburg Museum: 167 left; Werner Forman Archive/Liverpool Museum: 102, 179; Werner Forman Archive/National Museum of Anthropology, Mexico City: 100; www.anthroarcheart.org/Philip Baird: 28, 29, 36–37, 111.

Half-title page (1): *The barely excavated steps of the Great Pyramid of Cobá, the tallest in the Yucatán Peninsula, rise out of the low-lying jungle.*

Title page (2–3): *Fantasy montage from Yucatán: sky above Mérida, silhouette treeline from Cobá, pyramid from the city of Chichén Itzá.*

Facing: *Hieroglyphics of temple priests dressed in quetzal feathers and jaguar robes, taken from a Mixtec manuscript.*

CONTENTS

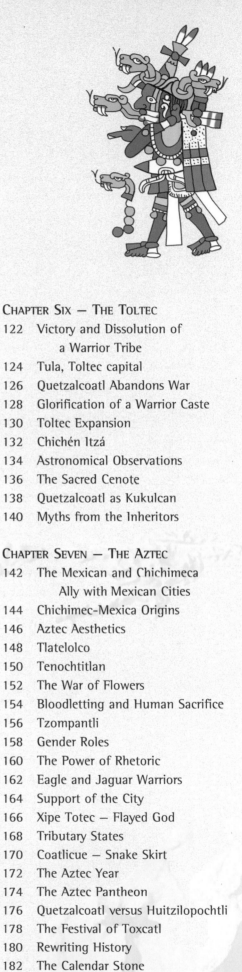

INTRODUCTION

*The ancient Americans had a close relationship with their deities. Among the most important was the Rain God, Tlaloc, **right**, who controlled not only rain, but also the four seasons of the agricultural year. Further links between the Sky World of the deities and the earthly home of the people were established through the erection of monumental pyramids, such as that of Kululcan at Chichén Itzá, **below right**, on whose summits sacrifices were made in homage to the gods.*

The term "Mesoamerica" was coined by the anthropologist Paul Kirchhoff to refer to that part of Mexico and Central America considered to be civilized at the time of the Spanish Conquest. It includes southern and eastern Mexico, all of Guatemala, El Salvador, and Belize, and southern and western Honduras. The people living here were dependent on agriculture and generally lived in urban communities, which had public art and architecture on a large scale. They also shared a number of common culture traits, which Kirchhoff has defined as including pyramids and temples, ritual bloodletting, a sacred calendar based on a 260-day cycle with a year of 365 days, hieroglyphic writing, and a complex pantheon of deities.

While these similarities suggest, at least, that there was interaction between the various Mesoamerican groups, there was nevertheless tremendous divergence in detail, as well as in time. The earliest civilization of Mesoamerica — that of the Olmec — came 3,000 years before the late Aztec, whose capital city of Tenochtitlan was destroyed by conquistador

Hernán Cortés and his men in April, 1521.

The entire Mesoamerican area lies within the tropics and can be broadly divided into Highlands and Lowlands. Parts of the Highlands are desert, particularly in the north, but there are also great valleys framed by both active and dormant volcanoes that provided fertile soils supporting large populations. For the Aztec, such volcanic peaks were home to the Tlalocs, or rain gods, whose influence over the river and lake systems and the pronounced wet and dry seasons of the region was fundamental to the success of their crops.

The Mesoamerican periods

In contrast, the Lowland Classic Mayan cultures developed in the jungle environment of Yucatán where, with the exception of the River Usumacinta, surface water is absent. However, water may be obtained from deep circular sinkholes, called *cenotes*, which on occasion served as the final destination for victims sacrificed to appease the rain gods.

Although the cultures of Mesoamerica are complex and diverse, it is possible to divide them into some approximate phases, which provide a chronology for the history of the area. The earliest phase is that of the Olmec, on the Gulf Coast plain, which begins c.1500 BC. Their major centers at La Venta, Tres Zapotes, and San Lorenzo were huge complexes of pyramids, platform mounds, and temples, with carved stelae and colossal stone heads, which, perhaps, were portraits of local dignitaries.

Although Olmec culture declined c.400 BC,

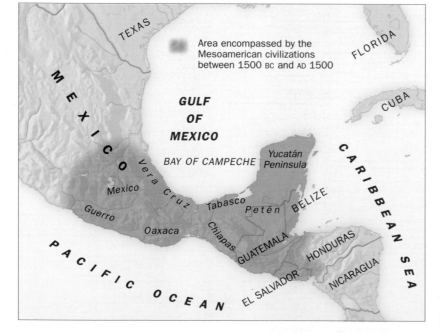

Area encompassed by the Mesoamerican civilizations between 1500 BC and AD 1500

GULF OF MEXICO

TEXAS

FLORIDA

CUBA

MEXICO

Vera Cruz

BAY OF CAMPECHE

Yucatán Peninsula

CARIBBEAN SEA

Mexico

Guerro

Tabasco

Petén

BELIZE

Oaxaca

Chiapas

GUATEMALA

HONDURAS

PACIFIC OCEAN

EL SALVADOR

NICARAGUA

35,000 BC
Asians migrate to Mesoamerican region on the tundra that once connected the continents

8000 BC
Hunter-gatherers begin to establish semi-permanent settlements

7000 BC
Beginning of the Archaic period; Hunter-gatherers begin domesticating plants

5000 BC
With the domestication of maize, permanent villages are formed

2000 BC
End of the Archaic period; larger permanent villages are established

1500 BC
Birth of Olmec culture

1200 BC
At San Lorenzo the first Olmec ceremonial center is built

753 BC
In Italy, Rome is founded

Conquest in the early 1500s. The most important early development of this period was the rise of the Toltec who, from their capital at Tula, expanded their influence into Mayan areas. The Mayan ceremonial center at Chichén Itzá in the Yucatán is, for example, a complex amalgam of Mayan and Toltec architecture.

The closing episode belongs to the Aztec, who rose to power in the 13th century and began a program of far-reaching military expansion. Like their predecessors, the Aztec also looked to the past and claimed descent from the legendary rulers of Teotihuacán and Tula.

it influenced all the later developments in Mesoamerica. The Classic Maya period, lasting from AD 300 to 900, for example, saw the fullest development of pyramid- and temple-building, as well as that of jade carvings, which had been inherited from the Maya's Olmec predecessors. During this period another great civilization, that of Teotihuacán, also came into eminence and exerted influence over the Maya area.

The third phase is the Post-Classic, lasting from AD 900 until the Spanish

400 BC	300 AD	400	500	850	900	1434	1521
Decline of Olmec culture	Beginning of Classic Mayan phase	Under influence of Teotihuacán, a new ceremonial complex is built at Kaminaljuyú	The Mixtec begin to take over the Zapotec power base	The Toltec led by Mixcoatl invade Mexico	End of Classic Mayan phase, beginning of Post-Classic phase	Triple Alliance formed between Tenochtitlan, Texcoco, and Tlacopan	Post-Classic phase ends with the Spanish Conquest

THE ORIGINS OF MESOAMERICAN CULTURE

Asian hunter-gatherers reach Central America

The origins of Mesoamerican cultures, like those of all Amerindian peoples, lie in Asia. The Americas were unpopulated prior to the migrations of nomadic bands of hunters and gatherers across a broad tundra that joined the American and Asian continents in the region of the modern Bering Strait.

Exactly when these first migrations took place is a matter of considerable academic debate, although a consensus is gradually emerging that this occurred some 35,000 to 40,000 years ago. Certainly, small bands of hunters had reached the Mesoamerican area long before the extinction of Ice Age mammals about 10,000 years ago, and radiocarbon dates suggest they may have been there for as much as 23,000 years. Their chipped stone spear points are found with fossil remains of animals such as the mammoth, mastodon, dire wolf, and saber-toothed tiger.

It is difficult to say what the lives of these people were like. There is little to suggest that they formed any permanent settlements, although some of them at least returned periodically to favored campsites. The

archaeological evidence suggests these were often located near springs or marshes, which attracted the larger game animals, as well as the hunters. Such locations would also have provided human families with an abundance of plant foods and a variety of fish and other aquatic resources, which must have formed a major part of the diet.

The seeds of agriculture

Despite their unsettled way of life, it is now emerging that these societies were far more complex and advanced than had hitherto been thought. Rather than being the New World equivalent of the Neolithic peoples in Europe, as scholars had previously supposed, they had highly developed technologies centered on stone-working and the use of the *atlatl* (spear-thrower), diverse languages, and rich and varied cosmology.

The end of the Pleistocene epoch in the Mesoamerica area marks a profound effect on the way of life of the early hunters, who

became dependent on smaller game, such as deer and jack rabbits. Also, as the ice fields receded in northern latitudes, the average temperature in what is now central and southern Mexico rose dramatically. It appears that the demise of the larger animals, coupled with changes in temperature, forced the people to return with greater regularity to favored sites and increase their reliance on the seeds, roots, berries, and fruits they were able to gather.

By 8,000 years ago the roaming bands of hunters had started to coalesce into larger groups and form semi-permanent settlements at which the selective planting of seeds was increasingly important. This consisted simply of selecting the better seeds from each season's yield and then leaving them to grow naturally.

Yet although they practiced no intensive agriculture, it is now clear that these hunting-gathering communities were laying the foundations for the great agricultural civilizations of the Olmec, Maya, and Aztec that were to follow.

Facing: *With the extinction of the larger Ice Age mammals, the people became more reliant on seeds, roots, and berries, and established semi-permanent campsites. They had not yet mastered techniques for cultivating food crops and did not use stone architecture. Archaeological evidence suggests that their houses were thatched huts of wattle and daub, **above**, similar to these homes of the Yucatec Maya.*

THE INTRODUCTION OF FARMING
Urban communities develop around the land

Above: *Cooperation between deities was essential to the people's survival. In this bas-relief the Rain God, Tlaloc, is paying honor to Cinteotl, the Goddess of Corn. It was believed that the gentle spring rains sent by Tlaloc fertilized the corn seeds for which Cinteotl was responsible and enabled her "corn children" to thrive and mature.*

The period after around 7000 BC until the formation of large permanent villages after 2000 BC is known as the Archaic, and marks major changes that were occurring throughout Mesoamerica. The early hunter-gatherers had already started to make regular seasonal visits to favorite campsites, where they carried out selective planting of wild seeds; the Archaic saw the development of this and the domestication of food plants that were to form the staple diet of later civilizations.

Exactly when plant domestication began is difficult to determine, although the pioneering work of Richard S. MacNeish is making the sequences clearer. His excavations in dry rock shelters and caves in the Tehuacán Valley in Puebla, Mexico, have uncovered the well-preserved remains of various plant domesticates, including avocado, chile peppers, squash, and cotton, which are tentatively dated at between 7000 and 5000 BC.

Domesticated maize, or Indian corn—which was to become the most important plant domesticate in the Americas—first appeared c.5000 BC. MacNeish discovered tiny cobs of primitive maize in the San Marcos Cave in the Tehuacán Valley. This significant find has raised a great deal of controversy and argument, since no wild progenitor of maize has ever been found. Archaeologists and botanists originally argued that maize was a hybrid form of teosinte, a closely related wild grass that grows as a weed in Mexican corn fields, although current arguments suggest that teosinte is an offspring of corn rather than its ancestor.

Domesticating maize crops

Whatever the outcome of these debates, it has to be acknowledged that there was a long period of experimentation and cultivation prior to 5000 BC, during which the intervention of Mesoamerican farmers enabled the domesticated form of maize to emerge. Whether this happened in the Tehuacán Valley or elsewhere is uncertain, since it may simply be that conditions at Tehuacán were such that remains were preserved, whereas elsewhere they have been lost.

Hand in hand with the domestication of maize came an increasing move into more permanent settled villages, since the cultivation of crops requires a local presence. A reliance on game decreased, since the formation of local communities tends to scatter animals from the vicinity, and, for the first time, there is evidence of the stone manos and metates (grinding mortars and pestles) needed for the processing of corn and other grains.

There is also evidence that other plant foods, especially beans, squashes, and pumpkins, were being cultivated; on the Pacific coast, there was greater dependency on other resources, such as fish and shellfish.

The increasing productivity of their crops meant that Archaic Mesoamerican populations expanded dramatically. The fields of crops could support much larger numbers of people than had been the case when subsistence depended on hunting and opportune gathering.

Together with this rise in sedentary populations came an upsurge in the material arts, as well as in the complexity of ritual procedures and observances. Pottery, basketwork, and small clay figurines are known from this period, as is the reverential burial of important members of the community. This latter point suggests that the processes of social stratification, which were to be so important later, also have their roots in the Archaic period.

Below: *The origins of maize are obscure, but it is believed to have been developed from a wild plant known as teosinte. This diorama shows early farmers cultivating maize in the Tehuacán Valley about 3400 BC.*

CHAPTER ONE

THE OLMEC

Evolving from agricultural communities

At some point around 1500 BC, the agricultural village communities started to evolve into large ceremonial and civic complexes. The first indications of this are from the Mexican Gulf Coast's lowland jungles and swamps in southern Veracruz and neighboring Tabasco. This is the heartland of Olmec culture, for all the major Olmec sites are located within this region.

It is unlikely that the Olmec centers were true cities. Indeed, most evidence points to the fact that the only permanent residents were groups of rulers, priests, and bureaucrats who were supported by a surrounding population of farmers practicing slash-and-burn agriculture. The structures and monuments erected at the sites attest to the fact that the ruling elite could nevertheless call on a large work force when required.

The Olmec built the first Mesoamerican pyramids, and although they did not have stone architecture, the labor required to shift tons of earth to erect platform mounds, which were then surmounted by perishable temple structures of pole and brush, must have been considerable.

They did, however, use stone for other purposes and are renowned for the gigantic basalt heads, some weighing as much as 20 tons, which were erected at the sites of La Venta and San Lorenzo. The stone for these and other monuments had to be imported by raft from the Tuxtla Mountains nearly 50 miles away.

In addition to their monumental works, the Olmec are famous for many smaller ritual carvings in jade and serpentine. This, too, had to be imported from outside the region, and to this end the Olmec established trade routes along the rivers, valleys, and mountain passes in their search for materials that could be used for ceremonial purposes. We can assume, therefore, that in addition to the nobility and the peasant farmers, there was also a class of specialized merchants and traders.

Olmec influence other cultures

The Olmec have been called the "mother culture" of Mesoamerica, for although their sites are in a relatively restricted area, there are clear indications of far-reaching Olmec influences. These extended as far north as Tlatilco (Mexico City) and south to Las Victorias in El Salvador and Los Naranjos in Honduras.

This influence was presumably maintained through their trade networks, and included the export not only of stylistic conventions, such as the snarling were-jaguar characteristic of Olmec carving, but also a whole complex of beliefs

Chupicuaro

VALLEY OF MEXICO

Tlatilco

Lake Texcoco

Xochicalco

Chalcatzingo

Above: The earliest Mesoamerican systems for dating are found in the Olmec area and spread around the region. Combined with glyphs, calendar dates became possible, as shown in this example from Xochicalco (see additional detail on page 31).

PACIFIC OCEAN

| **1500 BC** Agricultural villages begin to evolve into large complexes | **1400 BC** The emergence of Olmec culture | **1400–1100 BC** In the Mediterranean, Mycenaean civilization dominates sea trade | **1200 BC** At San Lorenzo the first Olmec ceremonial center is built | **1200–900 BC** Human-animal baby figurines made at San Lorenzo | **1070 BC** In Egypt, the New Kingdom comes to an end | **900 BC** San Lorenzo's sculptures and carvings are ritually destroyed | **800 BC** The Zapotec use hieroglyphics |

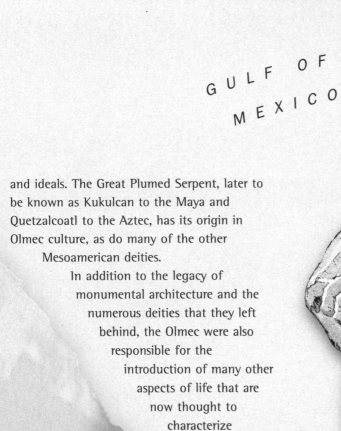

and ideals. The Great Plumed Serpent, later to be known as Kukulcan to the Maya and Quetzalcoatl to the Aztec, has its origin in Olmec culture, as do many of the other Mesoamerican deities.

In addition to the legacy of monumental architecture and the numerous deities that they left behind, the Olmec were also responsible for the introduction of many other aspects of life that are now thought to characterize

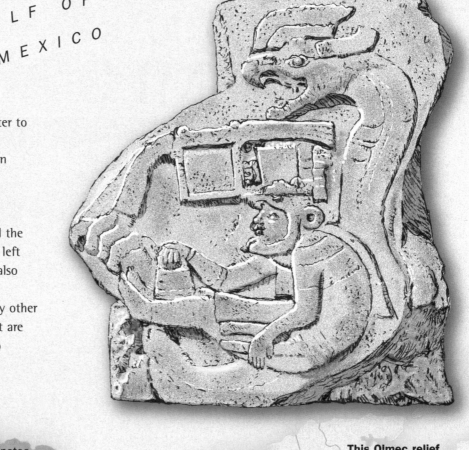

This Olmec relief carving from about the eighth century BC shows a priest making an offering. The serpent figure shown behind him is the guardian of water and fertility, which suggests that the offering may have been intended to ensure sufficient water to enable crops to mature.

Veracruz ●

OLMEC HEARTLAND

◆ Tres Zapotes

◆ Laguna de los Cerros   ◆ La Venta

◆ San Lorenzo

San José Mogote ●

ZAPOTEC

Monte Albán ●

SIERRA MADRE

● Izapa

Mesoamerican cultures. Among these is their theocratic system of government and the development of early writing and calendrical systems, which were to be brought to perfection by the Maya.

Between 400 and 100 BC Olmec culture went into decline. The reasons why this happened, or indeed where the Olmec went, remains one of the great mysteries of the region. Various

theories have been put forward, including that they migrated to the southeast and are the direct ancestors of the Maya. To all intents, however, by 100 BC Olmec culture had disappeared.

753 BC
In Italy, Rome is founded

600 BC
Monte Albán's first buildings are constructed

500 BC
Chupicuaro is established in the Valley of Mexico

400 BC
La Venta (Tabasco) is destroyed and abandoned

334 BC
In Asia Minor, Alexander the Great invades

300 BC
In North America, rise of the Hopewell Indian culture

100 BC
End of Olmec culture

31 BC
Date mark of Stela C at Tres Zapotes, indicating early calendric system

THE WERE-JAGUAR
Links with the Underworld

Right: *The were-jaguar is ubiquitous in Olmec culture and is easily recognized by its feline features and down-turned mouth. The cleft forehead was a symbol of status among the Olmec and identifies the were-jaguar as one of the nobility; it also appears in carvings depicting Olmec rulers and therefore links the were-jaguar with the ruling families.*

Facing: *This jade celt (ceremonial ax) depicting the were-jaguar only served a ritual function. Celts frequently accompanied the burials of royal personages or were used during sacrificial rites intended to appease deities.*

Mesoamerica has no record of artistic convention prior to the Olmec; the earlier products of the hunting-farming communities consisted almost entirely of utilitarian artifacts. Olmec art burst suddenly upon the scene — so suddenly that some scholars have described it primarily as an art style, rather than a culture.

It is replete with fully developed symbolism linking the natural and the supernatural worlds. An emphasis on the animals of the tropical forest and sea coast, such as the harpy eagle, rattlesnake, shark, and monkey, undoubtedly reflects an inheritance from the earlier hunters and fishermen who were dependent on local flora and fauna for their survival. Olmec art, however, brought in a fantastic new dimension in which the real and the unreal were combined.

A recurrent theme in Olmec carving is the were-jaguar, which combines the features of a snarling jaguar with those of a crying infant. In fact, so persistent is this image that for many years it was believed to be the only Olmec deity. However, more recent excavations have uncovered a host of representations of other deities, the jaguar appearing in several hybrid forms: the human-jaguar, jaguar-bird, bird-jaguar-alligator, and so forth.

Jaguar teeth and claws also appear in combination with other elements that identify various different gods, and in one memorable stone carving a figure appears to represent a kneeling shaman undergoing transformation into a jaguar.

Influence of the jaguar

The numerous references to the were-jaguar in Olmec culture suggest it may have been a prototypical deity that functioned as an early link between the world of the people and that of the supernatural. In particular, it provided a connection between the Middle World occupied by humans and the Underworld of the spirits and the deceased.

The full significance of the jaguar to the Olmec is open to speculation, but clues are provided from later cultures in which Olmec influence is apparent. Thus we know that the jaguar was conceived as a guardian deity of the entrance to the Underworld, as well as being a symbol of nobility. There were also close links with later rulers, the high priests, and the shamans.

It is likely the jaguar also functioned as a symbol for the lineages of ruling families who claimed supernatural sanction for their rule. Elaborate burials, which are clearly those of royal personages, contain numerous jade and serpentine *celts* (ceremonial axes) that are incised with the were-jaguar figure. Many of the royals who were buried at these sites still wear polished jade ear flares and pendants carved in the shape of jaguar teeth.

It is also notable that the Maya, who inherited many of their beliefs from the Olmec, frequently used the word "jaguar" as a royal name: Lady Une' B'alam of Tikal, for instance, translates as "Baby Jaguar," and the glyph for her name is that of an infantile feline, which has obvious Olmec antecedents.

Unfortunately, the exact meaning that the were-jaguar had for the Olmec will probably always remain a puzzle, since the early Olmec left no writing that might have revealed the origins of the mysterious cult figures that dominated their art.

ALTARS OF THE GODS
Sacrificial representations or gateways for the shamanic elite?

Below: *Although usually described as "altars," carvings such as this probably functioned as thrones during Olmec ceremonies, when the presiding priest or shaman sat cross-legged on the ledge above the carving of a figure emerging from the Underworld. The figure here holds a rope that encircles the altar and binds a prisoner carved on the reverse.*

Scattered throughout the Olmec sites are a number of rectangular platforms, typically about 5 feet tall, 10 feet long, and 6^1/$_2$ feet wide. They often depict a seated figure on one side, framed by the open jaws of a were-jaguar that forms a cave-like grotto. The function of these structures puzzled scholars for many years, but a general consensus was reached that they were probably altars. The iconography has been interpreted as representing the entrance to the Underworld guarded by the Jaguar God, from which the ruler/deity is emerging.

The best preserved of these structures is Altar 4 at La Venta. Here a life-sized human figure sits cross-legged in a niche, which is surrounded by a carving with a rope-like pattern. He is seated centrally between four symbols that represent maize, and a rope winds around the structure to a tied prisoner carved on one of the other sides.

The interpretation of this altar has long been that it shows an Olmec ruler holding a sacrificial victim, perhaps a ruler of a neighboring state, who is about to be killed. His heart and blood can be offered to the deities of the Underworld, thereby ensuring the fertility and growth of maize.

While such an interpretation has long been accepted, a closer reading of the carvings suggests that there may be an alternative meaning. A characteristic feature of the altars is an overhanging ledge carved with sky and earth bands, which acts as a model of the cosmos. This is associated with carvings that depict the entrance to the other world, reflecting the open niche beneath the bands in which figures are placed. The figures are frequently shown wearing bird masks, and it is almost certain that these represent the harpy eagle.

Ferried by jaguars and eagles
It is possible, therefore, that the altars act not only as portals to the Underworld and links between earth and sky, but also as a connection between night and day: the eagle is the dominant sky power, whereas the jaguar is a

lone night prowler. It is also significant that the eagle and jaguar act as guardians of the other world and can move freely between the realms. They can also carry those who have supernatural protection — the shamans, or priest-rulers.

If these conjectures are correct, the altars begin to have a far greater depth of meaning as signifying those places, or gateways, within the ceremonial complexes where direct interaction between the world of the deities and that of the people becomes a possibility. Since the only people who could travel with impunity between these worlds were those with ritual sanction to do so — that is, the priest-rulers and the shamans — it follows that the altars functioned as the focus of shamanic power. This is corroborated by the fact that many of the so-called altars have carvings that link them with the sacred World Tree, or *axis mundi*; an almost universal symbol of shamanism.

It might be more accurate to think of the altars as "seats of power" — perhaps, literally, as thrones — and the figures as priest-rulers about to undergo shamanic journeys with the assistance of his eagle and jaguar helpers. They thus become the stage on which this cosmic journey is performed, and the flat tops of the structures become representative of the middle ground: a space between sky and earth, or between night and day. This anomalous middle world has no specific spatial reference other than in shamanic terms.

Above: *In this detail of an altar from La Venta, the emerging figure is shown holding a child. The child is badly eroded and it may represent the were-jaguar baby being carried from its home in the Underworld into that of the people.*

SAN LORENZO
The earliest Olmec site?

Right: *Colossal stone heads depicting Olmec rulers have been found at La Venta and San Lorenzo. This head, from San Lorenzo, dates from about 900 BC and is preserved in the Anthropology Museum at Xalapa, where it was photographed while the museum was under construction in 1986.*

The earliest Olmec site to be thoroughly investigated is San Lorenzo, which was subject to intense investigation by the Yale Expedition between 1966 and 1969. San Lorenzo is located near a branch of the Rio Coatzacoalcos in Veracruz, where it covers the top of a 164-foot high plateau that has been artificially leveled and extends about 0.8 miles from north to south.

The excavations of the Yale Expedition revealed that the site had been occupied before 1500 BC by people belonging to the Ojochi culture. Although the population at this time was small – perhaps only one hundred people – status differentiation had already been marked. By 1200 BC the population had increased to over one thousand and eight colossal stone heads had been erected, presumably in honor of the ruling elite. Other monuments include stone "altars" and sculptures that identify the San Lorenzo rulers with a host of supernaturals that combine human and animal features.

San Lorenzo was almost certainly a ceremonial rather than a residential complex, and drew penitents from a large surrounding rural area. Intensive maize agriculture was practiced on the river lowlands to support these adherents, and there was heavy reliance on fish and turtles. Dogs were domesticated for food, and, ominously, human bones recovered from kitchen middens suggest some form of cannibalism took place.

Erasing sacred ground

They were skilled potters, representations of Olmec deities incised on neckless jars, which were highly sought after throughout the areas influenced by Olmec trade. While these jars apparently served utilitarian purposes at San Lorenzo, where they were used in the preparation of maize, other ceramics served a number of cult purposes. Among these are grotesque human-animal baby figurines that were made in considerable quantity between 1200 and 900 BC.

The buildings constructed at the site also indicate a ceremonial significance. Chief among

them are ball courts where a ritual game was played that symbolically pitted the sons of the ruler against the representatives of the Underworld. These are surrounded by some 200 raised earth platforms, which formerly supported brush and thatch houses or temples.

Systems of stone drains supplied water to artificial ponds in which ritual bathing took place. These drains are a staggering feat of

human ingenuity, since the stone had to be imported by rafts over a distance of 50 miles and each block carefully smoothed and shaped using only bone and stone tools.

In 900 BC a sudden calamity overtook San Lorenzo. In a frenzied burst of activity, all the stone monuments and carvings were deliberately mutilated and defaced by smashing, grinding, and drilling them. The remains of these once-proud sculptures were manhandled onto the surrounding mountain ridges, where they were aligned in rows and then carefully buried before the site was abandoned. While the ritual disposal of the monuments suggests a desacralization of the site, the reasons for this destruction and abandonment of San Lorenzo are unknown.

LA VENTA
Impressive works at an island site

Facing, top: *A tomb at La Venta constructed from basalt columns.*

Facing, bottom: *This carving from La Venta is simply described as "woman in a niche."*

Below: *A colossal head from La Venta.*

Located on an island surrounded by marshy swamplands near the Tonala in Tabasco, La Venta has the distinction of being the site of the largest Olmec pyramid. The Great Pyramid is 98 feet high and contains over 3,500,000 cubic feet of earth. It is so vast that some scholars claim it is the oldest true pyramid in Mexico. This huge monument acted as a ceremonial and political focus for the Olmec after the abandonment of San Lorenzo in 900 BC, until La Venta was in turn destroyed and abandoned in 400 BC.

Like San Lorenzo, La Venta was built on the foundation of extensive agriculture, which supported a large rural population and provided for itinerant worshippers and pilgrims. The weeping baby-jaguar figurines representing nobility and Underworld deities are again much in evidence, although it is clear that La Venta had expanded the trade networks first established by San Lorenzo. In addition to basalt and obsidian, which had been the primary materials used by the craftsmen at San

Lorenzo, La Venta traders located several sources of serpentine and jade.

Jade was to become a symbol of wealth to later Mesoamericans, and appears to have served this function at La Venta as well, since there are elaborate tombs and burials of nobles in which jade is much evident. Unique to La Venta, however, are jade and serpentine mosaic courtyards. Curiously, these were buried immediately after they were made, their positions marked by stone posts erected above.

Redirecting agricultural labor

The buried courtyards had no practical purpose and can only have served a ritual function; this is true of other constructions at the site. Recent studies increasingly suggest that the buildings, plazas, and courtyards were aligned according to astronomical observations, which linked them directly with Olmec cosmology and a pantheon of supernatural deities.

Archaeological detective work tends to throw some light on the function of the site. Given the agricultural practices of the time, the island could only have supported a population of about 45 families. It is clear that by themselves they could never have erected the gigantic buildings or imported the necessary materials for their construction.

The rural population of the area, however, was about 18,000. Since farming was a seasonal activity, they could have been co-opted by the priests and nobles living in La Venta as a labor force. Their work would probably have been considered part of their homage to the deities whose presence was symbolically located within the ceremonial complex.

Like San Lorenzo, La Venta suffered a paroxysm of destruction in 400 BC when 24 monumental sculptures, including some colossal heads, were defaced in a virtually identical manner. Again, there are numerous theories as to why this happened. In the case of La Venta, however, it seems likely that the population had increased to a point where agricultural methods of the time were no longer sufficient to support the expanding population.

ELABORATIONS INTO JADE
The significance of Mesoamerica's favored gemstone

Below: *Jade was revered as one of the most precious materials by all Mesoamerican cultures, who associated it with water and fertility. Using a combination of different techniques, blocks of jade were worked and polished to produce intricate and highly sophisticated carvings, such as the mask and figurine shown here. Many were manufactured purely as grave offerings and were buried soon after they were made.*

The Olmec, although best known for their massive and elaborately carved work in stone, were master craftworkers in many materials whose artisans set a precedent for the skilled work of the later Maya. In addition to their monumental carving, the Olmec employed precious stones and metals, many of which were obtained by trading out of the Olmec heartland of Veracruz and Tabasco.

Jade was the most eagerly sought of these precious materials, and its significance in Olmec and later Mesoamerican cultures is illustrated by the fact that the deity Chalchihuitlicue, or "Jade Skirt," was revered throughout the area as the wife or sister of Tlaloc, the Rain God.

By a combination of carving, drilling, incising, and polishing, the Olmec produced tiny jade beads and discs, ceremonial celts (ax heads), figurines, pendants, and other ornaments. Many of these were incised with intricate outlines of the characteristic were-jaguar, the offspring of humans and the gods, and were intended as burial offerings. Some of the ornaments, which were intended as ear flares and pendants, were carved in the shape of jaguar teeth and claws and worn only by the highest-ranking priests and officials.

Unfortunately the Olmec left no written or hieroglyphic accounts. It is therefore only through the archaeological record and by reference to later Mesoamerican cultures that we are able to surmise what jade meant to them. A connection with the dead is readily apparent, since a jade bead was placed in the mouth of the deceased at burial; but we can assume this was done as a symbol of life rather than death. The Olmec felt that their dead would be resurrected either in this world or the next, and jade refers to life and continued growth in later cultures of the area.

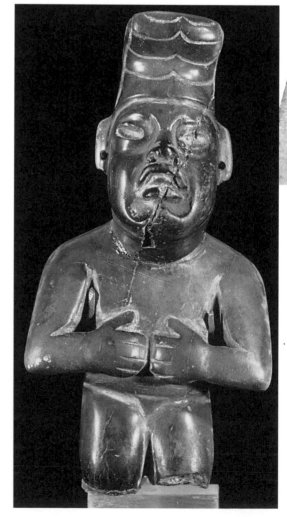

Water, growth, and fertility

The interpretation of jade as a life symbol is also suggested by the relationship between Chalchihuitlicue and Tlaloc. As the rain-bringer, Tlaloc was associated with the growth of plants and vegetation, and his wife or sister was felt to represent water and fertility. The Olmec, as we know from their architecture, believed in a cosmos in which life and death, the sky world of the gods, that of the people, and the Underworld, were all inextricably linked. That jade is frequently linked with the Jaguar god, which acted as the Guardian of the Underworld and was the antecedent of a water deity is significant; so, too, is the fact that many of the jade figures and mosaics recovered from Olmec sites were deliberately interred soon after their manufacture.

Perhaps the most famous of these is a group of 16 jade figurines and six celts found buried at the Olmec ceremonial center of La Venta. Immediately after they were made these were arranged in a pit in the center of the pyramid complex as a formal group performing a ceremony, and then covered with layers of earth. Exactly what function this burial served is unknown, although there is clearly a ritual link established between the world of the people and that of the Underworld deities. Also, since the spot where they were buried had been marked, it appears that successive rituals involved the uncovering and reburial of ritual jade offerings such as these.

Above: *This group of jade figurines is perhaps the most famous example of work in this material from La Venta. The figures appear to be involved in a ceremony. Shortly after they were made they were arranged as seen in this photograph and buried in the center of the pyramid complex.*

THE IDEAL OF NOBLE BIRTH
Colossal stone portraits?

Right: *Olmec carvings of figures almost invariably depict high-ranking officials and nobles. The man shown holding a child is identified as such by his elaborate headdress and the "mirror disc" worn on his chest.*

Facing: *This colossal head shows a helmeted ruler from San Lorenzo. Although the meaning of these helmets has been hotly debated, it is generally accepted that they represent the headgear worn by ball-players. The contestants were probably the sons of the ruling kings, and their helmets bear characteristic clan markings that identify the lineage to which they belonged.*

In 1862 a colossal stone head, carved from basalt, was discovered in the Veracruz district of San Andres Tuxtla. Scholars and writers at the time expressed bewilderment at the find, but it was to be another 63 years before further finds in the Laguna de Catemaco fueled intense speculation over their origin and meaning.

At first some refused to believe that the colossal heads — which weigh up to 20 tons — and finds of fine jade jewelry could be attributed to a culture that others claimed was older than that of the Maya. They suggested a non-American people had carved the heads or that they were related to the cultures of Easter Island, and refused to accept that they had an indigenous Mesoamerican origin.

Others pointed to the full lips, broad noses, and swarthy features of the faces and claimed they were the work of people of African descent and of more recent date. In a yet more fanciful vein, on the evidence of the "helmets" worn by the figures, it was proposed that the carvings belonged to antiquity but had been made by an alien race.

That the basalt originated from over 50 miles away also worked against those who claimed the makers were the indigenous predecessors of the Maya. They had no wheeled technology and no beasts of burden, and rivers and swamplands had to be crossed to reach the city centers. It was argued that the early Mesoamericans were not so advanced that they possessed the skills to originate the carvings.

Controlling the elements
We now know that they are the work of the Olmec and date back to c.1200 BC, although controversy still rages over what they are meant to represent and what purpose they fulfilled. While there are some adherents to the view that the carvings depict deities, the opinion is gradually being accepted that they are portraits of Olmec rulers. Indeed, facial characteristics are so carefully depicted that the unique features of individuals can be recognized. Jaguar symbolism in the form of incised markings suggests the lineages of these individuals.

Other elements of the carvings reinforce the view that they are portraits of noble lords. The "helmets" are now generally accepted as being the headgear worn by players in the ritual ball game, which set the powers of the ruling families against the forces of the supernatural. Each helmet is marked by a distinctive device, which emphasizes the individuality of the person depicted.

But even if the notion that these are indeed Olmec rulers is accepted, a puzzle remains: Why did the Olmec feel it necessary to undertake the extremely difficult task of rafting massive basalt blocks from the Tuxtla Mountains into their capital cities to provide the raw material for the carvings?

The answer, perhaps, lies in the origin of the basalt boulders themselves. They are found on the slopes of erupting volcanoes, where they have been flung by the force of fire from the bowels of the earth. The assumption must therefore be that by transforming these into portraits of their rulers, the Olmec were making a statement about their relationship with the sources of supernatural power. At the same time, they demonstrated the control their rulers could exercise over these forces and provided a spiritual link with the creation, the cosmos, and the cycle of life.

THE RELATIONSHIP BETWEEN DEITIES AND THE ELITE

Motivating the peasant workforce to build

Below: *Bas-relief of an Olmec king. His scepter is a symbol of his royal position.*

The discovery of colossal stone heads in the Olmec regions raised a number of problems of archaeological significance. Traditionally, archaeology focuses almost solely on material

remains, in terms of establishing dates, chronological sequences, the development of art styles, and so forth. Unfortunately, although such approaches tend to leave us with a significant amount of data, they tell us little about the people who lived and worked in these regions.

It is impossible, however, to study Olmec stratification without consideration of social, political, and ritual ideas that were evolving during this period. That there was much social inequality is apparent. A large population of peasant farmers was co-opted as a labor force, presumably of their own free will, during the periods when agricultural activities were slack. Given that the Olmec had no standing armies or other means of forcing co-operation, as far as we know, why did the peasant farmers freely give their time to efforts that elevated the status of a very small proportion of the population?

There had been major social and political changes during the move from hunter-gatherers, to farming communities, to a semi-urban population. Archaeology can be interpreted in ways that suggest what these changes may have been. In particular, the earlier hunting-gathering activities were opportunistic and depended largely on individual skills: Archaeology suggests that although there may have been favored sites, these did not provide guaranteed resources, so populations remained small and egalitarian.

As the groups coalesced into farming and then semi-urban communities, resources became more certain and populations grew. But these required greater co-operative effort and a consequent growth of able and respected leaders. The descendants of these leaders formed the basis for the Olmec elite. However, the erection of monumental architecture and the provision of a work force to do so was very different from earlier subsistence activities, and other forces must have been at work to encourage co-operation.

Assisting the gods

Undoubtedly many of these forces were ritual ones, in which participation was as essential to survival as the procurement of food: in a sense both the physical and spiritual selves required sustenance. Spiritual sustenance had previously been provided by local shaman-priests, and even the semi-urban communities were not so large that the activities of organized farmers and local priests would have been insufficient for these needs. In terms of population size and demography, there is no socio-political reason to explain the erection of the massive Olmec ceremonial centers.

In later Mesoamerican cultures the deities have similar hierarchical positions as those we assume for the Olmec. There are leading gods, their assistants, and assistants to the assistants, plus a host of subsidiary spirits and powers.

The prestige of each deity is marked by the amount of power he or she wields. Lesser gods readily acquiesced to the greater power of a superior deity. We can therefore assume that the ceremonial centers did not only have a ritual function but also served as symbols of power.

Given that archaeology tells us the centers contained both ritual buildings and elite residences, it appears that the elite may have been starting to claim more than just political status. They lived within the precincts of the gods, and accordingly may have been viewed by the rural population as being divine, or at least semi-divine. If this hypothesis is correct it sets a precedent for later Mesoamerican cultures, such as that of the

Aztec, and helps explain the structures of these complex hierarchical societies.

It also explains why the peasant farmers willingly gave time to the laborious tasks of transporting and preparing heavy building materials and erecting the elite residences. These may have been not only "palaces" but

Below: *The cape, headdress, neck ornament, and wide belt the figure known as "The Governor" wears functioned as symbols of authority.*

the homes of the gods and symbols of divine power, and their labor was therefore part of ritual activity and devotion.

BURIED TREASURES
Connecting the Middle and Lower Worlds

Below: *Mosaic pavement from La Venta depicting the Jaguar God. This pavement was laid on ground that had been carefully smoothed, covered with white sand, and then ritually burnt over and blessed; but immediately after its construction it was buried beneath more sand and fine gravel. It is likely that this was intended to reinforce ritual links with the Underworld of which the Jaguar God was the guardian.*

One of the most enigmatic aspects of Olmec culture is the presence at a number of sites, but particularly at La Venta, of buried artifacts. Why the Olmec chose to place objects in positions where they could not be viewed has long been a puzzle, and without written records any interpretation must, at best, be an educated guess. It is only through study of later Mesoamerican cultures that we can attempt to understand who the Olmec were and what their lives must have been like.

The buried treasures do not, however, have any direct parallels in later cultures, so their analysis must remain a matter of speculation. If, however, the ceremonial centers and elite residences were thought of as homes of the gods (*see pages 26–27*), the meaning of buried artifacts becomes a little clearer. Under this hypothesis we need to consider the pantheon of Mesoamerican deities and their relationship to the human world.

The deities may be considered as belonging to either the Upper or Lower realm. In this case, the pyramids and other monuments above ground reach toward the sky gods. It is perhaps significant that Olmec pyramids are inverted cones, the apex on which sacrificial fires were probably lit bearing similarity to the summits of volcanoes and the "heavenly fire" that issues from them.

Such an interpretation would be in accordance with the views of later Mesoamericans, to whom volcanoes were sacred symbols and where fire was associated with mountains. Via the pyramids, the power of the sky gods could be carried down the steps to the Middle World — that of the people.

Decorative drainage system?
The buried treasures reverse this relationship, toward the deities of the Lower World. These

deities are often associated with water, which runs in underground caves or issues from springs. The entrance to the Underworld is guarded by the Jaguar God, and, of course, were-jaguars depicted crouched at the entrance of cave-like openings is a very familiar Olmec motif. The Underworld itself is only reached by crossing a raging river.

When the buried artifacts are considered, their relationship to this later group of Underworld gods becomes clearer. There is an obvious connection with what have been described as drainage pipes. The usual explanation for these is that they were used to drain water from sacred artificial lakes in the plazas of the ritual centers. However, there is no reason to suppose that surface drainage would have been any less efficient. Also, the craftsmanship of these pipes is superb. If their function were purely utilitarian (although perhaps with some ritual association), it would seem unlikely that the finest craftsmen would have been involved in their manufacture. We should, perhaps, look for some kind of deeper significance.

This may be provided by other groups of finely worked objects. Among them are obsidian mosaic pavements. Obsidian is not native to the Olmec heartland, and in later cultures is associated with the sacrificial knife that sent its victims to Mictlan, the Land of the Dead. It may be significant that the waters of the Sacred Cenote at Chichén Itzá (*see pages 136–137*), from the later Maya-Toltec, contained a number of sacrificial knives. More significant, however, is that the mosaic pavements depict the Jaguar God, the Guardian of the Underworld. The other important group of objects is a group of jade figurines arranged in ritual postures (*see page 23*).

The buried objects are marked, and it is usually assumed that this was to enable their later recovery. However, it may be that this marking instead indicated a path back to the Middle World. If this is so, the markings may have had a similar function to the ceremonial stairways of the pyramids that connected the Upper and Middle Worlds, only reversing the order to provide connection with the Lower World.

Above: *Of the two pyramids erected at La Venta, only one retains much of its original form. It is believed that this Great Pyramid – the first true pyramid in Mesoamerica – was built to resemble the shape of a volcano. The name of the site – "The Vent" – is also an allusion to volcanoes.*

TRES ZAPOTES
Site of a parallel but longer lasting Olmec culture

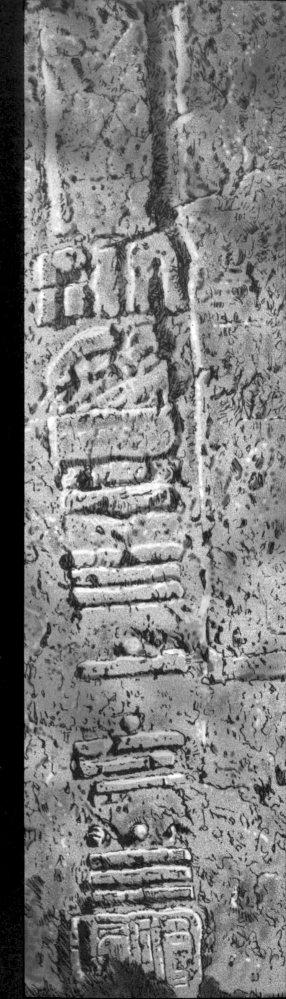

Right: *Stela C from Tres Zapotes is remarkable in that it bears the earliest known date markings from the Mesoamerican area. Although no earlier examples have yet been found, the dot and bar dates on this stela are part of an established tradition that must have originated in an earlier period. More detail on the Mesoamerican dot and bar counting system, developed fully into mathematics by the Maya, can be found on pages 72–73.*

The site of Tres Zapotes, on the slopes of the Tuxtla Mountains in Veracruz, was occupied by the Olmec during the same period as other major centers, such as La Venta, which ended c.400 BC. During this time the Tres Zapotes culture paralleled that of the other sites and was part of what we might term Classic Olmec.

The finds at Tres Zapotes are of types with which we are already familiar. They include some monumental sculptures with the familiar jaguar motif or with abstract designs, stone altars, and large engraved stelae. Jaguar claws and teeth are recurrent motifs. Tres Zapotes, therefore, seems to have adopted Olmec traditions practiced at other sites. The style of carving has been described as one of the greatest artistic achievements of ancient America.

Our understanding of these sites and of Olmec culture in general relies on what archaeologists can give us, and on different ways in which we interpret these facts. That Olmec culture was highly stratified is apparent from the elaborate burials of only a few individuals, who must have formed an elite of priests or rulers. Later Mesoamerican cultures provide some comparative examples, and we can assume that similar carved motifs from later cultures where the meaning is clearer also bear relevance for the Olmec period.

Numerous disciplines and various techniques contribute to this kind of analysis. Archaeology, art history, ethnology, and botany bring their own specialisms and a more complete picture of who the Olmec were begins to emerge. It is like a jigsaw puzzle; but one with many missing pieces. Although we know a great deal about the Olmec, and this knowledge is continually increasing, what we do not know is far greater.

Breaking the silence

The Olmec remain tantalizingly mute. At the time the great centers of Olmec civilization collapsed, they had not developed a writing system. The images they carved and the monuments they erected are often stunningly

This is a tremendous discovery for students of Mesoamerica, since it suggests that the late Olmec already had a basis for the highly sophisticated mathematical and calendric systems that were used by the later Maya and Aztec. It also has great emotional impact, in that it is the first "voice" to speak to us from the Americas.

For this simple carving to exist in the form it does has yet further significance. The lines and dots are arranged in a manner that can be read using the later Mayan system, and are not idle, unsystematic scratch marks. This means that they are part of an established, albeit simple, system that must have developed earlier.

Perhaps the Olmec recorded time on perishable materials that have not survived; or perhaps there are other stone carvings lying abandoned or buried somewhere in Veracruz. If any earlier

Although dot and bar dates continued to be used by later cultures, there were other developments. This Huastecan calendar (left) employs the "calendar round" that represents the cyclical events of the agricultural year. The Nahua and Zapotec linked calendar dates with glyphs representing the deities that ruled periods of the year. The example shown below is from Xochicalco, Tijuana.

beautifully, but they are silent.

Tres Zapotes, however, survived the collapse of the other centers and continued until just before the beginning of the Christian era. During this time it underwent many changes, some of them so great that some archaeologists claim this later period as proto-Mayan. Yet Olmec occupancy continued at Tres Zapotes and Olmec sculptural traditions continued to be practiced there, although at a much reduced level.

One of the Olmec carvings from this late period appears, at first, to be relatively insignificant. It is a stone post, known to us simply as Stela C, depicting the familiar jaguar mask on one side. On the reverse, however, is a deceptively simple abstract pattern of lines and dots. Overlooked for many years, this has now been reconsidered by Mayanists and found to be a date glyph. When the date is correlated with the Christian calendar, we arrive at 31 BC.

examples are found, it might be possible to trace the origins of writing in America.

CHALCATZINGO
Female rule over a dramatic landscape

Below: *This stone-lined tomb at Chalcatzingo also served as an altar where offerings were made.*

Chalcatzingo is located in one of the most spectacular and dramatic landscapes in the entire Mesoamerican area. It lies at the base of one of three great mountain peaks that dominate a flat valley in the eastern part of the Mexican state of Morelos, about 75 miles southeast of Mexico City.

It was discovered in 1934 by a Mexican archaeologist who found great boulders carved in a style that she immediately identified as

Below: *Chalcatzingo is set in a dramatic landscape at the foot of the mountains of the Valley of Morelos.*

Olmec, and later investigations confirmed that Chalcatzingo is contemporary with the great Olmec ceremonial center of La Venta. These huge relief carvings are among the most impressive examples of public art from before 900 BC.

Further investigations at Chalcatzingo revealed a wealth of data about the everyday lives of the Olmec that is not immediately apparent at larger sites, such as La Venta and San Lorenzo. There are extensive kitchen middens; analysis of their contents has shown that the Olmec occupants at Chalcatzingo

practiced intensive agriculture. Their basic diet consisted of corn, beans, and squash, which they supplemented with the meat of domesticated dogs, wild deer, rabbits, birds, and iguana. They also made tortillas, and had recourse to processed lime in its preparation.

Also found within the household context, and again generally in the kitchen areas, was a wealth of human and animal clay figurines. The bodies of the human figures are crudely shaped but the facial features are carefully modeled and painted, suggesting that they were intended as portraits of the household's occupants. Animal figures are mostly of ducks and dogs, but there are also some carvings of turtles, turkeys, deer, peccary, squirrels, and opossums. Curiously, carvings of monkeys are present – monkeys are not native to the central highland regions. Most of these zoomorphic figures are two-toned ocarinas or whistles.

Striking bas-relief carvings

A number of the carvings accompany burials that were made beneath the floors of houses, although it is apparent that these were of commoners, rather than nobles. The ruling elite were instead buried in stone-lined tombs on raised platforms, and their skeletons were surrounded by valuable grave goods.

The most striking features at the site are, of course, the large bas-relief carvings, and these deserve closer attention. Some depict the

nature/human relationship. In one a priest-ruler or man-god sits in a cave holding a box surrounded by clouds, water, jade, and vegetation, and carrying a stone that represents the earth. These symbolize all the forces of sky, water, and earth that formed a holy trinity in Olmec belief. Another depicts an ithyphallic bound captive who is threatened by two fully armed Olmec warriors. In another, two were-jaguar deities attack nude men.

The most important carving, however, indicates a peculiarity of Chalcatzingo lineages: it depicts a woman as a ruler, rather than as the consort of a male king. She wears a huge towering headdress as a symbol of her rank and sits within a cave-like opening formed from the jaws of a were-jaguar. Above her are rain clouds from which phallic raindrops fall toward her.

Although this carving is not accompanied by text glyphs, the symbolism seems clear. The woman wears the regalia of a deified ruler. The cave opening is the womb of the earth, protected by the were-jaguar as guardian of the Underworld, while the raindrops signify the fertilizing power of rain that impregnates the earth. The woman becomes both ruler and Mother Goddess, but it is unclear whether she represents a line of female rulers at Chalcatzingo or whether she inherited her position because there was no male heir.

TLATILCO AND CHUPICUARO
Sources of bright, expressive Olmec figurines

Olmec influence spread beyond the heartland and into the Valley of Mexico, although whether this was a diffusion of the Olmec style or actual occupation by migrant Olmec groups is unknown. Two sites in particular, Tlatilco and Chupicuaro, are of interest here, since burials at both have revealed hundreds of small clay figurines that are both charming and informative.

Tlatilco is by far the more important of the two as a settlement, and was probably a regional center in its own right. There are no pyramid structures, but there is indication of social stratification in that homes of the nobility were built on raised clay platforms.

It has two characteristics, both archaeological curiosities yielding important finds. One is the presence of deep bell-shaped underground storage pits, subsequently used for refuse disposal. The other is Tlatilco's long use as a brickworks, resulting in numerous finds of clay figurines with Olmec characteristics.

Important among these figurines are whiteware and hollow "babies" with jaguar mouths, and numerous intricately worked heads and figures. Pottery bowls with stirrup spouts and carved ceramic vessels are very similar to those made at the Olmec center of San Lorenzo, which has led to speculation that Tlatilco was an outlying trade post from which San Lorenzo goods could be distributed. Radiocarbon dates indicate that Tlatilco was contemporary with San Lorenzo.

It is likely, however, that these are local produce, since Tlatilco is an important source of clay, and that there was a resident Olmec community from San Lorenzo living here. This is also suggested by the numerous sub-floor burials, the presence of a jaguar mask complex, and Olmec bas-relief carvings. Such artifacts were made locally and do not represent traded items.

Change in the female form

While there aren't large amounts of carved stone and jade, usually associated with the Olmec, there is a tableau of jade figures arranged in a similar fashion to the better known array from La Venta. Both were found as sub-floor burials. While it is difficult to distinguish costume details on the figures from La Venta, those from Tlatilco can be clearly read. In the center is a man in magnificent attire, while standing or reclining around him is a group of 15 figures wearing less elaborate costume.

The burials that have received the most

Left: *Geometric fretwork patterns are familiar from the art of the early Mayan period but are not characteristic of Olmec style. This ceramic bowl, from a burial at Chupicuaro dated from 400–100 BC, is contemporary with other artifacts in which Olmec influence is apparent, suggesting that Chupicuaro may have been a transition point between the Olmec and Maya.*

attention, however, are the hundreds of hollow clay figurines. The majority of these are female and delicately modeled. Unlike the solemn jade carvings, many of them are cheerful and expressive figures of dancing girls and acrobats that give an insight into the lighter aspects of Olmec life.

They are painted with red and yellow ochre designs, and are remarkable for the variety of head coverings and hairstyles they have. Apart from head decorations, they are nude or wear minimal clothing, and are characterized by narrow shoulders, small breasts, tiny hips, and huge, flaring thighs.

Hundreds of small clay female figurines have also been found at Chupicuaro, which appears to have been more a cemetery than a settlement. There is, again, emphasis on extremely elaborate hairstyling and head decoration, as well as

expressive gestures and the use of bright paint decoration. Again, the majority are nude, although a few wear elaborate costume. The Chupicuaro vision of the female form is, however, opposite to that of Tlatilco: at Chupicuaro the figures have slender legs and hips, large rounded breasts, and wide shoulders.

There is less direct evidence of Olmec influence at the cemetery site of Chupicuaro, perhaps as a result of its later date, which is contemporary with the final years of the Olmec city of La Venta. Among the burial offerings are numerous clay bowls and utensils that incorporate non-Olmec design features contemporary with other developments in the Valley of Mexico during the period 500–100 BC. Chupicuaro may, therefore, represent a "melting pot" of cultural influences, rather than having a distinct style.

Facing: *This ceramic figure of a seated woman dating from about 1200 BC was found at Tlatilco. Unlike the formalized carvings of deities, nobles, and kings, the Tlatilco figurines depict real people in everyday – and sometimes erotic – activities, and convey a sense of playfulness.*

IZAPA
Olmec and Mayan cultures combined

The buildings at Izapa, located on the Pacific plain of the Mexican state of Chiapas, close to Guatemala, span the period between the Olmec and the Maya. Some scholars claim that Izapa is the key site in the development of early Mayan culture. They point to the presence of obviously Olmec influences combined with representations of deities that feature among the later Maya.

Others, however, feel that the development of early Mesoamerican cultures is too complex to be defined by any single event or placed in any specific locale, and claim the site represents a number of diverse influences over an extended period of time.

Most of the mounds at Izapa are earth, covered with a facing of river cobbles. There are a large number of these monumental buildings and 89 stelae have been found. Fewer than half the stelae are carved, the remainder undecorated stones, and those that bear carvings are generally paired with plain altar stones. Some of the non-carved stones may have had painted markings.

The carvings form a unique Izapan style that apparently features both historical and mythical themes, although exact interpretations of many of the figures remains to be made. They are often complex and at first glance give the impression of clutter, which has led to the coining of the phrase "Izapan Baroque," but most are nevertheless carefully constructed and follow a format. In this there is an upper band or frame representing the heavens or marked with cosmological symbols, and a lower band that depicts the earth or contains Underworld symbols. The action in the carving, whether the adventures of the Hero Twins or the exploits of an Izapan lord, takes place between these borders and is usually carved in low relief.

No glyphs, no contact

Although the Izapan style is highly distinctive, there is clear indication of Olmec inheritance in many of its figures. Thus there are depictions of the grinning jaguar deity, or were-jaguar, that was so highly characteristic of the Olmec, as well as the U-form (a U-shaped cleft in the head) used by Olmec

carvers to indicate royal lineage.

The prevalence of Olmec iconography has led Izapa culture to be described as neo-Olmec. There are, however, a number of Izapan gods that do not have Olmec precursors. Among them is a bearded god with tridents instead of eyes, who later appears in modified form at the Mayan site of Tikal, as well as figures reminiscent of the later Mayan Jester God.

No hieroglyphs or date glyphs associated with the Izapan carvings have been found, although it is generally assumed that at least some of the carvings represent historical figure-rulers, priests, and so on. If they could be deciphered, they would almost certainly provide an account of Izapan dynasties and the relationships this site maintained with neighboring groups, as well as give a clearer indication of which deities the Izapans considered important.

There is a suggestion, however, that the lack of date glyphs indicates that Izapa was relatively isolated. Other sites close to and contemporary with Izapa do have date glyphs, and it would be expected that these would have been incorporated within the Izapan carvings if regular contacts were maintained. While a reading of these other carvings might shed some light on Izapa's history, they are unfortunately in an as yet unknown text.

Left: *The relationship between Izapa and neighboring towns attracts a great deal of attention and argument from scholars. Some claim that Izapa was the birthplace of the Mesoamerican systems of time measurement, and as such is both neo-Olmec and proto-Maya. Others claim that its relatively isolated position prevented it from becoming a pivotal site in the region's prehistory. It is nevertheless clear that Izapa shared a number of traits with contemporary groups, including carvings that combine the features of rulers with insignia of animal-deities, as on this sculpture from nearby Kaminaljuyú.*

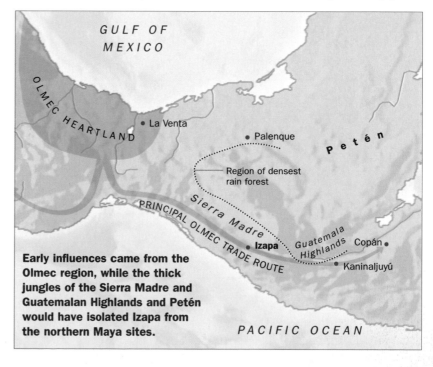

Early influences came from the Olmec region, while the thick jungles of the Sierra Madre and Guatemalan Highlands and Petén would have isolated Izapa from the northern Maya sites.

ABANDONMENT OF OLMEC SITES
The mystery of destroyed, deserted cities

Above: *When the Olmec sites were abandoned, their monuments were deliberately defaced. This detail of a colossal head from San Lorenzo shows drill marks to the left of the eye and on the bridge of the nose. By defacing their monuments, the Olmec were presumably taking away their religious and ritual significance, thereby minimizing their importance as depictions of deities or ruling families.*

One of the factors that has long been a cause of confusion and argument among scholars of Mesoamerica is the fact that many of the major cities were suddenly abandoned – often after an apparent attempt to destroy them. The large Olmec sites of San Lorenzo and La Venta were destroyed and abandoned, as were the later major cities of Teotihuacán and Tula. Although with less evidence of destruction, desertion is also apparent at a number of Mayan centers.

A peculiarity of these abandonments is that they do not appear to have been the result of a gradual decline, but were sudden and catastrophic. They occurred during periods when archaeological evidence suggests that they were thriving centers of ritual and commerce.

Numerous theories have been put forward to try to explain them. Among the theories that have the greatest current acceptance is that external pressures made the sites untenable.

According to this scenario, political intrigues between rival cities resulted in wars that caused ruling kings to lose authority, followed by a general exodus of the population.

Another theory suggests that internal dissension caused uprisings by rural communities against the ruling elites and consequent civil war. A third argument is that the populations simply outgrew themselves and became too large to be supported by local resources, which was followed by population dispersal and reorganization as smaller localized communities that required a less extensive subsistence base.

Each of these theories has its adherents, but none can be proven through archaeological record and so remain open to question. The third option is, however, unlikely for the Olmec, since populations were never large enough to exhaust local resources. Violent overthrow is also questionable, for a variety of reasons, so there may have been other factors at play.

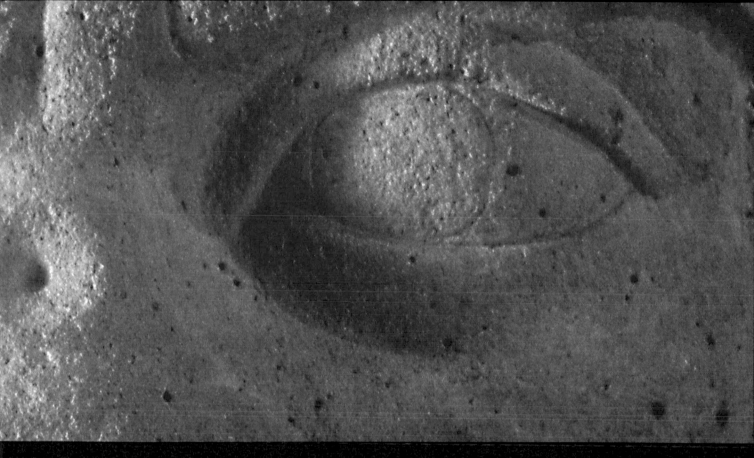

Ordered destruction

Neither San Lorenzo nor La Venta appear to have been destroyed by insurrection. If fighting of sufficient ferocity to utterly destroy a powerful ruling elite had taken place, the archaeological record should, at the very least, be in some disarray. This is what we find at the later site of Tula, where the Aztec invaded and burned the city. There the monuments have been thrown to the ground with such force that they have shattered. At San Lorenzo and La Venta, however, the destruction has the appearance of a systematic dismantling of the sites, rather than of a violent overthrow.

At both these sites the above-ground monuments have been defaced by slashing, grinding, slotting, pitting, and so forth. They were then carried out of the ceremonial centers and taken to the summits of nearby hills, where they were carefully aligned and buried. That an invading force, or even an internal uprising, would have left the mutilated remains in such a

carefully disposed order is unlikely: it is not in the nature of angry invading armies or civil war insurgents to treat the remains of their enemies with this degree of respect.

An option that remains open is that the sites were ritually destroyed. In later Mesoamerican cultures the closing of 52-year cycles was a period when ritual renewal was essential but uncertain. It is possible that the Olmec held similar beliefs, and if so the dismantling of the cities may have occurred because the ritual cycle had not been successfully renewed.

In this case, the mutilation of monuments and their careful removal would indicate a ritual removal of power from the centers. Their subsequent burial could also be significant. Buried monuments were not touched (*see pages 28–29*) and may have related to the Underworld. Burial of monuments may therefore have been a way of condemning them to the Land of Dead and of ritually disempowering them.

CHAPTER TWO

OLMEC INTERREGNUM

Sharing systems and decline with the "mother culture"

The reasons for the collapse of the great Olmec centers are only poorly understood, yet there is sufficient evidence for archaeologists and other scholars to present considered theories. Immediately after their collapse, however, the entire Mesoamerican region was thrown into turmoil; in many places there was an apparent rapid decline in artistic activity and cultural achievement.

The few centers that retained an Olmec culture, such as Izapa and Tres Zapotes, did so only in an altered and, in some senses, diluted form. Other cities, such as Tlatilco, were far from the Olmec heartland, and although exhibited some Olmec features, were also influenced by other cultural expressions.

Yet a number of features remained common throughout Mesoamerica and for which the Olmec had set a precedent. Some of these, including societies that were based on ranked hierarchies, might have been independent developments; but many factors point to the fact that they originated with the Olmec. That the ruling hierarchies combined the functions of both secular and religious leaders and were based in centers of power that served secular and ritual purposes might be coincidence. That the symbol of this power was almost always the jaguar argues against independent development or chance similarities.

The presence of many shared traits has led some archaeologists to label the Olmec as the "mother culture" of all later Mesoamerican groups. There are marked differences in later developments, particularly between the lowland cultures and those of the plateau, but the

similarities in many aspects of social organization and ritual practice are so strong that it is almost certain they share common heritage.

Lowland versus plateau life

The differences must nevertheless be considered. Most archaeologists agree that the lowland cultures of the Maya were definitely influenced by the Olmec. The arguments are only over the extent of influence. Some argue that the Maya are the direct linear descendants of the Olmec, others that the Maya developed out of rural populations that had previously been under Olmec control but that were not themselves Olmec. Neither hypothesis can be decided with any certainty, yet it is apparent that the Olmec system of many small ceremonial centers serving scattered rural populations was adopted by the Maya.

Developments on the plateau were different. Although the same hierarchical systems and

○ Colima

Map Key

Pre-Classic Western Mexican civilization 300 BC–AD 300

Teotihuacán AD 1–700

Zapotec AD 1–700

Classic Gulf Coast civilization AD 1–700

Maya AD 300–800

Cultural influences

 Teotihuacán

 Zapotec

Veracruz

PACIFIC OCEAN

2000 BC Date the Proto-Mayan language may first have been spoken

600 BC Monte Albán's first buildings are constructed

550 BC In Persia, Cyrus the Great founds the Persian Empire

500 BC The Zapotec occupy San Jose Mogote till this date

400 BC Decline of Olmec culture

250 BC Monte Albán is the largest civilization in the Valley of Oaxaca

50 BC Cerros begins to develop from a village into a city

100 BC End of Olmec culture

40

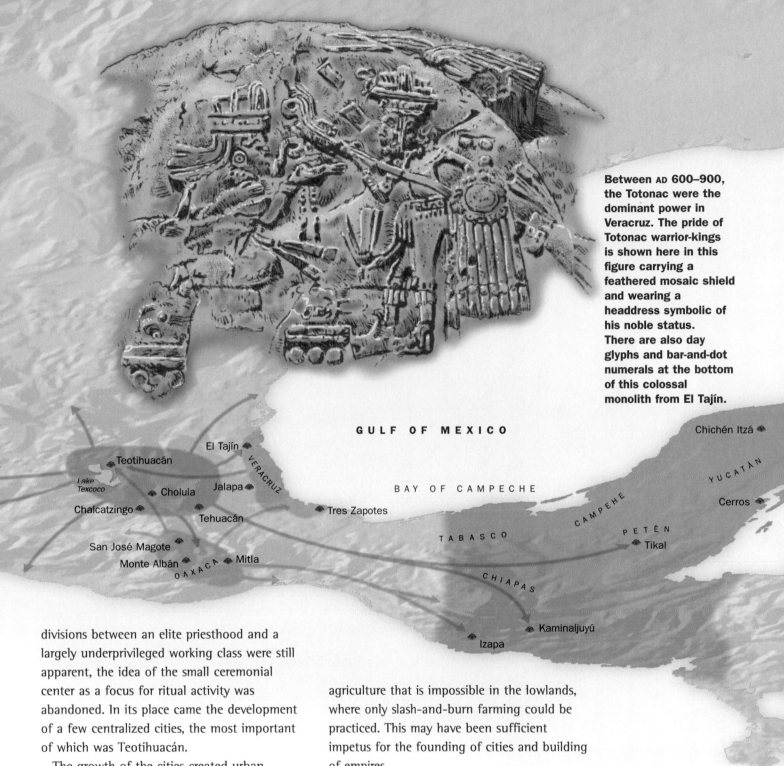

Between AD 600–900, the Totonac were the dominant power in Veracruz. The pride of Totonac warrior-kings is shown here in this figure carrying a feathered mosaic shield and wearing a headdress symbolic of his noble status. There are also day glyphs and bar-and-dot numerals at the bottom of this colossal monolith from El Tajín.

GULF OF MEXICO

Chichén Itzá

El Tajín

Teotihuacán

Lake Texcoco

VERACRUZ

YUCATÁN

Cholula   Jalapa

BAY OF CAMPECHE

Cerros

Chalcatzingo

Tehuacán

Tres Zapotes

CAMPEHE

PETÉN

San José Magote

TABASCO

Tikal

Monte Albán   Mitla

OAXACA

CHIAPAS

Kaminaljuyú

Izapa

divisions between an elite priesthood and a largely underprivileged working class were still apparent, the idea of the small ceremonial center as a focus for ritual activity was abandoned. In its place came the development of a few centralized cities, the most important of which was Teotihuacán.

The growth of the cities created urban populations that were quite different from the rural farming communities of the lowlands, and also set the framework for the growth of empires. Both Teotihuacán and the later Aztec maintained their hierarchies through the subjugation of other cities.

Exactly why these different developments should have taken place and what part Olmec influence played is open to debate. However, the plateau provided possibilities for intensive

agriculture that is impossible in the lowlands, where only slash-and-burn farming could be practiced. This may have been sufficient impetus for the founding of cities and building of empires.

As Michael Coe, Professor Emeritus and Curator Emeritus of Anthropology at Peabody Museum, has argued, the Olmec may have carried out a form of commercial expansion that introduced Olmec cultural forms among many groups of once-varied origin. The fertility of the plateau may then have encouraged centralization, while in the lowlands there was a continuation of small-scale farming more akin to the Olmec subsistence methods.

HUASTEC LANGUAGE
Divergence of speech as chronology markers

The long hiatus between the end of the Olmec era and the start of the Mayan has raised many problems for archaeologists seeking to establish chronology for ancient Mesoamerica. Neo-Olmec sites such as Izapa, which was occupied well into the historic period, blend some aspects of Olmec and Mayan symbolism, but offer intriguing possibilities rather than conclusive evidence. While Izapa may have been a link, it may also have been an isolated instant of cultural blending rather than solid evidence.

Archaeologists have turned to other disciplines in an attempt to discover what happened in the 500 or so years between the collapse of Olmec culture and the first clearly recognizable indications of a distinct Mayan expression at the beginning of the Christian era. One of the most important has been linguistics.

Modern Maya is composed of three distinct language divisions: Yucatecan, Huastecan, and Southern Maya. While they are clearly related, differences between them can be as great as that between, for example, English and Dutch. Linguistic theory suggests that the greater the divergence, the longer the period of separation. It should therefore be possible to trace these changes and discover a prototypical language, or mother language, for them all, and in turn this could enable us to identify the historical sequences and pinpoint the geographical region from which they stemmed.

Using these theoretical guidelines, Huastecan was the first to diverge from proto-Maya, since it shares only a small vocabulary with the other Mayan languages. This in turn suggests that the origins of the Maya can be found in the western Guatemalan highlands, followed soon after by Huastec migrations to northern Veracruz and Tamaulipas in Mexico. There followed a further separation into Yucatecan, the most widely spoken of the Mayan languages today.

Maize culture

A more recently developed linguistic technique known as glottochronology, which considers basic vocabularies that are relatively immune to borrowing, places a time depth on the divergence of Huastecan from proto-Maya of 4,000 years before present. This suggests that proto-Maya was spoken in 2000 BC, well before the collapse of the Olmec cultures and the emergence of a distinct Mayan identity.

Linguistic analysis thus suggests that the early Maya, or proto-Maya, were not the descendants of the Olmec, as has been suggested, but an independent group who probably spoke a different language. They are nevertheless closely situated in geographic terms, so it would be reasonable to assume that there were early borrowings of cultural forms and ideas and, probably, also of artistic styles and symbolism. While much of this undoubtedly was from the Olmec to the Maya, some reverse flow of ideas was likely.

From the evidence of existing languages it has been possible to reconstruct a proto-language which has significance in determining cultural and historical sequences. By tracing this back through Huastecan an amazingly complex series of words relating to maize agriculture was found, and this has given rise to speculation that the origins of maize lie within the original Huastec regions in the Guatemalan highlands.

Although the evidence is far from conclusive, it increasingly suggests that we should be looking to the Olmec for the origins of many cultural traits but to the Huastecs for the development of the economic base through which stable societies could be ensured. Without a strong economy built on maize agriculture, the "high civilizations" of

Left: *Quetzalcoatl does not feature heavily in Olmec sites, but was an important god to the Huastec and later Mesoamerican civilizations. This suggests that the cult of Quetzalcoatl, which was to become so important to the Aztec people, was already established in the early proto-Mayan period.*

Mesoamerica would have been unable to sustain the large ceremonial centers through which art and architecture was achieved on a monumental scale.

Many factors still need to be resolved. The reconstruction of proto-languages is based on languages with known sequences, such as Indo-European, and these may not be entirely appropriate for Mesoamerican studies. Geographic factors, which in Mesoamerica include the elevation at which settlements were located, may have a profound influence, as may the isolation of groups in mountainous regions where archaic forms of speech can be retained even into the present.

Facing: *Life and death were closely linked in late Mesoamerican cultures. The origins of these beliefs date back to an earlier period, as shown in this Huastec carving of a man representing the duality of life and death.*

ZAPOTEC
Mass tombs of a military-minded culture

Below: *The Zapotec rain god, Cocijo, is shown on a funerary urn from Monte Albán dated to* AD *400–500.*

It is not known when the Zapotec entered the Valley of Oaxaca. Until 500 BC they occupied San José Mogote, site of the earliest known Zapotec hieroglyphs, and this remained as their major population center until they established a base at Monte Albán. It was not, however, until AD 100–300 that they realized the full extent of their territorial power.

The most striking aspect of Zapotec cities is their military appearance. Unlike Teotihuacán or the Mayan centers, which served primarily ceremonial functions, Zapotec cities were constructed with defense in mind. As they expanded and conquered neighboring towns, they rebuilt and fortified perimeter walls, and established military posts to guard the frontiers of their territory: Ayoquesco was a defensive hilltop site at the southern extreme of the Valley of Oaxaca, while the northern frontier was protected by a garrison stationed at Cerro de la Campana.

During their expansion, the Zapotec adopted many of the familiar Mesoamerican deities. Their principal deity appears to have been Cocijo, who is equivalent to Tlaloc, Rain God of Teotihuacán. Pauahtun, the Jaguar God, and Pitao Cozobu, the Maize God, were also important. In this respect the Zapotec fit readily into the familiar pattern of gradual assimilation and change that gives Mesoamerican cultures their relatively homogenous appearance.

They were, however, unique in the emphasis they placed on cults of the dead and in the honorific positions afforded to

ancestors. Although other Mesoamerican groups honored their dead, and in some cases even deified important rulers, they did not construct the mass of elaborate burial tombs that are found at Zapotec centers. Literally hundreds of burials have been found, and the most characteristic form of Zapotec art is the burial urn, examples of which have been recovered from the tombs.

Ancestral concerns

The Zapotec did not think of the ancestors as deities, but as intermediaries between the worlds of the living and the dead. Thus we do not find depictions of ancestor-deities, but instead the burial urns are carved in the form of living human faces. It is evident from a study of these carvings that they are intended as portraits of individuals, who presumably belonged to the ruling elites that comprised about four percent of the population of Zapotec cities. The tombs were considered as family property: They were used for successive burials over extended periods, and it is highly probable that all the burials in a single tomb complex were members of a single lineage. The link these ancestors had with ceremony is also apparent in the fact that many of the carvings are covered with or accompanied by ritual masks.

Recoveries from these tombs suggest that the early Zapotec were almost entirely concerned with representational portraiture; but as their power grew, new considerations came into play. Later carvings, while still representing individuals, placed greater emphasis on status and indicated the necessity the Zapotec felt to state noble origins and make evident the political ties they established between leading families of the nobility.

At the height of their power, the Zapotec

controlled all the major trade routes through the Valley of Oaxaca from their center at Monte Albán. Extensive trade led to the establishment of provincial centers. As these grew in power and influence, Monte Albán's hold over them weakened, and after AD 500 their power began to be replaced by that of the neighboring Mixtec.

Even so, a Zapotec presence was maintained throughout the valley, although this began to emphasize ancestral rights far more than military supremacy. At the time of the Spanish conquest, the High Priest occupied a far greater position among the Zapotec than he did among other Mesoamerican peoples. Today there are about 300,000 people of Zapotec descent living in or near Oaxaca.

Above: *This Zapotec urn, dating from c.AD 200–350, was recovered from a tomb at Monte Albán. We do not know who is depicted, although the urn is clearly a portrait of an important person in the city's ruling lineage. Her elaborate headdress, neck ornament, and ear spools are all symbols of noble birth.*

MONTE ALBÁN
Hieroglyphics at an early city

The hilltop city of Monte Albán, in the Valley of Oaxaca, was the principal Zapotec site. The first buildings here were constructed between 600 and 100 BC, although most of them are now buried beneath later platforms. By 250 BC the population at Monte Albán had expanded to 15–20,000, making it the major regional civilization of the area.

The site had been artificially leveled to accommodate temples, ball courts, and palaces, as well as residential areas, surrounding a huge central plaza. Much of the residential area was built on terraces, which were cut into the rock, although there was also a large rural population of farmers. It is nevertheless true to say that Monte Albán was one of the first cities in Mesoamerica.

Among the most important buildings is the Mound of the Danzantes, a pyramid with walls that incorporate stone slabs carved with nude male reliefs in grotesque postures. Although it was formerly believed that these figures represented dancers, it is now known that they are sacrificial victims.

Several of these reliefs bear hieroglyphic dates, the oldest in Mesoamerica. This is the earliest writing in Mesoamerica and one can already determine the bar and dot numerals used by the later Maya, although the Zapotec texts have not yet been fully deciphered.

Unearthing burial goods

Zapotec culture was expansionist and the rulers at Monte Albán dominated several other towns during the early Classic period, until the site was abandoned by them c.AD 900. The majority of dates at the site appear to be associated with the names of towns conquered by the ruling elite at Monte Albán.

An unusual feature at the site is the vast number of royal tombs. During excavations in the 1930s, Alfonso Caso discovered 170 underground tombs, some of them very elaborate and painted with extensive mosaics. In one tomb alone over 500 objects of gold, silver, turquoise, pearl, onyx, marble, and jade have been recovered.

Numerous terracotta urns depicting various deities have also been found. Among them is the Jaguar, God of the Underworld, reflecting Olmec influence at the site. Other deities include the Rain God (*see previous pages*) and the Maize God, who were important to the Maya, as well as the Zapotec. Even after it was abandoned by the Zapotec, Monte Albán continued to be used throughout the post-Classic period as a focus for the royal burials of Mixtec kings, although there is no Mixtec settlement at the site.

The royal tombs are a major feature of late Monte Albán, but were begun earlier and are associated with the introduction of ancestor worship linked to kingly lineages. While many of the names are difficult to decipher, the family of Lord One Tiger appears to have been particularly prominent.

Right: *Monte Albán was the center of Zapotec civilization and supported a large resident population, but it also served as the focus for the religious devotions of a huge rural area. This view shows one of the terraced platforms that supported the temples.*

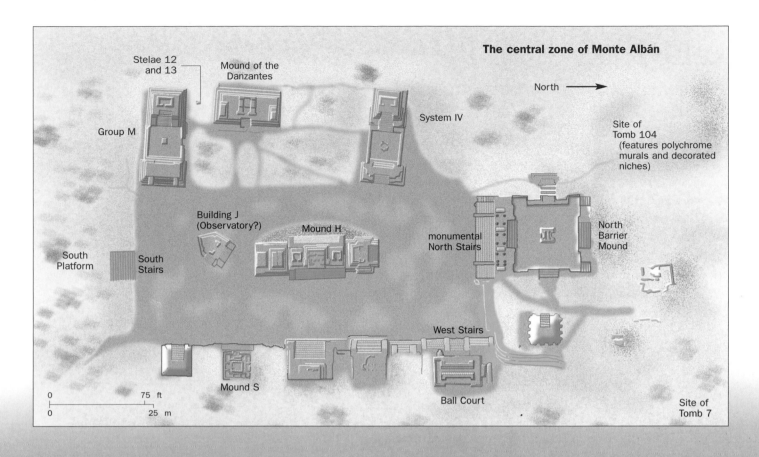

The central zone of Monte Albán

Stelae 12 and 13

Mound of the Danzantes

Group M

System IV

North →

Site of Tomb 104 (features polychrome murals and decorated niches)

Building J (Observatory?)

Mound H

monumental North Stairs

North Barrier Mound

South Platform

South Stairs

West Stairs

0   75 ft
0   25 m

Mound S

Ball Court

Site of Tomb 7

CERROS
A microcosm of Mesoamerican town development

Right: *The exposed position of Cerros overlooking Chetumal Bay means that erosion is a serious problem, and most of the carvings have been covered with plaster to offer some protection.*

The Pre-Classic town of Cerros is located at the mouth of the New River in eastern Yucatán, overlooking Chetumal Bay. The people living here were primarily seafarers and traders, who had established contact with peoples living in distant villages and towns. Although originally only a small village of clustered huts, Cerros is important archaeologically since it is possible to trace the transition from village community to city status, which at Cerros took place within about one hundred years.

This program of "urban renewal" began in about 50 BC. There is evidence that numerous animal sacrifices took place in the old village at this time. The vessels in which a great feast had been served were smashed with rocks, and the fragments, together with shattered pieces of precious jade jewelry, were scattered over the household foundations. The village was then abandoned and its homes rebuilt in a huge semi-circle surrounding the old location.

The old village became the focus of intense ritual activity. The ground was covered with layers of fine white earth, and strewn with broken pieces of pottery, more jade, and fruit tree blossom. The entire surface was then covered with flat slabs of rock to provide a foundation for a temple. Most of the building materials were obtained locally, and there are deep pits at Cerros from which limestone was dug.

Master craftsmen and masons from other districts supervised the building of the temple and the pyramid on which it was to be placed. Other masons carved four huge stone masks to flank the pyramid's staircase. When all was ready, the entire pyramid was covered with white limestone plaster and painted brilliant red. Details of the masks and other carvings that adorned the pyramid and temple were picked out in red, black, and yellow. The carvings and their glyph symbols related to the Jaguar Sun God.

Becoming divine
The village of Cerros had undergone transformation from a small trading port to the symbolic home of the Sun King, or *ahau*. The co-operation of the entire community was necessary for this process, during which the ruler of Cerros assumed semi-divine status. There is thus acknowledgement of his new status, performed as an act of community worship.

Several other buildings and plazas were

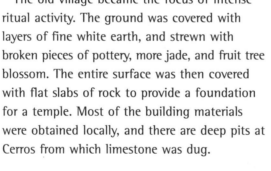

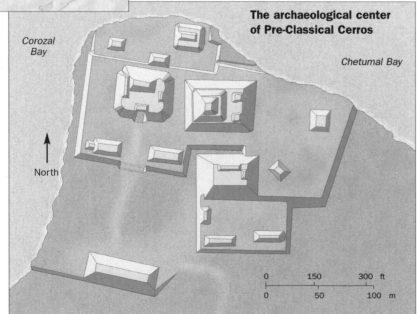

Corozal Bay

The archaeological center of Pre-Classical Cerros

Chetumal Bay

North

| 0 | | 150 | | 300 ft |
| 0 | 50 | | 100 | m |

erected at Cerros over the next 50 years. These included a vast palace complex, presumably the residence of the Cerros rulers, and a second pyramid, much larger than the first. Unfortunately, this pyramid is now badly damaged and little archaeological study has been made of it. Surveys suggest that it was built by the successor to the first king, and buried deep within its structure is a group of jade ornaments. These are the headbands and pectorals that stood as symbols of kingship and divinity, and the assumption is that the new ruler incorporated these symbols of his predecessor within the new pyramid to establish himself in the royal lineage.

The building program at Cerros was continued under a third ruler, who extended the center to include a complex of buildings and temple platforms surrounding a ball court where ritual games were staged. Much of the symbolism here relates to the Twin Heroes who, in Mayan myth, overcame the terrors of the Underworld to establish themselves as the Sun and Moon. A chamber was built deep within the acropolis, intended to be the last resting place of the third ruler but never occupied.

What happened to the third ruler is unknown, and his heir seems to have been a much weaker personality. Although he commissioned some new buildings, they were poorly executed. No offerings were made at their dedication, and shortly after their completion fires were banked against the masks and ornaments and the symbols of the ancestors were defaced and destroyed. Cerros was abandoned, and the people apparently returned to their former lives as fishermen and traders.

MITLA
Occasional capital of the Zapotec

The earliest archaeological finds at the town of Mitla date to c.500 BC, when it existed as a small farming community. By the start of the Christian era it had expanded considerably – more than 0.6 miles along both banks of the river that bisects the site – and had a ceremonial center covering approximately 0.8 square miles. Today it is incorporated within the largely Zapotec-speaking modern town that bears the same name, within the Valley of Oaxaca in southern Mexico. In the Late Post-Classic period it was the second most important town of the region.

Mitla's history is closely tied with that of its more powerful neighbor, Monte Albán. In fact, when Monte Albán asserted itself as the regional capital of the Zapotec, the occupied areas of Mitla seem to have been reduced to reflect its subsidiary status. Unlike Monte Albán, however, Mitla was never abandoned, and after the abandonment of Monte Albán the mixed Mixtec-Zapotec cultures may have restored Mitla as their capital and the focal point of their rituals.

Architecturally, Mitla is built in Mixtec-Puebla style, characterized by geometric fretwork patterns and underground cruciform tombs. Yet despite the Mixtec-Puebla identification, the construction of buildings is unique to Mitla and the neighboring Zapotec towns of Yagul and Zaachila. They consist of low buildings that flank open courtyards and had roofs that were carried on beams supported by stone columns.

The fretwork patterns on the façades are of raised stone mosaic. The most impressive example of this is on the Hall of the Columns, where 150 panels bearing geometric patterns are present on both interior and exterior walls. These decorations consist of eight basic forms arranged in horizontal bands, giving the architecture at Mitla a regular repeating pattern rarely seen at other sites.

Zapotec or Mixtec?

While it is probable that Mitla was always occupied by Zapotecan-speaking groups, the architectural features are derived from the Mixtec and Mixtec polychrome vessels were found in tombs. Some badly damaged frescoes contained within the buildings of the church group are executed in the realistic and narrative style familiar from Mixtec painted books.

The influences and occupations at Mitla are confusing, and it is unclear whether Mitla should be classed as a Zapotec or a Mixtec center, or even whether it had a mixed Zapotec-Mixtec population. The latter is certainly a possibility, since although the Mixtec and Zapotec were bitter rivals over much of the Valley of Oaxaca, they may have formed alliances. Shortly before the Spanish conquest of Mexico they united against the Aztec, and this may have been the case at Mitla too during an earlier period. It is also probable that Mixtec dominance of the Zapotec was achieved in part through strategic marriages that strengthened

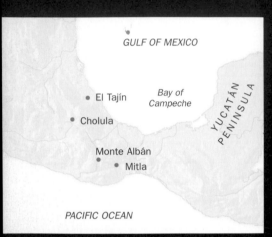

GULF OF MEXICO

El Tajín

Bay of Campeche

Cholula

YUCATÁN PENINSULA

Monte Albán

Mitla

PACIFIC OCEAN

Below: *Stone mosaics in geometrical fretwork patterns are characteristic of the decoration found on buildings at Mitla. The example shown here is from a wall in the Hall of Columns.*

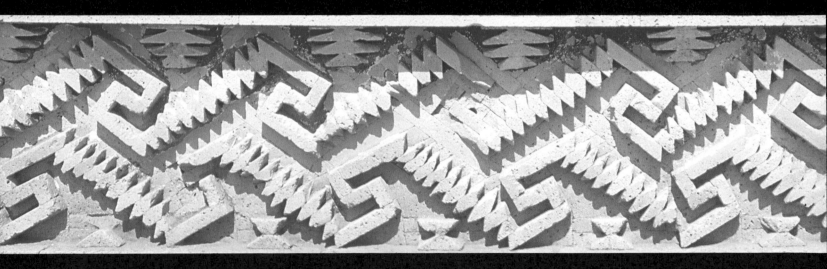

political ties, and if this were so at Mitla, Mixtec lords would have married women from leading Zapotec families who continued to reside there.

Legend only serves to compound the problem. The Zapotec claim that Mitla is the site of a secret underground chamber in which the most important Zapotec rulers and nobles have been interred — it seems unlikely that they would have chosen a place dominated by their rivals for this purpose. This secret chamber has not been found during archaeological excavations and surveys, and the tombs that

have been explored often contained artifacts of Mixtec origin. However, these negative findings cannot be considered as conclusive proof that no such chamber exists.

Above: *Interior view of the Hall of Columns. Large open courtyards with roofs supported by rows of stone columns are unique to Mitla and the neighboring towns of Yagul and Zaachila.*

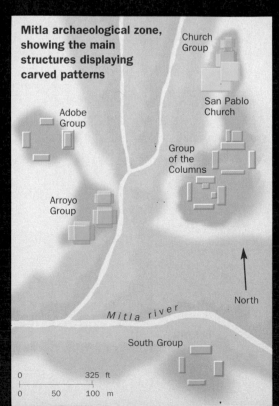

Mitla archaeological zone, showing the main structures displaying carved patterns

Church Group

San Pablo Church

Adobe Group

Group of the Columns

Arroyo Group

North

Mitla river

South Group

0   325 ft

0   50   100 m

THE MIXTEC
People of the Cloud Country

Among the finest achievements of the Mixtec was their skill in working gold to make intricate jewelry. Jewelry was worn by both sexes, and the quality of finish reflected the wealth and status of the individual. Examples of Mixtec gold pendants (top) and a gold pectoral, or chest ornament (below).

The Mixteca is a mountainous region in the western portion of the southern Mexico state of Oaxaca. It is a rugged, inhospitable but beautiful land, and the character of the people who lived here tends to reflect the nature of the environment they occupied.

Their main settlements were built on the tops of defensive ridges and the hieroglyphs for their place names usually include the glyph for "mountain." They called themselves Mixtec, the People of the Cloud Country. In addition to their warlike and aggressive responses to neighboring peoples, they are renowned for some of the most exquisite gold filigree jewelry to be made anywhere in Mesoamerica.

The late history of the Mixtecs is well known from eight screenfold books they wrote on deerskins, which record genealogical and historical information on the dynasties that controlled the Mixteca regions, but their early history is far from clear. No major archaeological work has been done, although it is known that Mixtec occupancy here is ancient.

By AD 750 the Mixtec had begun to expand into the Valley of Oaxaca and were in conflict with the Zapotec, whom they eventually conquered in the 14th century. The Zapotecs abandoned their principal city of Monte Albán by about AD 900 due to Mixtec aggression. Mixtec war progress and conquest is admirably reflected in the career of their most famous warrior-chief, Eight Deer Ocelot Claw, who is said to have been responsible for the downfall of some 75 other kingdoms in Oaxaca, including Monte Albán and Mitla.

Eight Deer Ocelot Claw was also the spiritual guardian of Lord Nine Ollins, a personification of the sun. A boy was chosen to represent Lord Nine Ollins in this earthly life; on his 52nd birthday, he was voluntarily sacrificed during the dedication of a *temazcalli* — a sweat house used for curing. His body was dressed as an Ocelot Chief and cremated.

Painting history

When the ashes were brought to Eight Deer, he adorned them with a feather headdress and a turquoise mask, and a quail — the symbol of sunrise — was sacrificed. Eight Deer himself was captured and sacrificed by his rivals at the age of 52, although this age (being the end of a *katun*, or ritual cycle) may have been a ritual one, rather than his real age. It is significant, of course, that Lord Nine Ollins was also sacrificed aged 52.

After the Zapotec abandonment of Monte Albán, the Mixtec used the

center as a royal cemetery. Tombs of Mixtec nobles containing over 500 items of great value have been found there. Later they moved into the Mexican state of Pueblo, where they built Cholula and created a new art style known as Mixtec-Puebla. Later still they were sometime allies with their old enemies the Zapotec in resisting Aztec domination.

Among the most notable artistic achievements of the Mixtec are intricate turquoise mosaics and elaborately worked gold filigree jewelry, although some scholars argue that these pieces should be judged on their technical wizardry rather than on esthetic achievement. It would be a mistake, however, to try to make value judgments on the basis of Euroamerican concepts of esthetics, since they are far removed from what the Mesoamerican peoples considered to be important in their artworks.

They also developed their own style of pictographic communication and sets of name glyphs. These are quite different from the Mayan hieroglyphs and were reliant on painting rather than carving. The Mixtec system was later adopted and adapted by the Aztec in the records they kept in their painted day books and ritual calendars.

Above: *A necklace made from sheet gold that has been hammered and beaten into shape.*

Left: *The skill of Mixtec goldsmiths is readily apparent in this finely worked example.*

CHOLULA
Scant investigation of a holy city

GULF OF MEXICO
- El Tajín
- Cholula
Monte Albán
- Mitla
PACIFIC OCEAN
YUCATÁN

Below: *Cholula appears to have always served as a place of pilgrimage, but when the Spanish arrived they destroyed many of the ancient temples and erected their own churches. The church of Nuestra Señora de los Remedios, shown here, sits atop the great pyramid where a Mixtec temple once stood. In the background is the volcano Popocatepetl, once believed to be the home of Tlaloc and other deities.*

Following the collapse of many of the Classic centers, bands of warlike tribes descended into the Valley of Oaxaca. Among them were the Mixtec, who may formerly have hired themselves out as mercenary warriors to the rulers of Monte Albán. They regarded the capital city as a holy center and later used it as a necropolis for their ruling lineages.

Although many of the new arrivals founded their own cities, they did, on occasion, occupy existing sites. One of the sites that was overthrown and occupied by invading tribes was Cholollan, now known as Cholula. Archaeological investigations at Cholula confirm the arrival of foreign conquerors in about the ninth century AD, when they founded a compact but strong military state that dominated many of its weaker neighbors.

One of the attractions of Cholula was that it had long been a place of holy pilgrimage. Its great pyramid, the largest in Mexico (although not the largest in Mesoamerica), had been built up, layer by layer, over many periods and by many cultures, until it stood nearly 200 feet high and covered an area of 25 acres.

It was perhaps because Cholula acted as a crossroad of cultures that it attracted the

Mixtec and other migrant groups, as well as the Toltec and Aztec. According to some studies, Cholula was even a colony of Teotihuacán during part of its varied history. Mixtec traditions tell us that Cholula contained over 400 temple precincts that drew worshippers from all over Mesoamerica, a fact that tends to be confirmed in reports written at the time of the Spanish Conquest. The great pyramid became a focus of Mixtec devotions.

Building new from the old
Curiously, it is Cholula's reputation as a place of pilgrimage that makes it one of the least known Mesoamerica sites for archaeology. It has been continuously occupied since the time of Teotihuacán (possibly earlier) until the present day, which has seriously hampered the extent of excavation that has been possible. Unlike abandoned sites that are buried deep in the jungle, where the archaeological problem is one of access, rather than limits on the excavations that can be done, in Cholula it is virtually impossible to investigate the ancient ruins without disrupting modern residential areas.

Archaeologists also face a problem that arises directly from Cholula's status as a place of

pilgrimage. As new arrivals came to Cholula they frequently used materials from existing buildings to erect new ones. Thus the buildings encompass a mix of styles and cultures that are rarely contemporary with one another. The layers of building styles from various dates discovered during investigations of the great pyramid are repeated throughout Cholula in the remains of its many ritual buildings.

When the Spanish came they, too, attempted to ensure the continuity of Cholula as a sacred city, albeit it one with a changed focus that reflected their Catholic faith. Hernán Cortés gave Cholula to his lieutenant, Pedro de Alvarado, who gave orders to pull down most of the temples that the Spanish found and to build churches on their foundations.

Today there are more than 300 Christian churches in Cholula, which replace the temples of the ancients and reflect this legacy of a Spanish past. In this sense, the architectural heritage of Cholula, which remains as a place of pilgrimage to the present day, is unique in Mexico. Even the great pyramid, now reduced to little more than a gigantic but shapeless mountain of earth and rubble, has a church perched on its summit.

Above: *This polychrome ceramic vessel dates to about AD 1200 and depicts the kneeling figure of the Mixtec Rain God.*

Left: *Among the most important documents recording the pre-Spanish period in Mesoamerica are Mixtec manuscript illustrations, or codices. The illustration here is from the Vienna Codex and depicts a Mixtec temple and temple priests.*

EL TAJÍN

Ceremonial and governmental center of unique artisans

Facing top: *Totonac ceramic figurine of an infant with raised arms, dating to about AD 700.*

Below: *This statue from El Tajín represents the deity Ouragon.*

El Tajín was the center for Gulf Coast civilization from AD 100 until it was destroyed by fire c.1100. Its principal ritual buildings and ball courts of this large site occupy an area of 150 acres, but there are numerous subsidiary mounds that extend this to encompass at least 2 square miles. Since much of the site has not been excavated, it is likely that future investigations will reveal its extent was even greater.

The preponderance of ritual buildings and ball courts suggests that El Tajín functioned primarily as a seat of government and a focus of ceremonial activity, rather than as a true city. It is located within an area of north-central Veracruz where there is extensive evidence of slash-and-burn agriculture, which suggests a large peasant population that looked to the nobles and warrior elites of El Tajín for physical protection and spiritual sustenance.

El Tajín was at the height of its power between 600 and 900 AD, when most of the major monuments were constructed, and it is evident that it was the dominant political force throughout eastern Mexico during this period. The art styles of its Totonac occupants influenced many other sites of the period, and it is clear that El Tajín enjoyed a status greater than the subsidiary centers.

The most characteristic – and most influential – aspects of El Tajín art are structural features. The use of niches, which at one time presumably contained images of deities, false arches, and columns supporting poured concrete roofs are typical of the site, as are interlaced scroll, fretwork, and key patterns.

The archaeological zone at El Tajín

North

Mound of the Building Columns

Tajín Chico

north Ball Court

Pyramid of the Niches

south Ball Court

GULF OF MEXICO

• El Tajín

YUCATÁN

Monte Albán
• Mitla

PACIFIC OCEAN

0   250   500 ft
0   100   200 m

Niche gods

The most impressive building at El Tajín is the Pyramid of the Niches, a stepped construction with four layers and an eastward-facing stairway. Probably the oldest significant building at El Tajín, each side contains niches 2 feet deep. This corresponds with the number of Day Gods in the Totonac year, and it is therefore likely that the niches contained representations of these deities, even though none remain today. This is supported in legends that have survived.

Other major buildings at El Tajín overlook the plaza of Tajín Chico, a complex of 18 buildings which have only been partially cleared. Among the most important structures in this complex is the Mound of the Building Columns, which is supported by six stacked columns of stone discs, an architectural feature which is unique to El Tajín. These columns are carved with relief images depicting priests, winged dancers, day signs, eagle warriors, and dot-and-bar numerals.

The Totonac occupants of El Tajín claimed to have built Teotihuacán, and were credited as such by the later Aztec. It may, however, be more accurate to claim that expatriate El Tajín artisans established a presence at Teotihuacán, from where they plied their craft. There is a temple platform at Teotihuacán close to the Avenue of the Dead predominated by polychrome murals with Veracruz scrollwork motifs, characteristic of El Tajín. El Tajín itself did not, however, appear to have come under Teotihuacáno influence. Whether this was because the sites were distant or El Tajín's political strength was able to resist the widespread dominance of Teotihuacán, or whether there is no evidence simply because so much of El Tajín is unexplored, is largely a matter of conjecture.

Below: *The Pyramid of the Niches is perhaps the most impressive building at El Tajín.*

THE BALL GAME

Rules, spoils, and rituals of ancient American sport

Above: *Panel relief showing a ball court scene from Juego de Pelot Sur at El Tajín.*

Right: *This ceramic sculpture of a ballplayer, made in Jaina (see page 100), shows him in one of the game's classic stances (other figurines have been found that exhibit a similar pose). He kneels on one leg to trap the ball on his hip, which is heavily padded to protect him against injury from the ball, which weighed several pounds.*

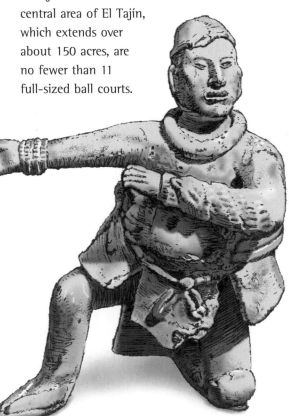

Although a ritual ball game was pan-Mesoamerican and in evidence from the early Olmec period through to the late Aztec — Teotihuacán is the only site where ball courts are absent — the Totonac ceremonial center of El Tajín is remarkable for its courts. Within the central area of El Tajín, which extends over about 150 acres, are no fewer than 11 full-sized ball courts.

Why there was such an emphasis on the ball game at El Tajín is not known; but a number of finely carved panels tell us much about the game and how it was played. Many of these are in the South Court, where two players in ritual costume are depicted cutting out the heart of a sacrificial victim under the watchful eye of a skeletal Death God.

Mythology tells us the game was a re-enactment of the epic battle between the Lords of the Underworld and the Hero Twins, so it was not staged purely as a display of athletic prowess, nor for its entertainment value. The alignments of ball courts suggest that they are cosmological diagrams. They also functioned as mythical entrances to the Underworld, while the game's rubber ball was said to represent the sun.

The ball courts are typically I-shaped structures. Sloping terraces with high perimeter walls set along the long sides of the court are common, and the walls frequently have a stone ring set into them at the center point. One of the objectives of the game was to drive the ball through the ring, winning the match and, according to late tradition, also the clothing and jewelry of the spectators.

The exact rules of the fast, furious, and dangerous game are poorly understood.

However, we do know that the players wore heavy protective costumes to guard themselves against the impact of the solid rubber balls. This clothing included a wide belt made from wood and leather, knee-pads, hip-pads, gloves, and sometimes a helmet. The players were not allowed to hold the ball during play — the most acclaimed shots being delivered from the hip.

Playing for liberty

Its link with myths of the Underworld and the heroic battles of the twins associate the game with human sacrifice, as shown in the panels at El Tajín. There has been a great deal of academic argument over who was the sacrificial victim. Some scholars claim that the captain of the winning side was killed to honor his great achievement in emulating the victory of the Hero Twins; but it is now generally accepted that it was the defeated captain who lost both the game and his life.

The significance of the ball game is indicated by carvings that often depict the players with the name glyphs for lord or noble. These, presumably, were the sons of the ruling elite and would also have been war captains in the more literal sense of the word. Thus there is the possibility that the opposing team were captured war captains, and that by victory in the ball game they may also have gained their freedom and avoided the sacrificial knives of the priests.

It is certain that the naming of players as nobles recognized the immense ritual importance that the ball game had in the lives of the Mesoamericans, as well as providing evidence that the ruling elites — who may themselves have claimed descent from gods or demi-gods — were charged with responsibility for maintaining both the secular and spiritual life of their community.

Above: *This reconstructed ball court at Yaqun is typical of many throughout the Mesoamerican area in scale and structure.*

Below: *During its later phases, the ball game was among the most important spectator events in Mesoamerica, and ball courts were expanded to accommodate large numbers of visitors. The example shown below is from Chichén Itzá.*

CHAPTER THREE

RISE OF THE MAYA

Garbled origins of a key Mesoamerican culture

Probably no other subject in the history of Mesoamerica has roused so much controversy, argument, and divided opinion than the question of where the Maya came from and how their civilization developed. The only fact to have received almost universal acceptance is that the great empire of Teotihuacán emerged in the north at the time as the parallel culture of the Maya evolved in southern regions.

For many years, Mayan culture, like that of Teotihuacán, was presented as a unified confederacy of city-states. In this scenario, Mayan merchants and traders carried ideas and art styles from one city to the next so that shared ideals and beliefs became part of Mayan consciousness. More accurate modern readings of Mayan hieroglyphs have shown this idea to be a fallacy, or at least a gross exaggeration of the supposedly peaceful nature of Mayan interactions.

Many of the carvings show the Maya were competitive rather than co-operative neighbors whose principal aim was often the capture and sacrifice of members of the neighboring ruling elites. Thus shared ideals may have been the result of forcible seizure of noble families' ritual privileges and property from townships and cities that were in opposition to each other.

It is also emerging that Mayan civilization had at least two clear forms of expression that were markedly different from one another. One was in the lowlands of the Petén-Yucatán peninsula, the other in the highlands of Chiapas and Guatemala. Lowland culture is marked by monumental public architecture and the high development of writing, whereas stone architecture and the recording of history had relatively little significance in the highland regions.

Olmec and Teotihuacán inspiration

The Maya did not develop in isolation from other Mesoamerican groups, but the lack of clear evidence of early connections has led to much speculation. Some scholars claim that they began as small, unsophisticated farming communities that coincidentally adopted traits from other Mesoamerican peoples, converting these to their own ends. Another view is that with the collapse of the Olmecs, small refugee Olmec groups found their way into the Maya

areas and introduced new traits. Yet others claim the Maya are the direct descendants of the Olmec and point to "neo-Olmec" sites such as Izapa as evidence of a transition from one culture to the other.

While Olmec influence is certainly apparent in early Mayan culture, the huge time gap between the demise of the Olmecs in 400 BC and the rise of the Maya at the beginning of the Christian era makes it impossible to trace any direct relationship.

Even more spectacular is the sudden efflorescence of Mayan culture between its incipient stages and the massive city-states they began building c.AD 200. Part of this can be traced back to sites such as Kaminaljuyú and El Mirador, as well as to ideas seeping south from Teotihuacán that affected not only the southern highlands,

but also the Mayan cities of the Petén such as Tikal and Uaxactún. Although many of the Teotihuacán-influenced buildings were later buried beneath Mayan constructions, the legacy of Teotihuacáno ideas and beliefs influenced Mayan thought and cosmology.

While it's now impossible to uncover all the intricacies of early Mayan history and provide an exact chronology for its development, it is possible to draw some conclusions from the archaeological records that remain available. One of the most significant of these is that the Maya drew their inspiration from very diverse sources, which included the Olmec and Teotihuacán. It can also be stated that there was

600 BC	36 AD	200	219	300–600	378	400	500
Tikal is established as a hilltop farming village	The first Mayan calendric inscriptions are made	The Maya begin building city-states	Yax Moch Xoc's reign at Tikal begins; the dynasty only ends with the city's demise	Teotihuacán is an influence on the Maya	Great Jaguar Paw of Tikal claims kingship of neighboring rival center Uaxactun	Copan is founded by Yax Kuk Mo (Green Quetzal Macaw)	In North America, the Anasazi construct cliff dwellings

never a unified Mayan state; there are too many regional variations in evidence, and it is expressly denied in carvings and in later records of Mayan mythology.

◆ **Izapa** important Pre-Classic site

● **TIKAL** dominant regional center

◆ **Nakum** important Classic site

• Xullún other Classic site

◆ **Naco** important Post-Classic site

• Lamanai other Post-Classic site

Isla Mujeres
Xlacah   Culuba
◆ **Dziblichaltún**
Tiho (Mérida)   ◆ **Izamal**
Y u c a t á n
◆ **Chichén Itzá**   San Gervasio
◆ **Mayapán**   ◆ **Cobá**
Oxkintok   Mani   Cozumel
◆ **Uxmal**   Chacchob   Tancah   Island
◆ **Kabah**
Jaina   ◆ **Sayil** ◆ **Labná**   Tulum
Xcalumkin   Chacmultún   Muyil
Kiuic
Xcocha
Xkichmook
Q u i n t a n a   R o o

◆ **Xtampak**
Dzibilnocac   • Huntichmool   Chacmool
◆ **Edzná**
Hochob

BAY OF CAMPECHE

C a m p e c h e
Y U C A T Á N
P E N I N S U L A

Pechal
Laguna de
Términos   Silvituk   ◆ **Becán** ◆ **Xpuhil**   Ichpaatun
Atazta Xicalango   Hormiguero   • Pasión del Cristo
                Uaacbal ◆ **Rio Bec**   Kohunlich Cerros
• Bellote   Candelaria Oxpemul   • La Muñeca   Nohmul
◆ **Comalcalco**   El Tigre   El Palmar   Cuello
              (Itzamkanac?) **CALAKMUL** ●   Colha
Grijalva   Jonuta   • Altamira Lamanai   Altun Ha
        Balancán   Ucal   • Balakbal
T a b a s c o Usumacinta   Moral   **El Mirador** ◆ Naachtún
• Tortuguero   Pomoná   Xullún ◆ **La Honradez**
        ◆ **PALENQUE** ● Chinikha   • Baking Pot
              El Porvenir P e t é n ◆ **Uaxactún**   Belize
                    El Peru **TIKAL** ● ◆ **Nakum** ◆ **Xunantunich**
        ◆ **Piedras Negras**   Uolantun   ◆ **Naranjo**
              El Cayo   **Tayasal**   Topoxte ◆ **Yaxhá**
◆ **Toniná**   La Mar   Flores Lake   Tzimin Kax
                          Petén Itzá (Mountain Cow)
◆ **Chiapa de Corzo** Lacanhá ◆ **Yaxchilán**   **Caracol** ◆ Pomona
              ◆ **Bonampak** Itzán   B e l i z e
        Poco Uinic Agua Escondida El Caribe • Ixkun
C h i a p a s   La Amelia Dos Pilas
              Altar of Sacrifices ◆ **Seibal** Ixtutz • Nim li punit
Grijalva   Aguateca ◆ **Machaquilá**   ◆ **Lubaatun**
                          Naj Tunich **GULF OF**
◆ **Chinkultic**   ◆ **Pusilha**   **HONDURAS**
        • Quen Santo   Cancuén
• Lagartero   Salinas de los
              Nueve Cerros
        • Chamá   Nito
                    Lake
                    Izabal Motagua   ◆ **Naco**
        ◆ **Nebaj**   **Quiriguá** ◆ H o n d u r a s
Zacaleu Negro   • Los Higos
G u a t e m a l a Motagua • El Paraiso
        ◆ **Izapa** • San Augustín **COPÁN** ●
PACIFIC **Utalán** ◆ **Mixco Viejo** Acasaguastlán
OCEAN
        Lake
        Atitlán ◆ **Iximché** ◆ **Kaminaljuyú**
◆ **Abaj Takalik**
        ◆ **Chukumuk**
              ◆ **Asunción Mita**
        • Tiquisate • Amatitlán
        • Pantaleon
              ◆ **Tazumal**
                    • Cerén
                    Lake
                    Ilopango

Lempa

C A R I B B E A N   S E A

A combined Calakmul-Caracol army overruns Tikal and kills its ruler, Wak Chan K'awiil

TIKAL
Steep pyramids of a competitive center

Above: *Tikal is characterized by its tall, steep-sided pyramids and temples that were mostly built at the height of its power in the eighth century. These rise to as high as 150 feet and tower above the forest canopy.*

Tikal lies in the very heart of the Petén rainforest, and began life c.600 BC as a village of farmers who settled on a hilltop between the swamps of the low-lying country. Their settlement was to grow over the next millennium to become one of the most impressive Mayan capitals.

At its greatest extent Tikal covered an area of 6.2 square miles, but also attracted a large urban population away from the ceremonial center. Its total population during its heyday is estimated to have been approximately 40,000. It is dominated by massive steep-sided pyramids, the steepest in Mesoamerica, their tops soaring high above the forest canopy, but has numerous smaller structures as well. So far

almost 3,000 structures have been discovered.

Much of the expansion and elaboration of the center had already begun by the first century BC, when large civic buildings and temple platforms were being erected and the excavation of vaulted tombs was well underway. The rich burials and wall paintings in these tombs point to a hierarchy of powerful rulers, but also give evidence of the sacrificial offerings and bloodletting that was part of Tikal's ritual practice.

Interestingly, the tombs also demonstrate the stability of Tikal's ruling families. Although not the founder of the city, a ruler named Yax Moch Xoc reigned between AD 219 and 238, and members of his dynasty continued to rule

buildings at Tikal was competition with a neighboring rival Mayan site, Uaxactún. The two centers are only about a day's journey apart, and rival kingships so close to one another provoked not only a series of wars but also a need for public architecture that would glorify the lineage's name. The aim of much of the fighting between Tikal and Uaxactún was to capture individuals of royal blood to offer as sacrificial victims.

This war came to an end when the Tikal king, Great Jaguar Paw, defeated Uaxactún. He is shown on a carved stela wearing his noble regalia and holding aloft a flint sacrificial knife. Kneeling before him with his wrists tied in a posture of submission is a bearded noble wearing regalia from Uaxactún.

Unlike former wars for captives, however, Great Jaguar Paw waged a war of conquest.

He finally overran and claimed the kingship of Uaxactún as well as that of Tikal on January 16, AD 378.

Below: *Competition between Tikal and the neighboring city of Uaxactún was severe, and ended only when Tikal defeated its rival in the fourth century. The ruins of Uaxactun, shown here, lie only 12¹/₂ miles northwest of Tikal.*

until the collapse of Tikal in the ninth century. This long succession of political and religious leaders dominated much of Tikal's history.

Gaining sacrifices

For many years it was believed that Tikal served only a political or ceremonial function. The precipitous pyramids are so steep that someone standing on the platform at the top cannot be seen from ground level. It is now thought the pyramids may represent sacred mountains rising through the cosmos, an interpretation that fits well with the lofty impression they give and the prestige associated with the name of Yax Moch Xoc and his successors.

Part of the reason for the elaboration of the

THE CONSOLIDATION OF POWER AT TIKAL

War and marriage to maintain supremacy

Below: *View of the Great Plaza and Temple I at Tikal. In addition to its function as a ritual focus for ceremonies, the North Acropolis was used as a burial ground for Tikal kings. Numerous underground tombs have been excavated here and these provide us with one of the most complete chronologies of Mesoamerican kings.*

Tikal is one of the most intensely investigated Mayan cities. Its North Acropolis reveals a complex sequence of constructions and, perhaps even more significantly, acted as a necropolis for Tikal's rulers. From excavation of tombs and translations of inscriptions at the site, it is possible to trace a clear succession of rulers extending over 800 years. The history of the Tikal kings chronicles the power struggles that typified many Mayan cities and provides insight into the machinations of the elite.

Tikal expanded from a farming village during the first century AD, and at that time was overshadowed by its mighty neighbor,

important of the Classic Mayan centers. Under the leadership of Chak Tok Ich'aak (Great Burning Claw), Tikal carried out long-distance trade with the Maya highlands to the south and with distant Mexico and the city of Teotihuacán. This expansion was not entirely peaceful – in one carving Chak Tok Ich'aak is depicted trampling a captured enemy noble to death.

He met his demise at the hands of Siyaj K'ak (Fire Born), a warlord from Teotihuacán who overthrew many cities of the Maya in the region and set Teotihuacáno rulers in place. Yax Nuun Ayiin (Curl Snout), the son of Spearthrower Owl – one of Siyaj K'ak's lieutenants – was set to rule Tikal, and during this period the dress of the

El Mirador. The relationship between them is unclear, although Tikal inscriptions on stelae from outlying settlements indicate that Tikal was independent and controlled an area of its own.

Tikal must have remained independent but secondary to El Mirador for many years, but by AD 300 it was the most progressive and

Tikal elite took on a Mexican appearance. There are indications, however, that Teotihuacáno power at Tikal was not achieved solely by military means, since Yax Nuun Ayiin's mother was probably a Tikal noblewoman married to Spearthrower Owl. Yax Nuun Ayiin was later married to a Tikal woman, thus ensuring the fusion of Tikal and Teotihuacán bloodlines.

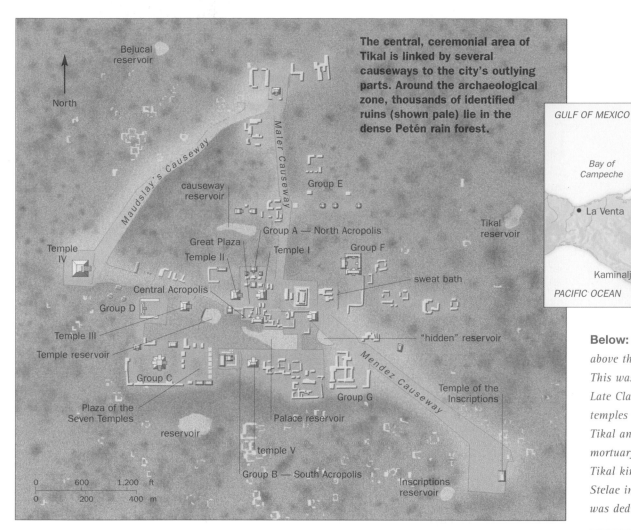

The central, ceremonial area of Tikal is linked by several causeways to the city's outlying parts. Around the archaeological zone, thousands of identified ruins (shown pale) lie in the dense Petén rain forest.

Bejucal reservoir

North

Maudslay's Causeway

Maler Causeway

causeway reservoir

Group E

Group A — North Acropolis

Great Plaza

Temple II

Temple I

Group F

Tikal reservoir

Temple IV

Central Acropolis

sweat bath

Group D

Temple III

"hidden" reservoir

Temple reservoir

Mendez Causeway

Group C

Temple of the Inscriptions

Plaza of the Seven Temples

Group G

Palace reservoir

reservoir

temple V

Inscriptions reservoir

Group B — South Acropolis

| 0 | 600 | 1,200 | ft |
| 0 | 200 | 400 | m |

GULF OF MEXICO

Bay of Campeche

YUCATÁN PENINSULA

La Venta

PETÉN

Tikal

Kaminaljuyú

PACIFIC OCEAN

Below: *Temple III rises above the Petén jungle. This was the last of the Late Classic pyramid temples to be erected at Tikal and served as a mortuary shrine for the Tikal king, Chitam. Stelae indicate that it was dedicated in 810.*

Losing favor

Tikal's fortunes shifted dramatically in AD 411 with the accession of Siyaj Chan (Sky Born), who asserted his matrilineal ancestry and is depicted in the elaborate costume of a Mayan noble of 150 years earlier. This was a conscious assertion of the antiquity of Mayan nobility and of orthodox kingship, and the next kings of Tikal, the son and grandson of Siyaj Chan, maintained the symbolism of matrilineal descent.

In an apparent attempt to reassert Mayan rule over the region, Tikal sent warlords to subjugate neighboring towns and began a campaign of political intrigue. This was complicated by the arrival from exile of Wak Chan K'awiil (Double Bird), who was to be Tikal's 21st ruler. In an aggressive campaign, he captured and sacrificed the ruler of distant Caracol in 556; a ruler he had installed on the throne only three years earlier. Caracol, however, had powerful friends at the city of Calakmul, and in 562 a combined Calakmul-Caracol army overran Tikal and captured and sacrificed Wak Chan K'awiil.

Little was heard from Tikal for the next 130 years. There are dates and names of rulers, few,

if any, from the original Tikal lineage, but no new monuments were erected; Tikal appears to have been in a state of decline. There was an attempted revival with a series of campaigns against Calakmul under the leadership of Nuun Ujol Chaak, culminating in his disastrous defeat in 679.

His son, Jasaw Chan K'awiil, reversed Tikal's fortunes, defeating Calakmul in pitched battle and restoring Tikal as a major military power. Interestingly, he did so not by reasserting Tikal's Mayan lineage, but by using the symbolism of Teotihuacán. His own son, Yik'in Chan, continued the campaign against Calakmul, defeating that city and its allies, Yaxa and Naranjo, and heralding a new building boom at Tikal that lasted until nearly 800.

The beginning of the ninth century, however, saw a sudden depopulation of the area that affected all Mayan cities. Tikal's rulers tried to maintain some semblance of their former authority, but the old lineages were broken. By the end of the century Tikal's glorious buildings and monuments were occupied only by a few wayfarers and squatters who erected thatched huts in the centers of its ceremonial plazas.

EL MIRADOR
Jungle site of the vast El Tigre and Danta pyramids

In 1926 explorations just south of the Mexican border in Guatemala discovered the jungle-covered ruins of El Mirador, but it was not until 1962 that controlled surveys and planning of the site revealed its extent. These surveys, by Ian Graham, indicated that El Mirador was one of the largest Mayan sites in existence.

On the evidence of a few pottery shards, Graham deduced that El Mirador belonged to the Late Pre-Classic period; a deduction that was immediately denounced by other scholars simply because no one believed that the early Mayans were capable of such massive constructions. Ian Graham has since been proved correct.

The extent of El Mirador has since been shown to be even greater than Graham had discovered during his surveys. Its central pyramid, which has been named El Tigre, is six times larger than the great pyramid at Tikal, previously the largest known construction from the Mayan world.

Excavations of El Tigre during the 1980s and 1990s found additional platforms and supporting structures at El Tigre that reveal it to be the largest known pyramid construction in the western hemisphere. A second pyramid at El Mirador, the Danta pyramid, has not yet been fully excavated, but early indications are that it may be even larger.

El Tigre forms the hub of a network of radiating causeways that extend into the *bajos*, or swamps, that surround El Mirador. One of these causeways extends 8 miles southeast to connect El Mirador with another Mayan center, Nak'be. How far the others go and where they lead is not

GULF OF MEXICO

Bay of
Campeche

YUCATÁN PENINSULA

• La Venta
Tikal •
• El Mirador

Kaminaljuyú •

PACIFIC OCEAN

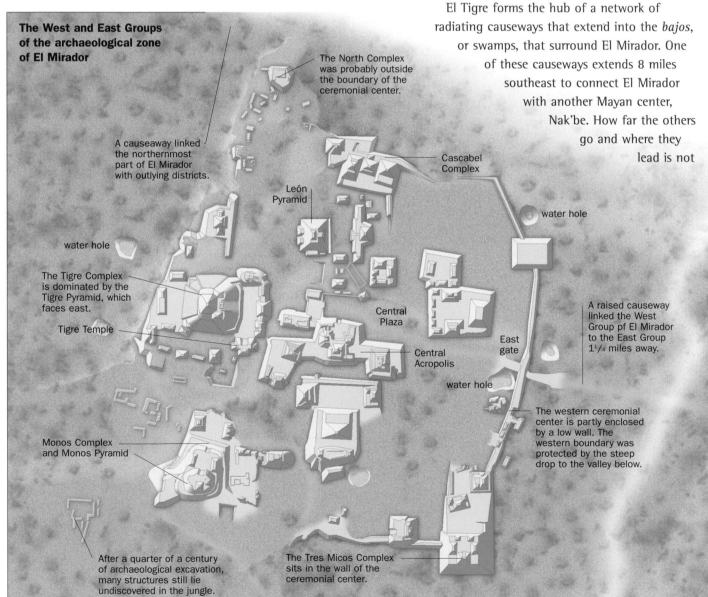

The West and East Groups of the archaeological zone of El Mirador

The North Complex was probably outside the boundary of the ceremonial center.

A causeaway linked the northernmost part of El Mirador with outlying districts.

Cascabel Complex

León Pyramid

water hole

water hole

The Tigre Complex is dominated by the Tigre Pyramid, which faces east.

Tigre Temple

Central Plaza

Central Acropolis

East gate

A raised causeway linked the West Group pf El Mirador to the East Group 1¹/₄ miles away.

water hole

The western ceremonial center is partly enclosed by a low wall. The western boundary was protected by the steep drop to the valley below.

Monos Complex and Monos Pyramid

After a quarter of a century of archaeological excavation, many structures still lie undiscovered in the jungle.

The Tres Micos Complex sits in the wall of the ceremonial center.

known; yet it is already obvious that El Mirador was of major importance and was perhaps the largest ceremonial center the Maya ever built.

Bird masks of Vucuub Caquix

The sheer size of the pyramids is staggering, and has great significance in our understanding of early Mayan culture in Guatemala. The labor force required was tremendous, and from this we can deduce that the people who occupied and built El Mirador had reached a level of social and political cohesion that was previously unknown.

Gigantic stucco masks found at El Mirador also tend to suggest that there was a considerable sharing of ritual beliefs during the early Mayan period. Many of these masks are of Vucuub Caquix, a bird deity, and are similar to others found at Nak'be, Tikal, Uaxactún, and elsewhere. Whether this represents an overall deity similar to the Jaguar of the Olmec is unknown, but Vucuub Caquix appear with great regularity and must, therefore, have been of major significance in early Mayan belief.

Investigations at El Mirador have revealed a great deal of information about how early Mayan societies were organized. The middle area of the site comprises the civic and ceremonial center. It is here that the pyramids and their supporting platforms are placed. Peripheral to these are a number of elongated mounds, usually in groups of four surrounding

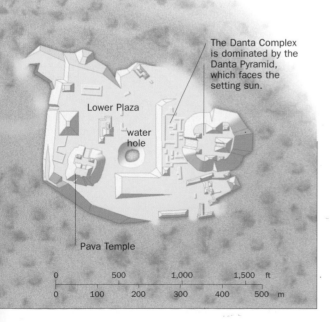

Lower Plaza

water hole

The Danta Complex is dominated by the Danta Pyramid, which faces the setting sun.

Pava Temple

| 0 | 500 | 1,000 | 1,500 | ft |
| 0 | 100 | 200 | 300 | 400 | 500 | m |

a small central plaza. Investigation of these mounds has shown that they were residential units, occupied during and after the major phases of construction at the site. The suggestion is that they were the homes of the elite families, occupied over several generations.

Further out are smaller residential units with fewer signs of long permanent residence. Again, home were raised on platforms, clear of the level of summer floods. These structures are, perhaps, where the families of lesser nobles lived, in buildings of less elaborate structure than those closer to the core of the site.

Numerous other residential units indicate only short occupancies, perhaps where workers lived temporarily during periods when building work was underway. The general impression at La Mirador, however, is one of gradual and relatively unplanned growth.

Above: *Giant stucco mask of the bird deity, Vucuub Caquix. Vucuub Caquix appears with great frequency at several sites in the Petén jungle, including El Mirador, Tikal, and Uaxactún, suggesting that a shared cult centered on this deity.*

KAMINALJUYÚ
Place of the Ancients

Kaminaljuyú, which translates as "Place of the Ancients," is a Late Pre-Classic center that links the cultures of the Izapa (or neo-Olmec) and the Maya of the Guatemalan highlands. The exact extent of Kaminaljuyú will probably never be known, since the site was almost completely destroyed by uncontrolled real estate expansion during the building of modern Guatemala City. Only a small area remains relatively intact, but surveys have shown that the civic-ceremonial center of the site once occupied an area in excess of 2 square miles.

At the height of its power, it contained at least 200 temple mound platforms that served as the bases for pole and thatch temple buildings erected on their summits and also functioned as burial tombs for the noble elite. Some estimates put the original number of mounds at several hundreds. Numerous other substantial sites in the Valley of Guatemala were almost certainly satellites of Kaminaljuyú and under its political and economic control and persuasion.

Although a reconstruction of this great ceremonial center is no longer possible, artifacts recovered at the site during rescue archaeology in the 1940s and 1960s give some indication of its power and influence. It is apparent that it served as a ritual, political, and economic focus for the entire region, and had established trade networks that extended into Central America and the Mexican plateau. Part of its influence was undoubtedly due to its advantageous position on the divide between the Atlantic and

GULF OF MEXICO
Bay of Campeche
YUCATÁN PENINSULA
La Venta
Tikal
PACIFIC OCEAN
Kaminaljuyú

Facing: *This stela from Kaminaljuyú shows a figure wearing an elaborate headdress in Pre-Classic style. Such headdresses were symbols of royal rank. They were carved and painted, often decorated with precious materials, and frequently bore plumes of the quetzal or other tropical birds.*

Grassy mounds rising from the midst of the tract housing sprawl to the east of Guatemala City mark the pyramids and other structures of the Mayan center of Kaminaljuyú, now an archaeological park.

Mound C-1-1
Mound B-I-4
Mound B-I-2
North
Mound C-I-6
Mongoy site (Mound B-I-1)
Mound C-II-3
Mound B-II-3
Mound C-II-4
Mound C-II-6
Mound C-II-8
Mound C-II-12
Mound C-II-14
Mound C-II-13

Pacific watersheds, from where it controlled the north-south trade routes.

Elaborate entombment

Burials uncovered during the digging of modern drainage ditches had almost all been robbed in antiquity, but what remains is sufficient to indicate that the Kaminaljuyú rulers enjoyed power and prestige greater than that from any previous kingdoms. Many of the temple mounds are elaborate tombs that have been cut down from the top in a series of stepped chambers. The deceased, painted red with cinnabar and decked in a profusion of ornaments of jade and other semi-precious materials, was lowered into the tomb on a wooden litter and a new clay floor made to seal the chamber. Much of the building at Kaminaljuyú was devoted to the erection of new stepped platforms on existing mounds to accommodate further burials.

Kaminaljuyú's strong trading position and its control of the richest obsidian quarries in the region, at a location known as El Chayan, drew the attention of Teotihuacán c. AD 400. Although most of the major building works had been completed before this date, a new ceremonial complex was erected at the site under Teotihuacán influence and shows the characteristic talud-tablero style of Teotihuacán city planners, where low sloping walls (taluds) supported carved and once-painted vertical panels (tableros). Also found at Kaminaljuyú and dating from this period were Teotihuacán-style pottery and other artifacts, much of it interred with the remains of deceased nobles.

The strong Teotihuacán influence has fueled speculation over whether these later inhabitants of Kaminaljuyú represented the older elite or a new influx of Teotihuacáno warrior-merchants had come to the city. If so, it is likely they would have married local noble women to legitimize their claims of control over Kaminaljuyú's former territories. Although there are stelae at the site that bear hieroglyphic inscriptions that could probably tell us the names and heritage of the ruling families from this period, unfortunately they have yet to be deciphered.

With the collapse of Teotihuacán and its loss of control over much of Mesoamerica, Kaminaljuyú also went into decline. No further buildings were erected, and although Kaminaljuyú was not destroyed by burning as at Teotihuacán, it was largely depopulated.

THE ORDERING OF SPACE AND TIME

The cycles of Mayan life

Below: *Terracotta incense burner of a priest wearing a costume associated with the Sun God. He stands on a turtle from which the chief god of the Underworld emerges.*

The Maya, like most Mesoamerican cultures, thought of time as a series of cyclical events, rather than a linear progression from the past, through the present, and into the future. For them, the world was governed by a cycle of creations and destructions, partially based on the cycles apparent in the agricultural year. At its simplest level, time passed from the sprouting of corn, through its maturity, harvest, and eventual replanting.

Similar cycles governed the passage of the day and the seasons of the year, as well as the life of a human being. But they also governed other events and longer timespans; thus every 52 years the world would stop and be renewed. Beyond this was a Great Cycle that governed the different periods of creation.

At the close of any cycle was a period of destruction: the sun "died" at the end of each day, corn was reaped after reaching maturity, and year's end was marked by extinguishing all the household fires. At the end of the Great Cycle the entire period of creation was destroyed, so that the next period might begin.

Each of these cycles had two parts. One was manifested in the human world, the other in the Underworld of Xibalba. Thus the sun's journey during the day was through the human world, whereas at night the sun journeyed through Xibalba and its place was taken by moon.

Again there is a parallel with the agricultural cycle. The farmer sends the maize seed into the Underworld via the hole he makes with his digging stick. The maize plant grows in the Underworld until it is resurrected as a young sprout by Chac, who brings the spring rains (*see pages 98–99*), so that the Upper World part of the cycle can be completed.

Hun Nal Yeh creates perpetual motion

Part of this concept of space and time is that everything is set in perpetual motion. Hun Nal Yeh (Resurrected Maize God) raised the Wakah Chah (World Tree) and set the stars in continuous movement around it. It is fitting that when Lord Pacal, the great seventh century leader of Palenque, died and descended into Xibalba, his face was covered with the green jade mask of the Maize God, so that he could later rise to the heavens via the World Tree.

This principle of continuous motion and interrelated cycles gave a sense of predictability and certainty to the Mayan world. The alternating movements of the sun and the moon — the celestial forms of the twin brothers,

Hunapu and Xbalanque, who defeated the Lords of the Underworld – are predictable and observable ones. Indeed, much of the activity of the Mayan priest-astrologers involved the observation of the movements of celestial bodies and determining their cyclic movements. It is, perhaps, in this search for predictable order that the priest-astrologers devoted much of their time attempting to plot the occurrence of future unusual events such as eclipses.

Order seems to have been the governing principle of Mayan concepts of space and time. Everything was fixed and had its place. If a predictable structure could be found, it was clear that even apparently random events had order and were under control. Even Xibalba had order and structure, although it was the reverse of that found in the real world.

The origins of these ideological concepts lie in the distant past, among the farmers and gatherers to whom the ability to predict when a particular plant or berry would be in season was paramount to their survival. Certain things in their world, such as the passage of the sun during the day or the alternation of the seasons, provided the guidance and security they needed. The Mayan priest-astrologers took these simple elements and built a complex cosmology from

them in which the Upper and Lower World orders were reversed and in which the sun, moon, and other celestial bodies were deified.

Above: *Relief carving of the Mayan Sun God, dating from AD 500–800. The sun was an important deity for the Maya and was believed to travel through the sky during the day before making a similar journey through the Underworld at night.*

Left: *Design on a Mayan vase. The painting shows the Maize God being born from a seed. Below him is a band containing water imagery, an allusion to the Underworld, while the upper band gives the name of the vase's maker or owner.*

AWARENESS OF MATHEMATICS
The underestimated system of Mayan traders

The elite Mayan priesthood used numerical symbols to record their observations of the movements of stars and planets as part of their divinatory activities. A similarly elite group of carvers and scribes also used number glyphs to document important events, such as the accession of kings or the dedication dates of major monuments and pyramids.

These systems frequently used anthropomorphic-deity glyphs where the date was represented by a symbol indicating one of the 13 deities of the Upper World. In doing this, the priests and scribes associated specific dates with those supernatural beings that controlled human destiny. By means of a complicated calendar involving cycles of 260 and 365 days, dates could be correlated with the cycles of time marked by the movements of the sun, moon, and the planet Venus.

Most studies focus on the use of complex mathematics by these elite groups, simply because the dates enable us to better understand important events in Mayan history or point to significant aspects of ritual belief. What is often left uncommented on, however, is the use of mathematics by the non-elite, especially by merchants, on a day-to-day basis. The merchants, using cacao beans as counters, were skilled practical mathematicians; yet the simplicity of their method has led many scholars to conclude that their skills were unremarkable.

A closer look at the mathematical system used by merchants nevertheless places it as one of the greatest achievements of the Maya. The system used only three symbols — the shell, dot, and bar — to represent the values zero, one, and five respectively. This was simpler and more efficient than the contemporary Roman system in use in the Old World, in which there is no "zero" and seven symbols (I, V, X, L, C, D, M), and the Arabic system adopted in Europe in the 13th century (zero plus nine symbols).

Positional numeration

Complex numbers were calculated according to the positions in which the shells, dots, and bars were placed — a principle known as positional numeration. An example of positional numeration in the Arabic system is where numbers with a value of one or greater are

Below: The counting system of the Maya, and (right) a simple addition example to show how it worked.

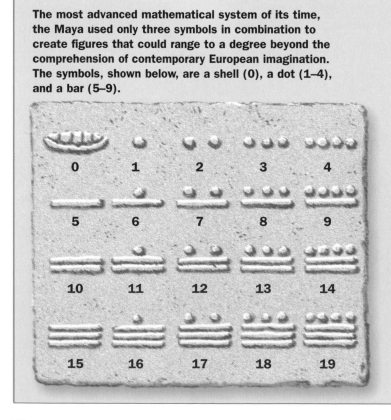

The most advanced mathematical system of its time, the Maya used only three symbols in combination to create figures that could range to a degree beyond the comprehension of contemporary European imagination. The symbols, shown below, are a shell (0), a dot (1–4), and a bar (5–9).

0	1	2	3	4
5	6	7	8	9
10	11	12	13	14
15	16	17	18	19

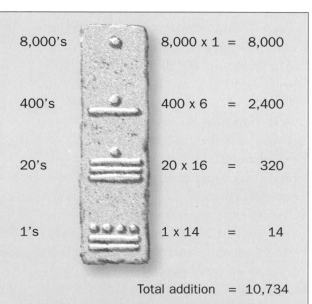

8,000's	8,000 x 1 =	8,000
400's	400 x 6 =	2,400
20's	20 x 16 =	320
1's	1 x 14 =	14
	Total addition =	10,734

Above is the figure 10,734, arranged in its vertical Mayan form. Each layer has a specific value, the top layer being 8000, the bottom layer being 1. Therefore, a single dot in the 8,000 layer equals 8,000, while a single dot over three bars (numeral 16 in the table on the left) in the 20 layer equals 320.

Left: *Mayan priests recorded events using a complex system of glyphs that represented the Day Gods, as shown here in this wooden lintel carving from Temple IV at Tikal.*

placed to the left of the decimal point; numbers less than one are placed to the right. The Maya counted from top to bottom rather than left to right and used a base of 20 rather than 10, but the principle is similar.

What is remarkable about the Mayan system is that their use of zero and positional numeration are the earliest known instances of these concepts. In other words, Mayan day-to-day mathematics used the most advanced and sophisticated system known anywhere in the world and share the same principles that govern modern mathematics. Its efficiency was a direct result of its simplicity, rather than simplicity

being an indication that it was undeveloped. When we consider that this system was already in place at the neo-Olmec/Mayan site of Tres Zapotes in AD 31 (*see pages 30–31*) the achievement seems even more astonishing.

The use of mathematics by the non-elite merchants and traders suggests that this method of counting was also understood by their customers. The common misconception that the majority of the population were ignorant peasant farmers must therefore be revised. While they may have been both peasants and farmers, they were probably educated ones.

THE MAYAN CALENDAR SYSTEM
Marking time and recording history

Below: *One of the most important positions in Mayan society was that of the scribe, who recorded events on bark paper books, or codices.*

The Maya developed complex writing and calendrical systems unique in the ancient New World. They were able to express every subtlety and nuance in their language and record time, from the smallest instant to depths of inconceivable antiquity.

Most Mayan writing and calendrics were not, however, concerned with the mundane, but instead marked moments of importance in the histories of the nobility and the lives of deities. The significance attached to this system is reflected in the fact that there was a special caste of scribes, known as *ah dzib*. Their patron deity was Itzamna, the Creator God, who was assisted by the monkey gods, who were themselves the half-brothers of the Twin Heroes who defeated the Lords of Xibalba, the Mayan Underworld.

Much Mayan writing is a record of the births and deaths, accessions, defeats, and triumphs of the ruling dynasties, and as such it acquired sacred meaning as a connection with the ancestral world through which these lineages were legitimized. At the same time, these records created social cohesion by ranking leading families according to their closeness to the original founding ancestor.

Equal in importance to the scribes was a class of priests, whose astronomical observations were surprisingly accurate. Their calculation of the synodic period of Venus, for instance, was 584 days, compared with the modern result of 583.92.

Living by the ritual calendar

The priests were not interested in simply marking time, however. Each date in the Mayan calendar had sacred significance and contained portents of success or failure. Indeed, many of the Mayan conquests were carried out on especially auspicious days, when the assistance of particularly powerful deities could be depended upon.

The Mayan priests relied on two distinct calendar notations. There was a year of 365

days that governed the agricultural year, but in addition there was a ritual calendar of 260 days. These, in turn, were considered within cycles of 52 years, enabling the Maya to accurately count back over several millennia.

Indeed, some of the dates go back to an impossibly remote past and refer to the divine ancestors of the ruling families, rather than actual events.

Even in the historical record there is evidence to suggest that singular events, such as the accession of a new ruler, were carefully timed to ensure that both the event and the person would receive help from the gods.

It is clear that much Mayan writing and the activities of the scribes and priests had astrological rather than astronomical functions. They had nevertheless developed a true science in their observations and records of the planets and the cycles of the sun and moon, including the ability to predict lunar eclipses. That these observations were tied to the actions of literally hundreds of gods who interacted in complex ways serves to highlight rather than diminish the achievements of the Mayan scribes and priests.

Left: *Large sculpture of the head of Itzamna, the Creator God, which was found at the ruins of Copán. Itzamna was the patron deity of scribes.*

Left: *Date glyphs carved on a fallen stela from the Mayan ruins of Yaxchilán.*

XIBALBA
Twin Heroes in the Mayan Underworld

Below: *Xibalba, the Place of the Dead, was the frightening abode of evil deities and monstrous demons. It was tremendously important, since the souls of the deceased were tested there before they could be reborn. Reminders of Xibalba are present at almost all Mayan sites, as in this skull carving from a wall at Chichén Itzá.*

The Mayan Underworld was a fearful place, peopled by demons and the death gods. The principal lords of Hun Came and Vucub Came (One Death and Seven Death) presided over Xibalba, a realm of monstrous beings who controlled disease and pestilence.

The Twin Heroes, Xbalanque and Hunapu, were destined to confront and defeat One Death and Seven Death when they were challenged by the death gods, who had been disturbed by the noise of the twins' ball-playing. Although their mother tried to persuade them not to go, they ignored her and descended from the ball court – which although on Earth is also the entrance to

Xibalba – to meet the challenge.

They crossed rivers of pus and blood toward Xibalba, until they arrived at a crossroads where carved wooden images of the death gods were placed to fool unwary travelers. Hunapu, however, plucked a hair from his shin and created a mosquito from it, which sought and bit the real death gods. They cried out their names, thus Xbalanque and Hunapu could surprise them by addressing each one personally.

In Xibalba the twins are confronted by numerous trials in the House of Gloom, the House of Knives, the House of Cold, the House of the Jaguars, and the House of Fire. They survived these trials but when they were sent to

the House of Bats, Hunapu peeked out from the hollow stem of the blowgun in which he had been hiding and the killer bat, Camazotz, struck off his head.

Resurrection tricks

By a ruse, Xbalanque replaced Hunapu's head with a squash, which miraculously attached itself to the body so that he could hear and speak, and the twins presented themselves for the ball game challenge. Here the death gods threw out the real head in place of the ball, but Xbalanque recovered it and restored his brother.

Although they were victorious in the game, the death gods still planned to kill their enemies

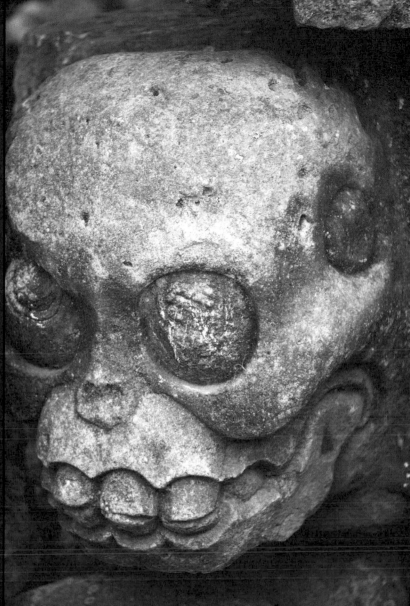

by building a huge fire into which the Twin Heroes were compelled to jump. They ground their charred bones to dust and cast it into the River of the Dead that runs through Xibalba. After three days the twins were restored again and returned to the death gods disguised as peasants capable of wonderful tricks.

The death gods told the disguised twins to sacrifice a dog and bring it back to life, which they duly did. They then sacrificed a man and, finally, Xbalanque decapitated Hunapu and tore out his heart before bringing him back to life.

Hun Came and Vucub Came were overjoyed at this display of miraculous power and begged the twins to kill and restore them. Instead, however, the Twin Heroes killed one of the death gods but did not restore him, at which the other Lords of Xibalba pleaded for mercy and promised that they would never harm people again.

Above: *Mayan skull walls are often composed from numerous blocks, each carrying its own individual carving. The skull block shown here was recovered from the site of Copán, Honduras.*

MAYAN TRADE CONTACTS

Jade, resin, salt, and cacao, by hand and boat

Mayan trade was established on the acquisition and exchange of goods and raw materials, and was determined, in large part, by the environmental diversity of the Mayan regions and their strategic position astride the trade routes connecting Mexico in the north with Central America in the south.

Within the Mayan area there was an exchange of goods between the highland and lowland regions. This was primarily of valued minerals from the highland region, particularly obsidian and jade, in return for products of the tropical forest, such as copal resin, which was widely used as a purifying incense in Mayan rituals. Much of this inland trade was carried on the backs of long lines of porters, since although the Maya were aware of the wheel – and, indeed, made wheeled toys – the terrain was unsuitable for wheeled vehicles and they lacked domesticated beasts of burden.

A larger part of the trade was along the coast and then inland using river systems, although

Below: Schematic drawing of Mayan social organization. At the top is the king, or ruler, apparent from his elaborate costume and regalia. Beneath him are priests, followed by members of the nobility. The fourth layer of the pyramid depicts Mayan officials, such as scribes; below them are traders and farmers.

salt. Yucatán was the largest salt producer in Mesoamerica, and the salt-evaporation pans at sites such as Dzemul date back to the pre-Classic period.

Salt and other luxury items, especially cacao from Santa Lucia and Yucatán sites, which was grown in the permanently damp bottom soil of dried-out *cenotes* (natural wells), supplemented a trade that was essentially of non-utilitarian items. Since these were also in demand well beyond the limits of the Mayan territories, much Mayan trade was long distance.

It has been argued that long-distance trade was fundamental to the development of Mayan city centers, such as El Mirador and Tikal, and that it was also through the influence of long-distance trading that elements of other cultures, such as that of Teotihuacán, entered the

even this was labor-intensive. Rivers required frequent portages of the dug-out canoes and their contents, and this necessitated a relatively large workforce capable of manhandling the heavy boats.

The coast was also important as a source of

Mayan area. It is believed, although not proven, that the pre-eminence of El Mirador was eclipsed when trade routes shifted slightly and brought Tikal into prominence.

Ek Chuah, patron of merchants

Long-distance trade was controlled by a small group of wealthy merchants who were under the protection of their own patron deity, Ek Chuah (Black God). The Mayans did not, however, have an organized class of merchants, such as the *pochteca* of the later Aztec (*see pages 164–165*), and most merchants were responsible only to the ruling elite of their own home town. It is likely that merchants were leading members of these elites and had responsibility not only for the commercial activities of the Mayan centers, but also for diplomatic contacts with neighboring cities and states.

While many traders would have been familiar with the great markets at centers outside the Mayan area, it is not clear whether regular markets were a feature of their own cities. There is no mention of them in the Spanish reports for the lowland Maya; although there is a reference to a "great and celebrated" market for highland Guatemala.

At Tikal, the most important of the Classic Mayan sites, there is an enclosed rectangular structure of multiple doorways that some archaeologists have identified as a marketplace; but this identification is speculative and such structures may have served other functions.

It is nevertheless likely that markets were organized to coincide with important days in the ritual calendar, when large numbers of pilgrims to locally important shrines might be expected to be in the city centers. Here local traders, rather than the elite long-distance merchants, might peddle their wares alongside craftsmen selling their goods and farmers bringing in their produce from the outlying *milpas*. Undoubtedly there were stalls selling tortillas and strolling musicians, acrobats, and other entertainers.

Below: *A Mayan mother nurses her child while waiting for tourist customers to buy the trinkets she sells along Lake Atitlán in Guatemala.*

CHAPTER FOUR

THE CLASSIC MAYA

Sudden end of a well-documented civilization

Facing: *Lintel 24, one of three panels from structure 23 at Yaxchilán, is considered one of the masterpieces of Mayan art. Shield Jaguar II, King of Yaxchilán, holds a flaming torch over his wife, the Lady K'ab'al Xook, as she performs a bloodletting ritual. This involves pulling a rope studded with sharp thorns through her tongue. Scrolls of blood can be seen around her mouth. The glyphs at the top of the lintel give the date of the ritual as AD 709. Other glyphs identify Yaxchilán and the name of Lady K'ab'al Xook.*

Northern influence over the Maya ended suddenly with the retrenchment and finally collapse and abandonment of Teotihuacán beginning in AD 534. After this date, Mayan culture in the lowlands flourished. Literally hundreds of pyramids, palaces, temples, causeways, and urban settlements were created, and existing sites underwent tremendous expansion. The city-states frequently supported urban populations of many thousands, who looked to the noble elites and priests for both physical and spiritual protection and guidance. Much of this had already been in place earlier, from the rise of Mayan civilization c.AD 300, but there was unprecedented growth during the Classic period. Then suddenly, about 900, Classic Maya civilization collapsed. The reason remains one of the greatest unanswered questions in Mesoamerican studies.

The Classic Maya period (AD 200–900), is the only fully literate culture in the New World, and rapid advances in the past 30 years in interpreting Mayan hieroglyphs has provided a detailed understanding of the history and beliefs of the period. The texts show a culture deeply concerned with issues of rank, status, and privilege. Lineage and royal descent, which was often traced back to a deity, was the driving force behind virtually all of Classic Mayan achievements.

Stelae were carved to commemorate the birth of a lord, his accession to the throne, and his triumphs over rival lords. Great palaces and temples were built to mark significant lineage dates, and were rebuilt and enlarged by successive rulers. Hieroglyphic stairways leading up to the temples on pyramids recorded successful wars and other important events in the lives of the rulers. Widespread trade was carried out, largely to supply the ruling families with the precious articles and materials they required to demonstrate their wealth and regal status.

Celestial lineage

Even the calendar was employed as a means of affirming the significant character of the royal lineage: The birth dates of princes were "adjusted" so that they fell on auspicious dates when the gods would favor them, and their battles with rival lords were fought only on days determined by priests from their observations of the movements and intentions of the star gods.

Artistic production reached a high level of achievement, since sumptuous and finely worked goods were required that matched the status of the ruling families. Accordingly, each city supported a large contingent of artisans and craftworkers, often with very specialized skills, who had their own quarters within the city precincts. Skilled workers were often brought in from other communities as migrant workers to enhance the range and variety of products available to the nobles and their entourages. Significantly, most of these goods were destined to accompany the nobles to their graves so that they could continue to enjoy the status they had known in this life during their sojourn in the Underworld.

By contrast, surprisingly little is known about the lives of the common people. They are not shown in any of the numerous carvings, and their burials were probably simple interments beneath the household floor. Many were engaged in farming, of course, since the city-states were supported by agriculture, and the presence of powerful gods of rain, corn, and fertility indicate the essential need for farm products to feed the vast populations.

After AD 900 the record stops. No more carvings were made, no more buildings erected, and no further elaborate tombs. Although small populations continued to live at some of the cities, the elite seem to vanish. Where they went or what happened to them is unknown.

COPÁN
Mayan record on its Hieroglyphic Stairway

Above: *This stela – which is also a carved figure – stands in front of the Hieroglyphic Stairway at Copán. The figures behind him, arranged at intervals along the steps, are portraits of Copán's various rulers.*

Copán is situated in a valley among the hills of western Honduras, in the Montagua Basin, and originally covered an area of 8 by 1.9 miles; only a fraction of this is visible today. The valley it rests in is one of the most beautiful of Mayan sites, and was described by John Lloyd Stephens in 1839 as "a valley of romance and wonder, where the genii who attended on King Solomon seem to have been the artists." It is famed for its buildings in green trachite (a volcanic rock), rather than the usual limestone of Mayan builders.

The earliest date for the site is the beginning of the fifth century AD, when it was founded by Yax Kuk Mo (Green Quetzal Macaw), and its oldest monument is a marker set into the floor in a deep tunnel beneath the Hieroglyphic Stairway. At its eastern edge the River Copán has carried part of the site away, cutting a vertical section some 100 feet high.

At its center is the Acropolis, supporting a complex of temples, courts, and terraces, many of which were erected under the direction of Waxaklahun Ubah K'awil, or Eighteen Rabbit, who was the 13th ruler of Copán. These are raised on an artificial platform within which several layers of earlier occupation are visible. Like many Classic Mayan rulers, Waxaklahun Ubah K'awil went to great lengths to proclaim his divine ancestry and stelae depict him in the jade-encrusted costume of the young Maize God.

The most impressive feature at Copán is the Hieroglyphic Stairway, which was completed in the eighth century AD. This descends from Temple 26 on the northeast corner of the Acropolis, and the risers of its 63 steps are covered by 2,500 glyphs that refer to the ruling dynasties. It is the longest continuous record known for the Maya, but many of the carvings were discovered in a jumbled and confused state and have been misplaced during reconstructions carried out in the 1830s. The balustrades are decorated with celestial bird-and-serpent monsters, and there are seated figures at intervals of ten steps.

A series of courts

North of the Hieroglyphic Stairway is a ball court with carved parrot heads set into the upper edge of the benches. This is the most perfectly preserved ball court known for the Classic Maya, and its carvings in the round give it a baroque appearance that is unique at Mayan sites.

Below this was an earlier court, in whose floor were three marker stones with representations of ball players. Buried beneath the second court was a third, contemporary with the early constructions on the Acropolis. In the main and middle courts stand sculptured altars and stelae, mostly dating to the seventh and eighth centuries. Their high relief and elaboration of detail are characteristic of Copán carving.

Left: *This view of Copán shows the site as it was during reconstruction work carried out in the 1980s.*

Bottom left: *This stela was found in the Main Court at Copán and depicts Copán's 13th ruler, Eighteen Rabbit.*

Unlike many Mayan sites, Copán flourished between its foundation in the Pre-Classic era until the Classic collapse. Most of the buildings at Copán were erected during the Classic period, and the site was abandoned about AD 800. Prior to this it served as a ceremonial center for the southern Maya, and post-Classic finds suggest the site was revisited later; but even during its heyday Copán's fortunes swayed between extremes of glory and misfortune. Waxaklahun Ubah K'awil, for instance, was captured and beheaded by Kawak Sky of the nearby and much humbler city of Quirigua on May 3, 738, but the following month Smoke Monkey took command and restored Copán's position as the dominant city of the region.

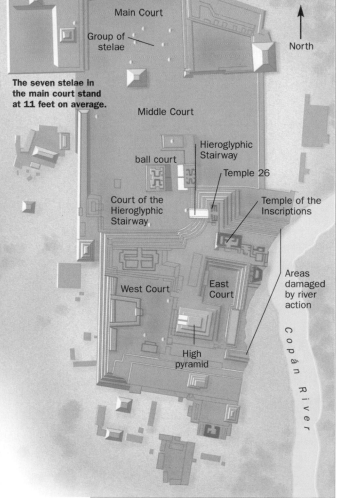

The Acropolis of the city of Copán

Main Court

Group of stelae

North

The seven stelae in the main court stand at **11 feet** on average.

Middle Court

ball court

Hieroglyphic Stairway

Temple 26

Court of the Hieroglyphic Stairway

Temple of the Inscriptions

West Court

East Court

Areas damaged by river action

High pyramid

Copán River

Catherwood and Stephens

The fathers of Mesoamerican archaeology

Two of the greatest names in Mesoamerican studies are John Lloyd Stephens and Frederick Catherwood. Stephens, an American, and Catherwood, an Englishman, met in London in 1836, where Catherwood was exhibiting his panoramic painting "Jerusalem." Catherwood had trained as an architectural draughtsman, but he had an abiding love of travel and exploration and had traveled extensively in Egypt in 1824. Stephens, a lawyer, had traveled even more widely and found a soul-mate in Catherwood.

They met again in New York in 1838, where they made plans to go to Central America and explore the ruins of the Maya. Only three Mayan ruins were known at this time – Copán in Honduras, Palenque in Chiapas, and Uxmal in the Yucatán – and few scholars attributed these to a single culture.

In October of the following year, they sailed from New York, hired guides in Honduras, and went to Copán – which Stephens purchased for $50 so that he and Catherwood could work there undisturbed. From Copán they went to Palenque, before returning to New York and publishing *Incidents of Travel in Central America*, illustrated with Catherwood's engravings and woodcuts.

Two years later they sailed again from New York, this time to the Yucatán. This trip was to be a milestone in Mesoamerican studies. Traveling under often extremely difficult conditions and beset by recurring bouts of malaria, Catherwood and Stephens spent ten months scouring the Yucatán for any signs of Mayan ruins.

They asked local people to guide them to these "homes of the ancients" and hired them to clear away the jungle and scrub. Stephens wrote down his views of the ruins and directed excavations, and seems to have acted as the ambassador for this little band of intrepid explorers, while Catherwood recorded the buildings and monuments in meticulous detail in thousands of drawings. Catherwood's illustrations are so accurate that it is possible to read the Mayan inscriptions from his engravings.

Scorned pioneers

When they returned to New York ten months later, they brought back drawings and descriptions of 44 cities of the Maya of which only one, Uxmal, had been previously known.

Stephens wrote *Incidents of Travel in Yucatán*, illustrated with 85 engravings by Catherwood, which became an immediate best-seller and stimulated popular interest in the Mayan cultures.

With good reason, Stephens and Catherwood have been called the "fathers of Mesoamerican archaeology." They were the first to claim a Mayan origin for the great city centers of the Mayan area, and the first to state that they were the work of the ancestors of the people who still lived in the area.

In 1843, when *Incidents of Travel in Yucatán* was first published, there were still some academics who refused to believe that any indigenous peoples had the skill or culture to build such monuments. They called Stephens and Catherwood "amateurs" and dismissed their theories as "fanciful imaginations." Time, however, has shown just how correct they were.

Stephens and Catherwood both met tragic ends. Stephen's last project was to superintend the building of the first railroad in South America, across the Isthmus of Panama (the foundation of the route of the Panama Canal), in 1852. One day he was found unconscious beneath a ceiba tree, and taken in a coma back to his home in New York where he died without regaining consciousness on October 13.

Just two years later, Catherwood was returning from London to New York in the *S.S. Arctic* when she collided with another ship off the coast of Newfoundland. The *Arctic* sank almost immediately with dreadful loss of life. The New York papers, after listing the names of the lost and saved, ended with a poignant last line: "Mr Catherwood is also missing."

Above: *Catherwood and Stephens' visits to Mayan sites required hiring local workers to clear vegetation before the extent of the sites was revealed. This illustration shows local workers clearing debris from in front of the "castle" at Tulum, the city on the Yucatán Peninsula's east coast.*

Facing: *Catherwood and Stephens were the first explorers to record the Mayan sites of the Yucatán. Their work in the mid-1800s inspired others to make detailed studies of the Maya and established Mayan culture as an indigenous Mesoamerican expression. The illustration shown here is Catherwood's "Pyramid of Kukulcan" (see also photographs on pages 7, 134).*

PALENQUE
Realization of a great dream

Above: *Aerial view of Palenque, with the Palace in the center and the Temple of Inscriptions immediately beyond to the right.*

Facing above: *An interior stairway leads through the middle the Temple of the Inscriptions to a tomb that contained the remains of Lord Pacal.*

Bay of Campeche

YUCATÁN PENINSULA

El Mirador

Palenque • Tikal

Kaminaljuyú Copán

PACIFIC OCEAN

Right: *The Palace Complex served as the residence for all of Palenque's historically known rulers.*

According to Maya legend, the mysterious Votan left his own village of Valum Chivim and traveled up the Usumacinta river to found a great metropolis in the forests of the Sierra de Chiapas, overlooking the plain of Tabasco and Campeche in the Yucatán province of modern Mexico. Here he built a vast ceremonial complex that was to serve as the focus for the religious devotions of the Lowland Maya of the Yucatán area.

Votan's realization of his dream of a great city has been identified by archaeologists as the site of Palenque, a Late Classic Maya complex of temples, pyramids, ball courts, and plazas whose principal buildings as seen today were erected between the seventh and tenth centuries AD. It is nevertheless clear that there were earlier buildings on the site. Scattered finds throughout Palenque indicate occupation prior to the Classic period, while the three-tier pyramid built as a support for the Temple of the Inscriptions and bearing a stela date of AD 692 was built over a much earlier eight-story platform mound. The buildings as they now

stand, however, serve primarily as a memorial to the great Lord Chan Balum (Snake Jaguar) and many bear inscriptions recording his accession to rule Palenque in AD 683.

Chan Balum identified himself with the Jaguar God of the Underworld, and it is therefore fitting that the large pyramid at the east of the site (the most sacred position in Maya cosmology) bears a temple, the Temple of the Sun, which is dedicated to this deity. The archaeological zone represents only a fraction of the once sprawling metropolis. In it are several more temple-pyramids, a vaulted aqueduct, and a ball court, as well as various plazas and the foundations of other buildings and courtyard complexes surrounded by double galleries divided into small rooms whose functions are largely unknown. Among the more important buildings are the Temple of the Cross, the Temple of the Foliated Cross, the Temple of the Sun, Temple of the Inscriptions, the Temple of the Count, and the Palace; the latter perhaps serving as the Royal Court and residence of the rulers and high priesthood.

Cleared from the jungle

In common with many other Mayan sites, Palenque was abandoned shortly after AD 800 for reasons that are not altogether clear. Although revisited from time to time by small groups of pilgrims paying homage to the old

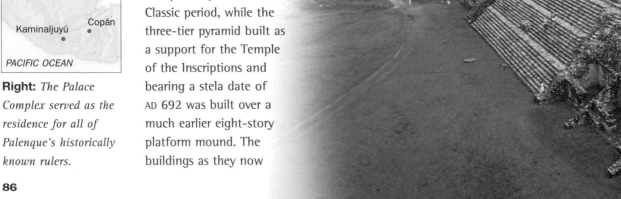

deities, it ceased to function as a major ceremonial center and many of the buildings and pyramids became overgrown as the jungle encroached. Thus Palenque lay largely undisturbed for some 900 years until it was "discovered" by Mexican Indians in 1773.

It was visited by Captain Guillaume Dupaix between 1805 and 1807, and then by Juan Galindo in 1831. Since then there have been intensive archaeological investigations, the central area has been cleared of jungle overgrowth, some of the buildings have been partially restored, and the site now boasts its own museum housing a representative collection of sculpture and pottery. Prominent in this collection are a number of incense burners depicting the Jaguar God of the Underworld, which serve as a lasting testimony to Lord Chan Balum and a permanent reminder of the skills of the Classic Maya artisans.

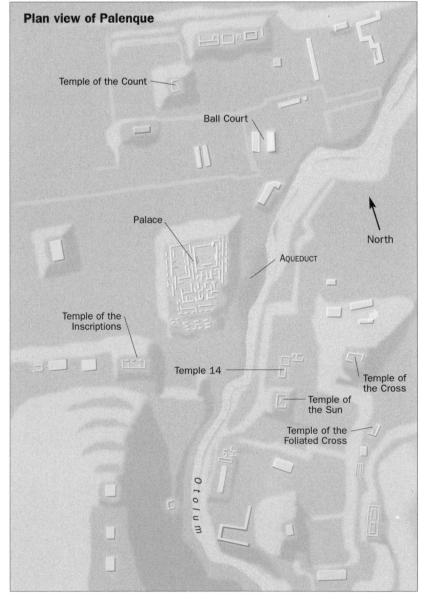

Plan view of Palenque

Temple of the Count

Ball Court

Palace

North

AQUEDUCT

Temple of the
Inscriptions

Temple 14

Temple of
the Cross

Temple of
the Sun

Temple of the
Foliated Cross

Otolum

LORD PACAL
Religious center of Aztec culture

Below: *An unusual find at Palenque was this death mask of Lord Pacal. It provides an excellent view of the physical appearance of the early Maya.*

In 1949 the archaeologist Alberto Ruz was carrying out investigations at Palenque. He intended using the Temple of the Inscriptions as a base room during his visit, and consequently ordered that the floor be swept clean of debris. To Ruz's surprise the floor was not a solid block of concrete as in most other

Mayan temples, but contained a large stone slab with inset rings.

Curious at what lay beneath, Ruz had his workmen prise it free. Beneath it he could make out signs of a steep stone staircase descending into the interior of the pyramid, but the way forward was blocked by tons of rubble. Over

three years the rubble was carefully removed and in 1952 Ruz stepped into a small burial crypt similar to others he had seen. One of his workmen, however, noticed that one of the crypt's walls sounded hollow. By cutting a small hole Ruz was able to shine a flashlight into the hidden room, and so became the first person to look on Lord Pacal's tomb since he had been interred there in AD 683.

In the center was Pacal's sarcophagus, still containing his remains covered with a jade mask, necklaces, ear spools, rings, and mother-of-pearl ornaments. Stucco reliefs covered the walls, and the floor was strewn with fragments of pottery and the skeletons of five sacrificial victims. The most significant aspect of the find was the stone sarcophagus lid. Measuring 12 by 7 feet, it is covered with elaborate imagery depicting the Maya vision of the cosmos and Lord Pacal's movement through it. It shows a fantastic cosmic tree laden with jewels, mirrors, and blood-letting bowls, with a celestial quetzal bird perched on top. Also shown is Pacal, falling backward into Xibalba, the Underworld, through the jaws of two skeletal serpents. Through this imagery, Pacal is linked and identified with the Feathered Serpent, who emerged from the Underworld under the protection of the Jaguar gods to become the patron deity of Mesoamerican priests and rulers.

According to inscriptions in the tomb and on *stelae* recording Pacal's career, he is reputed to have ruled over Palenque from the age of 12 until his death at 81 years old. But tests on the skeleton found in the tomb reveal this to be that of a male aged about 40 years. Skeptical archaeologists and anthropologists initially deduced that the skeleton could not be Pacal's, but a closer reading of the glyphs suggests that the dates have been chosen for their cosmological and ritual significance rather

than referring to an actual birth date. Pacal is thus shown as being born on a day that coincided with the mythical birth date of the First Mother, the mother of the gods.

Divine right

It is significant here that the name of Pacal's biological mother, Lady Zac Kuk (White Macaw), who ruled Palenque before him, is also written with the glyph sign for the First Mother. The dates recorded for Pacal at Palenque therefore appear to confer on him a divine right to rule and refer to his deification as one of a host of Maya gods. His inauguration as ruler is shown as being made on a significant calendrical date that provided auspicious omens for future prosperity.

Since its discovery by Ruz, Pacal's tomb has provided a wealth of information for Mesoamerican scholars. Unlike virtually every other Maya tomb, it had not been desecrated by grave robbers seeking to exploit the lucrative but illegal trade in Mayan artifacts. As such it has given us a complete record of Pacal's birth, accession, leadership, and deification, from the world-view of the Maya, that is unavailable from any other source.

SACRED ARCHITECTURE
The Temples of the Cross, Foliated Cross, and Sun

Below: *The Temple of the Sun. Carvings within the* pib na, *or sanctuary, depict a shield adorned with the Jaguar Sun, supported by crossed spears resting on a throne decorated with jaguar and serpent heads.*

The world of people and that of the gods was inextricably linked in Mayan thought, and the buildings and carvings erected at their ceremonial centers often act as architectural expressions of this basic unity. Although this is apparent at the majority of large Mayan sites, and particularly at those of the Classic period, it is nowhere more evident than in a group of buildings commissioned by Chan Balam (Snake Jaguar) at Palenque.

At the eastern edge of the site is a plaza surrounded on three sides by stepped platforms, a small temple set on each. These are the Temples of the Cross, Foliated Cross, and Sun. Each of the temples is similar in construction and consists of an outer and inner vaulted room surmounted by a mansard roof — four-sided and double-angled, the upper angle sharper than the lower. Against the back wall of the inner room of each temple is a sanctuary, in effect a miniature representation of the temple itself, where there are low relief tablets bearing long hieroglyphic inscriptions.

A reading of the inscriptions makes it clear that the temples were dedicated to the accession of Chan Balam in AD 683. Carvings on the tablets and the exterior pilasters of the temples depict him as a boy of six years old and as a mature man of 49 years on the date of his accession, and link him with the Jaguar God of the Underworld, Vucuub Caquix (the monstrous Quetzal Macaw), and a deity today only known as God L (patron of warriors and traders).

Aligned with the Sacred Directions

There is, however, more to be read into the inscriptions and the placement of the temples than the familiar theme of linking the ruling families with powerful deities and ancestral figures. The northern temple — Temple of the Cross — is raised slightly higher than the others and records the Creation and the history of the Palenque dynasty, which surrounds the World Tree. At the east, in the Temple of the Foliated Cross, are depictions of the Mountain of Sustenance and the Tree of Maize; while in the western Temple of the Sun are images of war and the Jaguar God.

This arrangement and the details of carvings in the temples accord closely with Mayan concepts of the structure of the universe. The elevated northern temple is in accordance with the importance and significance of north in Mayan cosmology, and it is therefore appropriate that this should contain the World Tree, or *axis mundi*, of Mayan belief. The Temple of the Foliated Cross is at the east, the position of the rising sun and of growth and

renewal; whereas the western Temple of the Sun marks the setting sun and is associated with warfare, death, and the blood of ritual sacrifice.

Although these temples are often referred to as the "Palenque Triad," the fourth, open side of the plaza complex has significance too, since it points in the direction of emptiness and

In the diagram:
Temple of the Cross
Temple of the Foliated Cross
Temple of the Sun
Temple 14
The Palace

Above: *Viewed from a high vantage point on the Palace, the arrangement of artificially raised platforms for the east temple complex becomes more evident.*

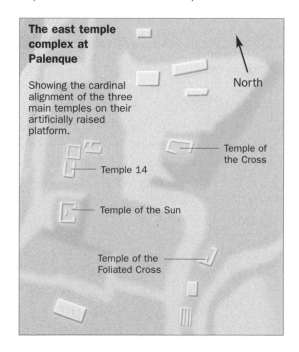

The east temple complex at Palenque

Showing the cardinal alignment of the three main temples on their artificially raised platform.

North

Temple of the Cross

Temple 14

Temple of the Sun

Temple of the Foliated Cross

midnight; a period when the sun is considered to be dead in Xibalba (the Underworld). The three temples and the open space are therefore concrete representations of the Mayan world and of the four Sacred Directions.

In addition to these meanings, the sanctuaries within the temples are referred to by the Maya as *pib na*. A direct translation of this is "sweatbath." Maya priests used sweatbaths as a form of ritual cleansing and purification, and their identification with the temple sanctuaries is therefore an appropriate one.

However, they were also important in rituals that immediately preceded and followed childbirth, and it has been suggested that the presence of the *pib na* is symbolic of the birth of the god to whom each temple was dedicated.

JAGUAR THRONES
And the descent into the Underworld

Above: *For the visitor to Chichén Itzá who can withstand extreme heat and humidity (as well as claustrophia-inducing spaces) the climb up the steps inside the Pyramid of Kukulcan reveals this jaguar throne. The platform on which it rests is actually the top of an earlier, lower pyramid, which was built over.*

Kukulcan (Quetzalcoatl), the Feathered Serpent and creator of the people, ascended into the Upper World through the jaws of the Jaguar God, and at the close of each day K'inich Ahau, the Sun-Faced Lord, descends into the Underworld at the west and begins his southern journey through the night in the form of the Jaguar.

According to Mayan myth, the Jaguar, as Lord of the Earth and Guardian of the Underworld, and the Eagle, Lord of the Sky, were chosen by the gods because of their outstanding bravery. They were the first to leap into the sacred fire from which Sun was born, and thereafter bore the signs of courage in their pelts and plumage. To honor the Jaguar, the deities charged him also with the guardianship of the Maya priest-rulers and linked both Eagle and Jaguar with the Twin Hero Gods, Hunapa and Xbalanque. Hunapa, or Sun, became the symbol of life and celestial power; Xbalanque, as the Morning and Evening Stars (Venus), was the deity of the Underworld and of death and resurrection. Between them they represent the divine duality that is linked to both Sky and Earth, and are thus the twin aspects that underlie all Mayan belief and cosmology.

The priest-rulers, as the earthly incarnations of the deities and through whom the people's prayers and offerings might be made, therefore associated themselves with the planet Venus in both its Morning and Evening Star aspects as well as with the Jaguar which was Xbalanque's earthly form. As jaguar priests they were able to communicate with Xbalanque's twin brother, Hunapa, so that the wishes of the people could be reconciled with the demands of the deities.

It is nevertheless important to remember that the Jaguar is the guardian of the Underworld and of death and resurrection, and it was with these that the Mayan priests were most concerned. For them, life stemmed from death: the maize plant grows, flourishes, and then dies, only to be reseeded and to bring forth new life. Similarly, the sun completes its daily round but then descends each evening into Xibalba, from where it is reborn with the dawn.

Protection of the Jaguar

The passage between life, death, and rebirth is, however, fraught with difficulty and needs to be protected. Jaguar, because of his courage, was assigned this role and, through him, the priest-rulers were given responsibility to ensure that rituals were correctly performed and that acts of personal penance and sacrifice which would bring benefit to everyone were strictly adhered to. In this the priest-rulers re-enacted the journeys of Hunapa and Xbalanque to the Underworld, from which they were theoretically reborn. Such acts were under the guidance and protection of the Jaguar God, and at Tikal there is a carved wooden lintel depicting Ah Cacau, the ruler of Tikal, seated on a throne in front of a gigantic Jaguar protector.

Perhaps the most decisive link between the

priests and the Jaguar as Guardian of the Underworld is found at Chichén Itzá. Buried deep inside one of the pyramids which was erected in pre-Toltec times is a small chamber, and within this is a carved and painted jaguar throne. Its deep internment has obvious Underworld connections, but until other similar thrones are found its exact function is impossible to determine. We can only guess

Below: *The Jaguar God demanded human sacrifice to appease his appetite for souls and ensure his continued protection of the entrance to the Underworld. This carving in bas-relief shows a jaguar eating a human heart.*

that the priests retired here to reassert their identification with the Lords of the Underworld and to request the intervention of the Jaguar God in this hazardous undertaking.

UXMAL
The Nunnery and Pyramid of the Magician

Below: *The Adivino, or Pyramid of the Magician, dominates the center of Uxmal. It consists of a high round-cornered platform that supports two temples. The lower of these represents a giant monster mask whose mouth forms the doorway and is reached via the steep western staircase shown here. The upper temple is accessed via another stairway on the east side of the platform.*

The Puuc, a range of low hills in southwest Yucatán, was the setting for a Late (or Terminal) phase of Classic Mayan architecture characterized by cement and rubble core buildings, faced with a thin veneer of finely carved limestone slabs. The majority of Puuc buildings have exterior façades that are divided into two horizontal bands, the upper half decorated with rows of columns and relief designs forming fretwork patterns, human figures, sky serpents, and stylized masks of the Long-Nosed Rain God.

The largest and most impressive of the Puuc sites is Uxmal, which flourished from the seventh to the eleventh centuries. The outstanding features at Uxmal are two massive pyramids, the Great Pyramid and the Pyramid of the Magician, which dominate the site.

Today the Great Pyramid is largely in ruins, but the Pyramid of the Magician is well preserved. Standing on an elliptical platform, its upper temple is entered through a monster mask doorway that marks its sacred significance and links it to the gods of the Mayan Underworld.

Adjacent to the Pyramid of the Magician is the Nunnery Quadrangle. The Spanish coined its imaginative name, and it is evident that the Nunnery was, in fact, a palace group of four buildings arranged around an interior courtyard, entered via a great corbeled arch on the southern side. The Nunnery Quadrangle is unique in that many of its carvings depict the simple thatched huts of a peasant population, but further studies have suggested that its layout also has cosmological significance.

Cosmopolitan Mexican influence

The north building is placed higher than the others and has 13 exterior doorways, reflecting the 13 layers of the Mayan Heaven; serpents surmounting the huts also identify it with the celestial sphere. The west building has seven doorways — the mystic number of the earth — and depicts the Earth God in the form of a turtle, while the east building bears carvings that link it with the war gods of Teotihuacán. The southern building is placed lower than the others and has nine doorways, corresponding to the nine layers of the Underworld.

Below the Great Pyramid and standing on an artificial raised platform of its own is the House of the Governors, which bears some of the finest carvings in Puuc style. The House of the Governors gives the impression of one long, low building, but is in fact three interconnected structures covered by a fantastic mosaic of fret and lattice work and monster masks.

Uxmal may have been a ceremonial and political center for outlying communities, and an 11-mile causeway connects it with the smaller sites of Nohpat and K'abah, where, again, monster masks are much in evidence. Unfortunately, there are only a few poorly executed stelae at Uxmal and no mural paintings that might provide clues to the relationship between these different centers.

In its later period, Uxmal was dominated by a dynastic family, the Xiu. Although the Xiu claimed ancestral rights at Uxmal, and are traditionally cited as its "owners." They could not have been its founders — Xiu origins are Mexican rather than Yucatecan and indicate late occupancy of the site by peoples from the Valley of Mexico.

Their occupancy nevertheless gives Uxmal a cosmopolitan feel which, at its height, embraced a population of perhaps 20,000 people living in an urban core of some 1¹/₂ square miles, although there must also have been a rural population of many thousands more.

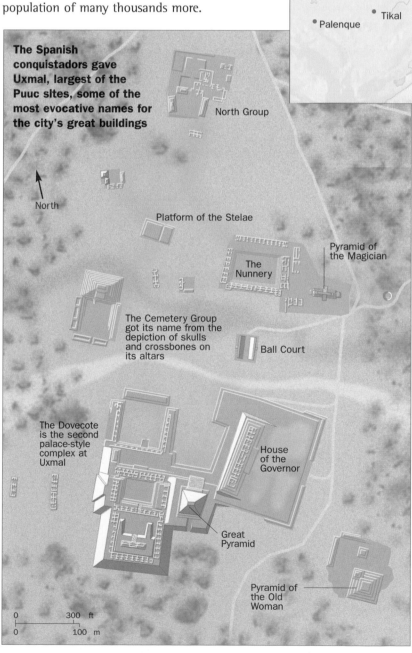

The Spanish conquistadors gave Uxmal, largest of the Puuc sites, some of the most evocative names for the city's great buildings

GULF OF MEXICO

Chichén Itzá

P U U C

Uxmal

Bay of Campeche

YUCATÁN PENINSULA

CARIBBEAN SEA

Palenque

Tikal

North Group

North

Platform of the Stelae

Pyramid of the Magician

The Nunnery

The Cemetery Group got its name from the depiction of skulls and crossbones on its altars

Ball Court

The Dovecote is the second palace-style complex at Uxmal

House of the Governor

Great Pyramid

Pyramid of the Old Woman

0   300 ft
0   100 m

BONAMPAK MURALS
A story of battle and celebration

Below: *Detail of a battle scene from a mural at Bonampak. This vivid mural shows the warriors of Bonampak and Yaxchilán under the leadership of Chan Muwan and Shield Jaguar II during an expedition to capture enemies for sacrifice during the naming of Chan Muwan's heir.*

In February 1946 Lacandón Maya Indians took two American adventurers to a remote ruin on a tributary of the Usumacinta. This site had been important during the Early Classic period but had fallen under the political control of Yaxchilán in its later days. Three months later, photographer Giles Healey was taken to the same site and became the first non-Maya to see the magnificent murals that covered the walls in one of Bonampak's structures.

These murals tell the single story of a battle, the capture of rival lords, and their subsequent sacrifice during Bonampak's victory celebrations. The murals give us a wealth of information about Mayan customs. In them we can see the elite warriors of Bonampak arrayed in their splendid costumes, setting out to battle and encouraged by musicians who blow long war horns of wood or bark.

Their success is recorded in a mural which depicts the stripped prisoners having the nails torn from their fingers. An apparently important captive has been tortured to exhaustion and sprawls on the steps of a Bonampak pyramid. The severed head of a defeated noble lies nearby on a bed of leaves.

At the center of this mural is the great lord Chan Muwan, King of Bonampak, who is dressed in his jaguar skin warrior cloak and surrounded by his principal war leaders.

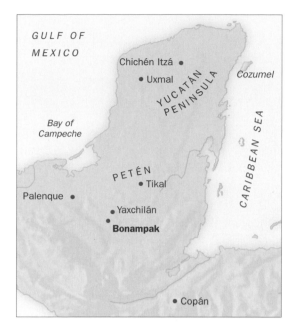

He presents a magnificent figure, and is obviously admired by the Mayan audience that surrounds him. Among the audience we can identify Chan Muwan's principal wife, as well as a group of dancers from Yaxchilán who are disguised as water gods. They are accompanied by an orchestra of rattles, drums, turtle shells, and trumpets.

Maya clashes revealed

The final scene in this mural is the great sacrificial dance. White robed Maya ladies are seated on thrones, but they draw blood from their tongues in homage to the deities that brought Bonampak this moment of glory over its rival states. Their dance is performed to the accompaniment of trumpets played by Bonampak lords wearing gigantic headdresses of quetzal plumes.

Prior to the discovery of the Bonampak murals, the Maya were thought to live in peaceful co-existence with each other. Scholars had missed or ignored their warlike proclivities and dwelt instead on the trading relationships between the major centers. In this scenario, Mayan customs were shared between centers as mutually co-operative partners.

The Bonampak murals tell a different story, one of battle, rivalry, and conquest, and shed new light on the warlike interests of the Maya leaders. From them it becomes clear that the ruling families were in constant turmoil and that each sought to justify and maintain its position through the subjugation of neighboring groups. The capture and ritual sacrifice of a rival lord became a means whereby one's own position could be validated.

Although the Bonampak murals glorify the ruling dynasties at the center, it is clear that Bonampak's leaders were unable to meet the opposition offered by the lords of Yaxchilán. Bird Jaguar was captured by the Yaxchilán king, K'inich Tatb'u Skull I; his successor, K'inich Tatb'u Skull II, enjoyed considerable success in his wars against Bonampak, Lakamtuun, and Calakmul.

Bonampak ended its days as a satellite of Yaxchilán and was finally abandoned during the Late Classic period before the murals were completed.

Above: *This Bonampak mural depicts a row of Mayan nobles. They are presiding over rituals at which the royal heir to the ruler Chan Muwan was presented to the assembled court.*

CHAC – THE RAIN GOD
The many faces of an enduring deity

For the ordinary Mayan farmer, the most crucial concern of the year was adequate rainfall. *Milpa* (slash-and-burn) farming is precarious, and too much or too little rain can rapidly prove disastrous. Although there were great annual ceremonies to ensure a good year, the farmer also had recourse to his own private rituals that were intended to appease Chac, the Rain God. The importance of Chac is attested to by the fact that he has endured in the Mayan area since at least the time of the late Olmec, where he appears at Izapa as the Long-Lipped God, through to the present day.

Even when foreign deities were introduced, as at Tikal by the Teotihuacános or Chichén Itzá by the Toltec, Chac continued to be represented and venerated. Occasionally he appeared as the counterpart of a foreign rain god, Tlaloc, but generally his Mayan form and symbolism remain intact.

Chac was appealed to and his benevolent intercession on the people's behalf sought more frequently than

Left: *A column of three Chacs decorates the corner of this building at Xlapac in the Yucatán. In profile it is easy to see the curling snout characteristic of the deity in Yucatec Mayan depictions.*

that of any other Mayan god, and Chac or his representatives featured prominently in many of the ceremonies dedicated to other deities. Significantly, he is also one of the few ancient Mayan deities that survived the suppression of the Spanish.

In codices and temple carvings, Chac is depicted as reptilian. He has a characteristic and unmistakable curving nose or snout that distinguishes him from other Mayan deities, and long curving fangs that extend downward from the corners of his toothless mouth. His hair is made from a tangle of knots, and he is usually accompanied by serpents and depicted with weather symbols and glyphs of the four cardinal directions.

Despite his somewhat terrifying appearance, Chac is almost always a benevolent god who is associated with creation and life. But when angered, he strikes together his great stone axes to create lightning and is capable of wreaking vengeance in a spectacular manner.

A compound god

Although Chac is generally referred to in the singular, he is a compound god, his four aspects linked with the cardinal directions. In the east is the Red Chac, Chac Xib Chac; in the north is the White Chac, Sac Xib Chac; west is home to the Black Chac, Ek Xib Chac; and in the south is the Yellow Chac, Kan Xib Chac.

As well as being an aspect of the Rain God, Chac Xib Chac is associated with Venus in its aspect as the Evening Star and is also an emblem of rulership. Collectively the Chacs are paired with the Four Bacabs (Four Winds), each of which has control over one quarter of the 260-day ritual calendar and is linked to a similar color: Chac is the Red Bacab of the east; Zac, the White Bacab of the north; Ed, the Black Bacab of the west; and Kan, the Yellow Bacab of the south.

The great annual spring festival devoted to Chac was called Ocna (Enter the House). This was a festival of creation and renewal, during which the temples devoted to Chac were renovated and their carvings and incense burners renewed. The Four Bacabs were present,

in their guise as the Four Balam (Sky Bearers), and were consulted by the priests during their divinations to determine a propitious day for the ceremony to be held.

The Chacs were also honored during the March festival of Itzamna who, in his form as Hunab Ku, was the Creator of the Universe and the chief patron of the Mayan ruling lineages. Itzamna's name glyph, means "king, monarch, or great lord," and the importance of the Chacs is reinforced by their close attendance upon him during the festivities held in his honor.

Above: *Although described as a Toltec-Mayan statue of Chac, this figurine probably represents a priest wearing a Chac mask or helmet.*

JAINA
The island cemetery

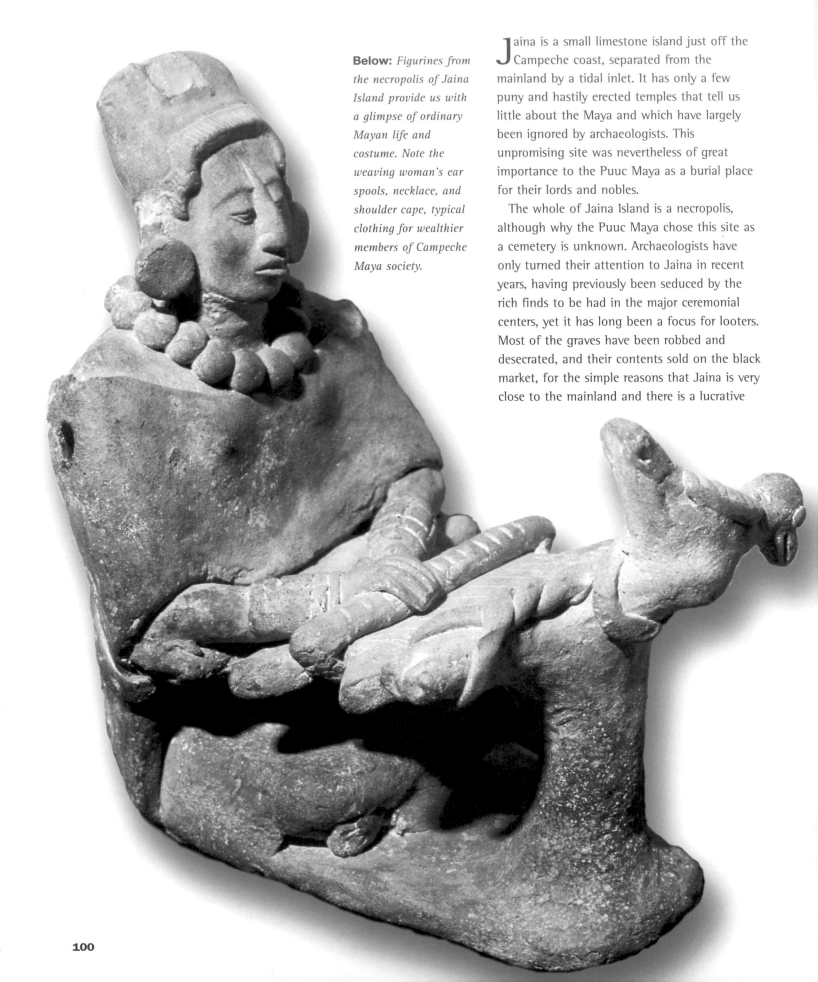

Below: *Figurines from the necropolis of Jaina Island provide us with a glimpse of ordinary Mayan life and costume. Note the weaving woman's ear spools, necklace, and shoulder cape, typical clothing for wealthier members of Campeche Maya society.*

Jaina is a small limestone island just off the Campeche coast, separated from the mainland by a tidal inlet. It has only a few puny and hastily erected temples that tell us little about the Maya and which have largely been ignored by archaeologists. This unpromising site was nevertheless of great importance to the Puuc Maya as a burial place for their lords and nobles.

The whole of Jaina Island is a necropolis, although why the Puuc Maya chose this site as a cemetery is unknown. Archaeologists have only turned their attention to Jaina in recent years, having previously been seduced by the rich finds to be had in the major ceremonial centers, yet it has long been a focus for looters. Most of the graves have been robbed and desecrated, and their contents sold on the black market, for the simple reasons that Jaina is very close to the mainland and there is a lucrative market for Mayan artifacts.

Jaina is now protected — Mexican gunboats warn off intruders — and archaeologists have at last begun to unravel its secrets. Their investigations have revealed numerous figurines that appear to be portraits of the occupants of the graves. These are real people: haughty nobles, proud warriors, beautiful young women, and fat old matrons. Through them we catch a glimpse of what the daily life of Maya was like.

Almost all of these figurines are hollow and fitted with whistles at their backs. Just why the Maya associated their dead with the whistle is a matter of conjecture, although it may be that this was reminiscent of the hoot of the owl, the harbinger of death. The figurines might therefore link the deceased with the Underworld.

Images in Maya blue

At another level the figurines may represent a connection with deities. A figurine showing a woman sheltering a grown man could be a representation of the Mother Goddess, and images of the Fat God who was popular among the Maya of Campeche frequently appear.

Many of the figurines are nevertheless portraits of ordinary people, expressed with an unusual liveliness and animation that was not allowed the artists who carved the monuments at the major public ceremonial sites. Among them we find portraits of women weaving, nobles sitting cross-legged in contemplation, and orators in the midst of an ecstatic dance.

The Jaina figurines are important in that they give us a good impression of Late Classic Maya costumes and occupations, and bring these to us in vivid and realistic detail. Most of the figurines are remarkably well preserved and often retain the brilliant colors given to them by the Mayan artists.

Among the colors is the famous "Maya blue," which was produced by mixing indigo with a special clay and is extraordinarily stable. Unlike modern blue pigments, Maya blue is highly resistant to the effects of acids, light, and time, so it retains its brilliance over long periods.

The indigo used in this process is found at

only one site in Yucatán — Sakalum — and was traded from there to other centers along the Campeche coast. Its presence at Jaina suggests that the necropolis was used by the occupants of several Puuc Maya centers and was not under the exclusive ownership of any one Mayan king.

Above: *The makers of the Jaina Island figurines were adept at capturing the expression and poise of their sitters. This figurine has an aloof and haughty posture in accord with the high status of a Mayan noblewoman.*

THE MAYAN CODICES
Folded books of painted knowledge

Above: *The Mayan codices were made on long strips of bark paper painted on both sides and could be read as a continuous narrative. They were folded for ease of storage, as shown in this photograph of the Codex Fejervary-Mayer.*

One Howler and One Monkey were the supernatural patrons of the *ah tz'ib*, or scribes, of the Mayans. Through their patronage the *ah dzib* occupied positions of status and authority second only to that of the *ahau*, or king, himself. Under the guidance of the Monkey God, the *ah dzib* set down the histories, genealogies, prophecies, and sciences of the Maya on bark paper in long, screen-fold books known as codices.

Each codex was made by preparing a long strip of bark paper. This was covered with a lime gesso, on which the scribes painted their records, folded in a concertina pattern, and bound between animal-hide covers. Entire libraries of codices were kept by Mayan rulers, under the charge of an *ah k'uhun* (keeper of the holy books), who functioned as the royal librarian but was also responsible for negotiating royal marriages and diplomatic treaties.

Unfortunately, these libraries did not survive the Spanish Conquest. Bishop de Landa noted that:

> *"We found a large number of books in these characters and, as they contained nothing in which there were not to be seen superstition and lies of the devil, we burned them all...."*

Only three pre-Columbian Mayan books are known today, the Dresden, Madrid, and Paris codices, named after the modern cities that hold them in their museums.

All three deal with matters of Mayan ritual and contain no historical references. The largest, the Madrid Codex, is 22 feet long and contains detailed horoscopes and almanacs that were used by Mayan priests in divination. The shorter (11$^1/_2$ feet) Dresden Codex is of far superior workmanship and is concerned primarily with astronomy. It contains a complete Venus cycle across five of the folded pages, which plots the movements of Venus against the background of the stars, correlated with the solar year.

Fragments of knowledge

The Paris Codex is only a fragment of the original and is in poor condition, but it is still apparent that this, too, deals with ritualistic matters. One side refers to patron deities and ceremonies, while the other contains fragmentary information about the poorly understood Mayan zodiac.

A fourth codex is known as the Grolier Codex, after the Grolier Club in New York, where it was first put on public display. It is in a very damaged condition and its provenance is in dispute because the style of the drawings is simplistic and quite different from the other known codices.

However, tests on the bark paper indicate this is pre-Columbian, dating from AD 1230. If genuine, this would be the earliest codex to survive; it may well be that the different drawing style simply indicates a different place of origin within the Mayan area. Many scholars are convinced that the style is fully consistent with that of the Toltec-Maya. The Grolier Codex is entirely concerned with the Venus cycle, but adds little to the information that is already known from the Dresden Codex.

None of the existing codices was recovered archaeologically, and any buried books of this kind will have become mildewed and destroyed by the moist climate over most of the Mayan area. But several fragments of others have been found in Mayan tombs. The most complete of these is the Mirador Codex, now in the Museo Nacional de Antropologia in Mexico City. The paper has rotted away but the lime gesso survives. This is, unfortunately, congealed into a solid mass, but although this codex cannot be opened, experiments on fragments of it indicate that the painting inside is still intact.

Scholars are hopeful that other complete codices may be found. Stores of unused bark paper on which codices would have been written and dating from the pre-Columbian period have been discovered in dry caves, and this leaves the possibility open that a similar cache of painted screen-fold books may be awaiting discovery somewhere.

Below: *This page from the* Codex Cospi *shows Tlauixcalpantecuhtli, the planet Venus, using a spear to pierce the heart of an ocelot warrior. Tlauixcalpantecuhtli was thought to use his spears to attack various social orders at certain periods of the Venus cycle.*

MAYAN SOCIETY

Impractical temples, spacious palaces, and pole-and-thatch homes

Above: *The Temple of the Warriors at Chichén Itzá is similar to Pyramid B at the Toltec capital of Tula (see page 125); although it is larger and more finely built, it is probable that the Tula pyramid served as a model for the one at Chichén Itzá. The Hall of Colonnades, seen at the right of the Temple of Warriors, was originally covered with beams and mortar and probably served as a council hall.*

The typical Mayan city of the Classic period was dominated by its pyramids, surrounded by series of stepped platforms on which important buildings were constructed in stone. In larger centers, such as Tikal, there might be several of these pyramid-temple complexes, connected to one another by raised causeways. That these temples served a purely ritual function is suggested by the narrowness of their rooms. Although tall, their dimensions are such that it would be impossible to live in them.

By far the larger number of buildings are so-called "palaces": single-story buildings erected on lower platforms than the temples and often containing a dozen or more rooms. These rooms are larger, and are frequently arranged around open central courtyards which, in the absence of windows, permitted light to reach interior spaces. It is likely that the walls of these buildings, both inside and out, were covered with stucco and painted, although unfortunately only a few fragments of this decoration survives.

There are, however, numerous painted vases that indicate what life in the palaces must have been like. They often depict a ruler seated on his jaguar throne and holding court, or show a great noble receiving offerings of supplication from a person of lesser rank. From these we obtain the impression that a palace was something like a royal court or administrative center for the site; certainly the nobles are

shown acting royally and displaying their emblems of rank and prestige.

That they had royal entourages is also obvious from the vase paintings. There are groups of dancing girls who perform provocative dances to the accompaniment of large bands of musicians playing conch shell trumpets, waving rattles, and beating drums. Quite often there is an orator, or perhaps a singer, and seated behind the noble are his poets and scribes. The overall impression from these paintings is one of pomp and pageantry.

Domestic layout

Missing from the paintings are depictions of domestic activity, which has led some scholars to conclude that the palaces served only an administrative function and the noble elite actually lived in much less grandiose buildings elsewhere. This has led to speculation that Mayan centers served only political and ceremonial functions.

Excavations have, however, found considerable quantities of domestic detritus within the palace complexes. There is evidence of domestic utensils and food remains, suggesting that at least some eating took place here; although perhaps they were feasts held to impress visiting ambassadors and dignitaries from other Mayan cities.

The question of whether the nobles lived in these palaces is difficult to answer from the

archaeological record. If they did, there would presumably be evidence not only of private living quarters for the nobles themselves, but also for an array of cooks and other domestic servants; but sleeping quarters, royal kitchens, and so forth are not apparent.

There are nevertheless numerous house mounds close to many of the palace complexes. The buildings that were erected on these were presumably made of poles and thatch and have failed to survive, yet

a study of the post holes that contained supports for the walls of the buildings gives a good impression of their layout. They were divided into a number of separate rooms which, presumably, served different functions. Some of them were clearly kitchens, since there is evidence of cooking fires, and these were usually sited away from the other rooms, at one edge of the building and close to an area where refuse could be disposed of.

The general impression of a Mayan city

center is therefore one of a ceremonial core surrounded by administrative buildings, with a residential zone for the nobles and their retainers beyond. But defining exactly how the city was structured is not always easy. Mayan cities were not planned and built according to any grand plan, but grew slowly over many generations. As new occupants arrived, they built over existing structures — often demolishing part of them to incorporate as rubble in their own constructions.

Above: *Stone-built architecture was probably reserved for buildings that served a ritual function or for palaces of the nobles. Most ordinary Maya lived in pole and thatch houses similar to this example near Mérida in modern Yucatán. They were often oval in shape and supported by two main beams,* **left.** *They were usually divided into separate areas for living and preparing food; hammocks were slung for sleeping.*

CHAPTER FIVE

BUILDING EMPIRES
The evolution of Cuicuilco, Teotihuacán, and Tenochtitlan

The Olmec tradition of many small, scattered ceremonial centers supported by *milpa* (slash-and-burn) farming reached its fullest development among the Maya of the lowlands. Developments on the plateau of Mexico were very different. In this area there was growth of a few large cities that served both secular and ritual functions, which were supported by intensive agriculture.

The first clear archaeological indications of the growth of large cities come from Cuicuilco, south of modern Mexico City. The large pyramid erected here is well known, but recent excavations have revealed the presence of

innumerable buildings between this and another smaller pyramid almost 2 miles distant. The indications are of a large settlement, rather than of a small ceremonial center, as had previously been thought.

Cuicuilco was destroyed by an eruption of the Xitli volcano, and attention shifted to the Valley of Teotihuacán in the northeastern part of the Valley of Mexico. Sometime between 100 BC and the first century AD, the population of Teotihuacán dramatically increased. At this time perhaps half the total population of the Valley of Mexico was concentrated at Teotihuacán.

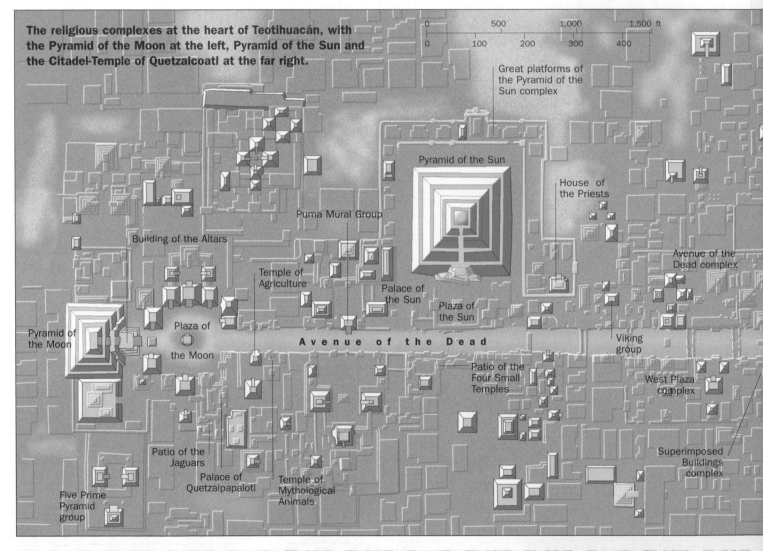

The religious complexes at the heart of Teotihuacán, with the Pyramid of the Moon at the left, Pyramid of the Sun and the Citadel-Temple of Quetzalcoatl at the far right.

Great platforms of the Pyramid of the Sun complex

Pyramid of the Sun

House of the Priests

Puma Mural Group

Building of the Altars

Avenue of the Dead complex

Temple of Agriculture

Palace of the Sun

Plaza of the Sun

Pyramid of the Moon

Plaza of the Moon

Avenue of the Dead

Viking group

Patio of the Four Small Temples

West Plaza complex

Patio of the Jaguars

Superimposed Buildings complex

Five Prime Pyramid group

Palace of Quetzalpapalotl

Temple of Mythological Animals

200 BC	100 BC–100 AD	50 AD	200	300	350	431	750
Settlements develop in the Teotihuacán Valley	Surge in Teotihuacán's population; expansion continues until the 7th century	Teotihuacán has control of the Valley of Mexico	The Pyramids of the Sun and the Moon are constructed at Teotihuacán	Beginning of Classic Mayan phase; Teotihuacán ceremonial center is built	Teotihuacán gains control of lowland Yucatan area	Founding ruler of Palenque, Bahlum Kuk (Jaguar Quetzal), accedes to the throne	Teotihuacán is destroyed in combat and fire

Although most of the monuments at Teotihuacán have a ritual theme, the city clearly served other functions, too. There is evidence for market places, artisans' quarters, and administrative buildings. Teotihuacán-influenced art has been found at numerous sites far from the Valley of Mexico, some of them at a distance of many hundreds of miles.

Unfortunately the Teotihuacános left us no written evidence, but the archaeological record suggests that the city was larger than Tenochtitlan, the capital of the later Aztecs, and that it continually expanded from the first century AD until the seventh. At the height of its power the population resident in the city center was at least 25,000, but if the urban population is included then Teotihuacán may have been home to as many as 150,000–200,000 people.

Unrivaled cities

That Teotihuacán built an empire is evident from the archaeological record at distant sites, where the presence of,

at least, a diplomatic force from Teotihuacán is apparent. Trade played a large part in this, and Teotihuacán specialized in the export of finished products in the form of small carvings, pottery, and the like. Imports to the city were most probably in the form of raw materials or foodstuffs from nearby settlements.

The domination of Teotihuacán was such that no cities of comparable size existed in the Valley of Mexico. The only rivals to Teotihuacán on the sub-continent were Cholula in the Valley of Puebla, which was a site of religious pilgrimage, and Atzcapotzalco on the shores of the lakes in the central part of the valley. Both of these were much smaller and did not exert comparable influence.

The building of empires was to continue later, with the establishment of Tenochtitlan by the Aztec. Again there is a clear record of an expansionist state exerting its influence over a very wide area. Although the Aztec claimed an origin in Teotihuacán, the city had long been in ruins when Tenochtitlan was established and it is unlikely the Aztec knew very much about its administrative and bureaucratic functions. Despite this, Tenochtitlan appears to have ruled its dominions in a very similar manner, and it may be that the ecology of the Mexican plateau was one of the determining factors for both Teotihuacán and Tenochtitlan.

The cities attracted an urban population because of their size and power, much as modern cities do today. Lacking any natural products for trade (most of their local resources were readily available elsewhere), they adopted the policy of wholesale export of finished products and, perhaps more importantly, of political and ritual ideas. With the growth of the empires, their hold over the smaller outlying regions became crucial to their survival, and both cities developed military strategies by which this hold could be secured.

GULF
OF
MEXICO

El Tajín

Lake Cuitzeo
Lake Texcoco
Teotihuacán
Tenochtitlan
Cuilcuilco
Chalcatzingo

BAY OF CAMPECHE

North

Temple of Quetzalcoatl (the Feathered Serpent)

Citadel

North Quadrangle

Great Compound (market)

SAN JUAN

TEOTIHUACÁN
In the shadow of Cerro Gordo

Although the Maya began to assert themselves in the lowlands following the decline of the Olmecs, the Valley of Mexico remained a cultural backwater until the beginning of the Christian era. This situation was dramatically reversed with the founding of the thriving metropolis of Teotihuacán.

Below: *This host figurine from Teotihuacán has a hollow chest cavity in which small objects dedicated to the household gods might be kept.*

Teotihuacán is located on a well-watered plain on the northeastern side of the Valley of Mexico, close to the site of modern Mexico City. The San Juan river and its tributaries drain into Lake Texcoco here, and perennial springs made the area amenable to intensive irrigation that was capable of supporting large populations. Perhaps for this reason, farmers of the Late Formative period gathered in this region and gradually established trading relationships with other parts of Mesoamerica.

The Teotihuacán ceremonial center, however, was not the result of a gradual growth in influence but appears to have been planned and built in one massive operation c.AD 300.

While the impetus for this sudden building is unknown, archaeological investigations make it clear that the ceremonial center and its urban zones were built within a few decades.

At the height of its power, Teotihuacán's ritual center covered an area of 7.7 square miles, far larger than most Old World cities of the time, and had a population that has been conservatively estimated at 25,000. This is larger than any of the Classic Mayan centers and rivals Tenochtitlan, the great metropolis of the later Aztec that so astonished the Spanish conquistadors with its splendor and extent.

At the center of Teotihuacán is the ceremonial complex, dominated by the massive pyramids attributed to the sun and moon. The Pyramid of the Moon is at the northern end of the Avenue of the Dead and is placed so that its shape echoes that of the volcanic mountain Cerro Gordo. When viewed from the south, the Pyramid of the Moon is framed by Cerro Gordo. The larger Pyramid of the Sun faces a point on

the western horizon where Tianquitzli (the Pleiades) lies directly in front of it; but it also provides some clues as to why this site was considered so important.

Class divide

Excavations beneath the Pyramid of the Sun have uncovered an underground lake which earlier occupants modified to create a clover-leaf configuration. It lies beneath the exact center of the pyramid and may have been seen as the "Place of Emergence": the womb-cave from which the ancestors of the tribes are said to have emerged.

Scattered throughout the site are other buildings of ritual significance. At the center of the city is the royal palace, the Ciudadela (citadel), which consists of a broad sunken enclosure containing the Temple of Quetzalcoatl. In this temple, relief figures of the Feathered Serpent alternate with those of Fire Serpents, expressing an opposition between the gods of greenness and fertility and those of the Mexican deserts.

Teotihuacán's religious center attracted migrants and pilgrims from a wide area, few of whom carried any means of subsistence. It appears that both the permanent and transient populations of Teotihuacán grew too fast for the city to support, and while the nobility ate in excess and lavish ritual feasts were maintained, the poorer residents and visitors often went hungry. Teotihuacán collapsed violently during the eighth century AD: its major buildings were burnt and destroyed, giving rise to speculation that the poorer masses rose against the hierarchy.

Yet Teotihuacán remains as an enigmatic symbol of Aztec ancestry and of the first true Mesoamerican empire. Despite the fact that only a small part of the city has been excavated and restored, its ruins today evoke a sense of awe and respect, and convey the power and authority invoked by the ancient gods.

Above: *View of Teotihuacán taken from a platform on the Temple of the Moon. The main thoroughfare through the ritual center of the city was known as the Avenue (or Street) of the Dead, flanked by numerous small pyramids and temple platforms. To the left of the Avenue of the Dead is the massive Pyramid of the Sun, the largest structure at Teotihuacán.*

TEOTIHUACÁN CITY PLANNING
Design and influence of a center of trade

Above: *A terrocotta mask from Teotihuacán, together with the mold from which it was formed.*

that came under the influence of Teotihuacán. These precincts were devoted entirely to the produce of skilled craftspeople.

Obsidian, a volcanic glass obtained from the Pachuca mines that Teotihuacán controlled, was worked into spear and ceremonial points in workshops located in the eastern part of the city. Thin orange ware was produced elsewhere by a colony of ceramicists from Puebla, and these were traded widely to cities within the Mayan districts as offerings to the dead.

Foreign merchants and artisans had clearly established themselves as resident communities within Teotihuacán, and the rapid building of the city suggests that these incursions were welcome. While there is evidence that Teotihuacán occasionally engaged in warfare, its contact with neighboring groups was usually peaceful and relied on barter and exchange, rather than the tribute and tax systems that marked relationships at the Aztec capital of Tenochtitlan.

From its inception, Teotihuacán sought to establish itself as a major center of trade and the planning of the city reflects this. Thousands of artisans worked within the city limits and the goods they produced were traded throughout the regions now known as Mexico, southwestern United States, and Guatemala. In return, Teotihuacán traders obtained cacao, rubber, jaguar pelts, caiman skins, marine shells, stingray spines, and brightly colored feathers.

Investigations at Teotihuacán suggest that it was the focus for far-reaching trade, as well as the largest ceremonial center of its time. Its principal monuments — the Pyramids of the Sun and Moon and the Temple of Quetzalcoatl — are linked by a long causeway that bisects the city, but the outskirts contained the residences and workshops of craftworkers from many areas

Satellite cities

Unfortunately, the Teotihuacános left no written records and the extent of their influence can only be surmised from finds uncovered during archaeological research. Such finds are nevertheless sufficient to indicate that Teotihuacán products were widely traded and that many of the Mayan sites show some degree of Teotihuacán influence. Even Tikal, the largest Mayan city, was for a time under Teotihuacán's control, as were the major sites of Cholula, El Tajin, Kaminaljuyú, and Monte Albán. The later Aztec were to claim that their gods came from Teotihuacán, and the city site remained as a place of pilgrimage even after its destruction by burning c. AD 750.

Excavations reveal that the majority of the artisans' workshops and the homes of merchants were located between 1 and 1¹/₂ miles outside the ceremonial center of the city and the residences of the noble elite. In these areas there are clearly identifiable potteries, obsidian workshops, and the remains of looms. Here too are small temples, some of which have been restored, that are dedicated to the various deities who had control over the arts. These temples are

often decorated with colorful murals and reflect the cosmopolitan nature of Teotihuacán, since many of them are dedicated to local gods from outside the Valley of Mexico.

The layout of the artisans and merchants quarters nevertheless follows the general plan of the city. Their houses were still constructed according to the grid that determined the main form of the ceremonial and noble districts, and it is therefore unlikely that the merchants came later to the city.

The lack of written records means that we do not know who built Teotihuacán or even what the original name of the city may have been, since "Teotihuacán" is an Aztec word. The ruins of the city stand as a memorial to the genius of the Mesoamerican cultures that preceded the Aztec.

Below: *Among the many temples and palaces that flank the Avenue of the Dead is the Palace of Quetzalpapaloti, or the Quetzal-Butterfly. The inner courtyard shows some of the carving and painting with which the pillars and walls were originally decorated.*

TEOTIHUACÁN AND URBANIZATION
Ritual, residential, industrial, and agricultural zones

Teotihuacán was the first metropolitan city in Mesoamerica and the first to control a true empire. Its trade and religious influences spread far to the north, east, south, and west, and in size the city exceeded anything that had ever been built before and probably exceeded even that of the massive city of Tenochtitlan (Mexico City) that was built by the later Aztec.

It is clear that Teotihuacán was intentionally built to be a major trade and ritual center, since there is no evidence of gradual accretions of buildings or of rebuilding over earlier structures, as is evident with the Maya. The entire city was carefully planned and executed as a single building operation, and is laid out according to a grid. This is based on a building unit of one-story square-sided apartments measuring 164–197 feet on each side and surrounded by

high exterior walls.

Streets intersect at intervals of 187 feet and aerial photography immediately shows that these are planned around the north-south orientation of a main avenue – the Avenue of the Dead. This is bisected by the San Juan river and by a secondary main street that runs from west to east.

There are clearly delineated zones within the city plan. At the center are the pyramids and temples of ritual significance, such as the massive Pyramids of the Sun and Moon and the Temple of Quetzalcoatl.

Surrounding this center are numerous "palaces": the residential units of the nobles and priests, which consist of windowless buildings surrounding open inner courtyards. The outsides of these buildings were elaborately

Below: *Stone-built homes for the nobility and priests were erected close to the Avenue of the Dead. This photograph shows the remains of some of the retaining walls on which these residences were constructed.*

adorned with carvings and the interior walls bore brightly colored frescoes; they were festooned with ornaments and caged birds, and set against the red ocher lime-plaster stucco of the pyramid surfaces. Cedar lintels and carvings from aromatic woods scented the air.

Feasting on taxes

Stretching beyond the homes of the nobility were those of the artisans, where potters, silverworkers, and obsidian-, shell-, and basalt-carvers each had their own specialized locale. Craftworkers from outlying regions such as Oaxaca had their own distinct residential areas and workshops within the artisans' quarters of the city, and it is apparent that they enjoyed a considerable degree of autonomy since many of these districts contain small temples. Here, too, were noisy and bustling markets.

Yet further out were the homes of farmers who provided Teotihuacán's subsistence base. Although these houses were little more than wattle-and-daub thatched huts and lacked the elaboration and studied aesthetics of the city center, they were nevertheless built according to the grid plan. The streets in this quarter were far narrower, often becoming little more than alleyways between the crowded buildings. Beyond these were the farmers' fields.

Although few of the farmworkers' houses and none of the fields have been excavated, recent research suggests that many of the fields were *chinampas* (raised fields) in which sludge dredged from rivers and swamps was piled to create small, highly fertile "islands." The farmworkers went to their fields in flat-bottomed canoes and brought produce back for the regular street markets. It is likely that part of their produce was paid to the ruling families and nobles in the form of taxes — which could be used to maintain the lavish feasts that often accompanied the nobles' ritual performances.

Unlike any other Mesoamerican city — and indeed, unlike most modern cities — there is nothing haphazard about the layout of Teotihuacán. There must have been a dedicated team of city-planners, but we do not know who these people were or what status they held in the Teotihuacán hierarchy. However, it seems likely that they were scribes working under the direction of the high priests, since much of the city is constructed along astronomical alignments that were dedicated to various deities.

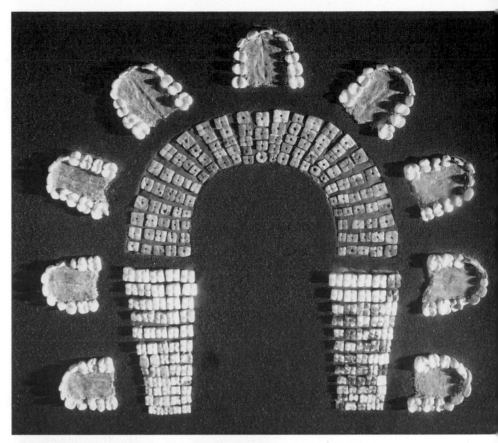

Above: *This necklace found at Teotihuacán is made from numerous pieces of shell that have been fitted together. The pendants attached to the necklace are human jaw bones.*

Left: *Figurine of a standing man from Teotihuacán*

113

WHERE THE GODS CAME FROM

Teotihuacán's deities and their monuments

The name "Teotihuacán" was given to the city by the Aztecs and means "The Place Where the Gods Came From." When the Aztec first became acquainted with the monumental archaeological zone of Teotihuacán it was already in ruins; many of the important temples and pyramids, as well as the homes of the

regeneration. Quetzalcoatl was also the Lord of Healing and Magical Herbs, and the God of Learning and Poetry.

Quetzalcoatl's major monument is in the center of a sunken courtyard within a complex called the Citadel which flanks the Avenue of the Dead. Here there is a small pyramid with

Above: *The Temple of Quetzalcoatl, within the courtyard of the Citadel. The sculptures show the feathered serpent from which the temple derives its name, as well as a fanged deity with huge circular eyes that may represent Tlaloc.*

nobles that formed the city center, had been burned and looted. Even so, the buildings were impressive enough to make the Aztec believe that the city had been built by a race of giants, and for them to claim ancestral links with the Teotihuacáno rulers.

Teotihuacán was to provide the Aztec with some of their most important deities. At Teotihuacán the major deity was the Feathered Serpent, Quetzalcoatl, who was associated with water and acted as a symbol of fertility and

carvings of feather-covered serpents as the image of Quetzalcoatl, together with grotesque carvings of a fanged deity who has been identified as Tlaloc, the Rain God.

Tlaloc appears with astonishing frequency throughout Teotihuacán. In addition to the carvings, he appears in various murals in different temples and palaces and is often associated with rivers. In a remarkable painting in a house known as Tepantitla, formerly the residence of a high priest, he is shown with drops of rain falling from his fingertips. He looks out over a lake from which two rivers run, where people are bathing and swimming. Amid fruit trees, other figures catch butterflies, cut flowers, dance, and sing. This scene of joy and abundance represents Tlalocan, Tlaloc's earthly home.

Late dedication

Also important at Teotihuacán, and again echoing the theme of water as a religious motif, is Chalchihuitlicue, the Water Goddess. She was both sister and wife of Tlaloc and

are placed according to astronomical observances. The great stairway of the Pyramid of the Sun, for instance, faces a westerly point on the horizon where Tianquitzli (the Pleiades) lies in front of it.

There is, however, no evidence that the pyramids were dedicated to the sun or moon. This attribution was given them by the Aztec, who also believed that the pyramids contained the burials of Teotihuacán kings. In fact, extensive excavations carried out since the 1960s have proven conclusively that neither pyramid contains any tombs. Instead, they

among her many duties she was the patroness of marriage and babies. It is said that Chalchihuitlicue invented the rainbow as a spiritual bridge between Earth and Heaven. She is often depicted by symbols of maize and snakes.

The most imposing religious buildings at Teotihuacán are, of course, the massive Pyramids of the Sun and Moon. The Pyramid of the Sun stands nearly 246 feet high and each side of the base is 738 feet long. The pyramids

served as temple platforms, although the flat-roofed temples that stood at their summits no longer exist.

Also regularly featured is the god Mictlantecuhtli, the Lord of the Underworld, or Mictlan, and frescoes depicting Eagle and Jaguar Warriors. In common with other Teotihuacán deities, Mictlantecuhtli was to be adopted by the Aztec, and the Eagle and Jaguar Warriors were to become elite soldiers in Aztec armies.

Above: *Tlalocan was the earthly paradise of Tlaloc and is depicted in murals at Teotihuacán in the residence of a high priest. This detail from the murals shows people playing and catching butterflies.*

COSMIC MYTHS

Remote and terrible, creative and rejuvenating gods

Above: *This mask represents Xochipilli, the Flower Prince. He was associated with dance, spring, and pleasure, and was the God of Love and Sport and patron deity of gamblers and gambling.*

Facing: *Teotihuacán's architects used different-colored materials for decorative effect, as shown on this stone carving.*

In contrast to the monuments erected at Mayan cities, where we find innumerable depictions of the exploits of the ruling lineages, the art at Teotihuacán is almost entirely religious in character. There are no carved stelae commemorating important dates in a ruler's life, and there are no indications that the ruling elite identified themselves directly with the deities.

The gods at Teotihuacán are "remote and terrible" and the art often has an austere quality. The Teotihuacános left us no record of the names of these gods, but by comparison with the deities worshipped by the later Aztec, we can begin to identify them. The principal deities appear to be versions of the Old Fire God (Huehueteotl) and the Rain God (Tlaloc). There are a number of carvings of a feathered

serpent, possibly indicating the influence of Mayan ideas as a representation of Kukulcan, who was later to become the Quetzalcoatl of Tula and Tenochtitlan.

It is perhaps significant that, despite their solemn appearance, these deities are all creative ones. They are the gods of renewal and rejuvenation, and of fertility and growth. Sun brings the new day and breathes life into everything; he is the Animating God who makes things happen, and in the Aztec pantheon he is also the oldest and most revered of the deities. Tlaloc, of course, brings the rains that fertilize crops, and in this respect is the god of fertility and good harvests.

The artistic expression of the Teotihuacános is, therefore, an optimistic one. This would be in accord with the archaeological record, which suggests that the growth of the city prior to its last few years was boundless and energetic. People were attracted to Teotihuacán in their thousands because of the promise it offered, and Teotihuacán's traders traveled across all of Mesoamerica to build what was possibly the greatest empire the New World has ever known.

A holy trinity

There are no depictions of any destructive deities at Teotihuacán. The gods of war are entirely absent, as are any monuments dedicated to a warrior caste or military achievement. This has led some scholars to deduce that Teotihuacán's expansion was an entirely peaceful one — although, of course, the absence of war symbolism is not the same thing as an absence of war. In fact, at some sites, such as Tikal, there is archaeological evidence to suggest a sudden incursion of warriors from Teotihuacán and the overthrow of existing regimes.

In addition to the carvings, there are numerous painted frescoes on the walls of the various temples and other buildings at Teotihuacán's center. Many of these have, unfortunately, been badly damaged; but sufficient remains for us to begin to interpret the images. In striking contrast to the carvings these paintings are of happy scenes, with lush landscapes and joyous figures engaged in all kinds of pleasant pursuits.

Closer inspection, however, reveals that this happiness is not being expressed in the human realm but in a land beyond the grave ruled over by the Rain God. In one remarkable painting, there are vast meadows aglow with flowers and surrounded by fields of maize and maguey. Gentle rivers cut through this enchanting landscape, and men, women, and children are shown eating maize, chasing butterflies, and bathing in the rivers (*see page 115*).

While it is impossible to say so with absolute certainty, the presence of these three elements — the Sun, the Rain God, and the Underworld — implies a kind of Holy Trinity at Teotihuacán which combines the forces of the Upper, Middle, and Lower Worlds.

DEATH OF A CITY
Civil uprising topples mighty Teotihuacán

From the first to the eighth centuries AD, Teotihuacán was the greatest power throughout Mesoamerica. No other city approached it in size, and none wielded comparable power and influence. Teotihuacán products were traded everywhere, and their priests and diplomats had established themselves at cities thousands of miles from their homeland.

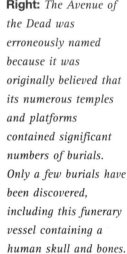

Right: *The Avenue of the Dead was erroneously named because it was originally believed that its numerous temples and platforms contained significant numbers of burials. Only a few burials have been discovered, including this funerary vessel containing a human skull and bones.*

Then suddenly Teotihuacán went into decline. No new monuments were erected for about one hundred years, and although the craftworkers maintained their output, the quality of their work declined. A large part of the population, perhaps as much as a quarter of the total, drifted away to other areas.

Then, in the eighth or ninth century, a dramatic event occurred. The archaeological evidence points to fierce fighting in the city center, monuments thrown down and destroyed, and temples desecrated. This was not a ritual deconsecration of the sacred sites, but a cataclysmic war. Then, the entire center of Teotihuacán was put to the torch and burned.

We do not know what really happened. Most theories suggest some form of internal strife, for the simple reason that Teotihuacán was so powerful that it could presumably have repulsed any attack from outside. Archaeologists do not think that Teotihuacán had external enemies powerful enough to be considered a threat, since the city had no fortifications of any description.

The decline in architecture and the arts implies that something had happened to disrupt the city's internal functioning. Teotihuacán's emphasis on trading may also have served to undermine the control of the priests, turning the city into a commercial rather than ritual center.

It may be significant that the heaviest fighting took place within the ceremonial center itself. It is here that we find signs of deliberate destruction, desecration, and burning. As well as being a sacred precinct, this part of Teotihuacán was home to the nobility and priests and contained the important administrative buildings. No fighting or burning took place in the artisans' quarters or in the suburbs, where the greater part of the population had their residences.

War against taxes

These archaeological facts have given rise to speculation that Teotihuacán experienced a brief but disastrous civil uprising. We can guess, but with some certainty, that the growth of Teotihuacán had seen the establishment of a state bureaucracy with ever-increasing power. Aside from the organization required to oversee and implement Teotihuacán's massive building programs, it would have been necessary to control agricultural production and administer an empire that embraced thousands of square miles. To support what must have been a small army of bureaucrats would have meant imposing some kind of tax or tribute on the productive members of society.

As trade increased – and with it the power

Left: *These skeletons of nine sacrificed warriors were found buried beneath the Avenue of the Dead. Note the shell-and-human-jawbone necklaces with which they are adorned, similar to those on page 113.*

Below: *This stone funerary mask was found at Teotihuacán. It is embedded with carefully cut and polished pieces of turquoise mosaic.*

wielded by traders, merchants, and artisans — resentment may have arisen at the increasing amounts of tax necessary to finance the ambitious programs of the nobility, priests, and bureaucracy. The cessation of the building program during the last years of Teotihuacán could simply be a consequence of the merchants exerting their rights and refusing to meet tax demands. If Teotihuacán was becoming a commercial center, the threat of supernatural retribution from the priests may not have been sufficient to keep internal dissensions in check.

This does not explain why Teotihuacán was virtually abandoned by the entire population, but we should remember that continuity was provided by the nobility and priests. It was they who ensured that the ritual elements of the calendar were adhered to and decided the auspicious dates for ceremonies to take place, and the record of most cities is the record of the ruling lineage. Without this stabilizing element it is likely that the structures that kept Teotihuacán functioning as a city would have quickly broken down.

JALISCO, NAYARIT, AND COLIMA
Unknown purpose of grotesque clay figurines

Below: *Nayarit figurines are often found in male-female pairs, as shown here. They were probably intended as caricatures of their owners, rather than realistic portraits.*

Although the development of great city-states and ceremonial centers with their associated sacrificial rituals is most often emphasized in Mesoamerican studies, large pottery figurines from the western states of Nayarit, Jalisco, and Colima reveal a strong sense for caricature and humor. These were interred in family tombs cut down through the sub-surface volcanic tufa sediment and reached by deep shafts.

Unfortunately, the popularity of such figurines in the tourist and collectors' markets means that no undisturbed tombs have been found. All of the excavated tombs have been looted, and although the skeletons of their occupants were left undisturbed, unbroken figurines were removed for illicit sale. The figures are nevertheless common in museum and private collections, but usually without any data concerning the manner of their acquisition. This makes dating them difficult, although it is generally assumed they are contemporary with Teotihuacán.

The earliest are thought to be from Nayarit, in a style known as Chinesco. Grotesque females with colossal genitals and slanting eyes are frequently depicted. Many have long noses but ridiculously stunted arms. Later Nayarit figures are in male-female pairs, depicted in various group activities. There are lovers, dancers, warriors, ball players, and banqueting scenes, often complete with miniature clay houses and temples. Some of the figures depict

sexual intercourse or women giving birth, and in others the human form has been distorted to give the appearance of hunchbacks and dwarfs.

The figurines from Jalisco are probably a little later in date; in these the modeling is more sophisticated. They still have exaggerated human forms, such as elongated heads and sharply pointed noses, and thus serve as a form of caricature, but they lack the grotesque effect of the Nayarit figures. They may have been a transitional form between the figurines of Nayarit and Colima.

Hairless dogs

The most refined figures come from Colima and it is generally assumed they are also the most recent — although this is a most unreliable method of setting a chronology. They may simply be a separate but contemporaneous tradition.

Again, an extraordinary variety of human activities are depicted, but a new form also appears, known as *techichi* (hairless dogs).

These are figurines of a special breed of dog common in ancient Mexico. They were fed on corn to fatten them, since they were an important source of meat. Curiously, the *techichi* dogs are modeled as if they were human: they dance and wrestle, are shown seated or standing on their hind legs, sleeping, as pairs of lovers kissing and licking each other, or in ridiculous contorted poses with their feet in the air.

There has been a great amount of discussion over what these figurines meant to the people of Nayarit, Jalisco, and Colima. The previously prevailing point of view was that they were merely grave goods to keep the deceased amused during their journeys to the next world, and this view still has many adherents.

Anthropologist Peter Furst has, however, suggested another function. He points out that the contorted poses are reminiscent of those adopted by shamans when engaged in battles with the spirits, and that dogs were thought to accompany the deceased on their journeys across the River of the Dead on their way to the Underworld.

The desecration of the tombs means that our knowledge of these enchanting figurines will probably never be complete. Even so, they provide a unique record of everyday activity in Mesoamerica, as well as details of costumes, face painting, and so forth. They are mostly admired, however, for their lively charm and expressive energy.

Above: *Although often more sophisticated than the figurines from Nayarit, those from Jalisco are still caricatures.*

Left: *Carvings of* techichi *were a speciality of Colima ceramicists. The hairless dogs were fattened on corn, as has been well illustrated here.*

CHAPTER SIX

THE TOLTEC
Victory and dissolution of a warrior tribe

In the ninth century AD a warrior tribe from the north invaded the central Mexican plateau. The cultures of this region, already weakened by internal dissension, offered little resistance to the invaders. Under the leadership of Mixcoatl (Cloud Serpent) and his successors, they pushed further south, and within a century had conquered not only the plateau, but also the Yucatán. These invaders were the Toltec.

Where the Toltec came from and what their background may have been is uncertain. It is nevertheless clear that they were not northern nomadic hunter-gatherers, since they had a fully developed warrior ethos and highly organized armies. This has led to speculation that their original home was at La Quemada, a fortress town close to the modern city of Zacatecas.

The incursion of the Toltec introduced a new element in Mesoamerican history. Prior to this, the societies had been governed by hierarchical priesthoods, and even their wars had been planned by the priests who consulted their almanacs to ensure that they took place on auspicious days within the Venus cycle. Under the Toltec, however, the state was ruled by a military aristocracy.

The cities they built were decorated with the emblems of a warrior caste and with representations of warriors, and the great murals they painted at the Mayan center of Chichén Itzá are depictions of their invasion and conquest of the Yucatán. The myths about the Toltec are varied and often contradictory, yet they point throughout to the suppression of the priestly cult of Quetzalcoatl (Feathered Serpent) and its replacement by a cult centered on Tezcatlipoca (Smoking Mirror), who was later adopted as War God of the Aztec.

Fragmenting coalition
The Toltec did, however, need to adapt to the new circumstances in which they found themselves, and to this end they adopted many of the existing symbols of the old Mesoamerican deities, particularly those from Teotihuacán. Their capital city of Tollan (Tula) was modeled in part on Teotihuacán, and it appears that it was through this adoption of existing frameworks that the Toltec sought to

legitimize their rule. Curiously, and despite their suppression of the priesthood, the Toltec ruler of Tula, Ce Acatl Topiltzin, renamed himself Quetzalcoatl and the Feathered Serpent was considered to be the patron deity of the city.

The Toltec were few in number, and the state they established was actually a coalition of groups over which there was little central control. In this respect they were quite different from the empires that were built by Teotihuacán and by the Aztec. Dissension and argument, leading to further warfare, seems to have marked the Toltec period.

Eventually the various groups within the Toltec state began to reclaim their independence, until the Toltec themselves were pushed south by new waves of northern invaders. In AD 1156, Tula was attacked and destroyed, probably by Aztec raiders.

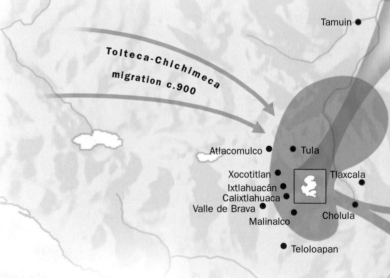

The Toltec legacy should not, however, be underestimated. The Aztec later claimed Tula as their legendary birthplace. They described it as a city of jewels, and Aztec families married into the royal Toltec families to unite their bloodlines. It is also clear that many Aztec beliefs, such as the cult of Tezcatlipoca, can be traced to a Toltec origin, and that the practice of mass human sacrifice for which the Aztec are infamous probably began at Tula.

100 AD	**534**	**683**	**800**	**850**	**900**	**950**	**1156**
The first pyramids are erected in the Valley of Mexico	Teotihuacán's abandonment begins	Revered Pacal ruler and father of Chan Balam, Hanab Pacal , dies aged 80	Metalworking techniques from South America are adopted in Mesoamerica	The Toltec led by Mixcoatl invade Mexico	Tula, capital of the Toltec Empire, is founded	Toltec influence has spread throughout Mesoamerica	The Toltec capital of Tula is invaded and destroyed

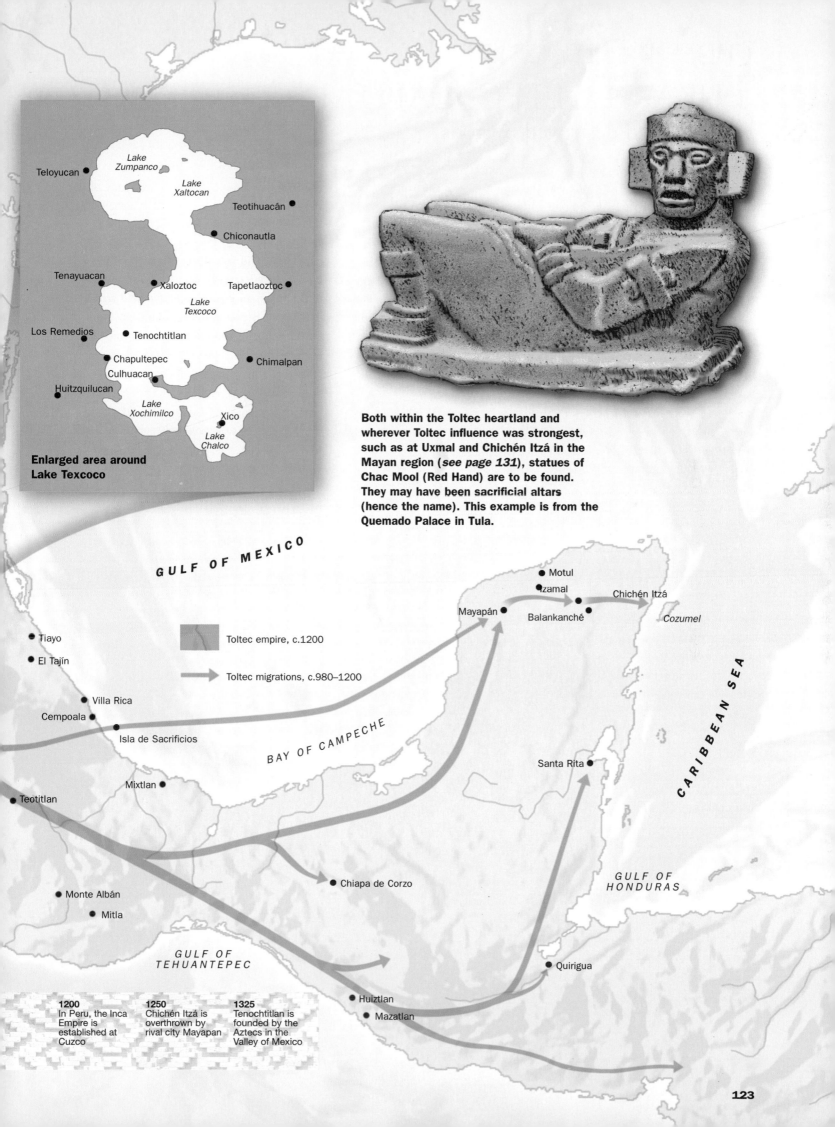

Enlarged area around Lake Texcoco

Teloyucan
Lake Zumpanco
Lake Xaltocan
Teotihuacán
Chiconautla
Tenayuacan
Xaloztoc
Tapetlaoztoc
Lake Texcoco
Los Remedios
Tenochtitlan
Chapultepec
Chimalpan
Culhuacan
Huitzquilucan
Lake Xochimilco
Xico
Lake Chalco

Both within the Toltec heartland and wherever Toltec influence was strongest, such as at Uxmal and Chichén Itzá in the Mayan region (*see page 131*), statues of Chac Mool (Red Hand) are to be found. They may have been sacrificial altars (hence the name). This example is from the Quemado Palace in Tula.

GULF OF MEXICO

Motul
Izamal
Chichén Itzá
Mayapán
Balankanché
Cozumel

Tiayo
El Tajín

	Toltec empire, c.1200

→ Toltec migrations, c.980–1200

Villa Rica
Cempoala
Isla de Sacrificios

BAY OF CAMPECHE

CARIBBEAN SEA

Santa Rita

Mixtlan
Teotitlan

Chiapa de Corzo

GULF OF HONDURAS

Monte Albán
Mitla

GULF OF TEHUANTEPEC

Quirigua

Huiztlan
Mazatlan

1200
In Peru, the Inca Empire is established at Cuzco

1250
Chichén Itzá is overthrown by rival city Mayapan

1325
Tenochtitlan is founded by the Aztecs in the Valley of Mexico

TULA, TOLTEC CAPITAL
Founded and destroyed by gods

Below: *The most outstanding feature at Tula is the Temple of Quetzalcoatl, which is surmounted by a number of stone columns carved to represent Toltec warriors. These originally supported the beams for the roof of the temple erected on the pyramid's summit.*

Tula was the capital city of the Toltec Empire and is located just north of the Valley of Mexico in the modern state of Hidalgo. Modern scholarship has now established beyond doubt that Tula is the site of the legendary Tollan, or Place of Reeds, which the Aztec thought of as a magical place where palaces were made from jewels. Indeed, the Aztec emperor, Moctezuma Xocoyotzin, claimed descent from these Toltec.

Archaeological investigations reveal that Tula was founded c.AD 900 during the Post-Classic period, and that it is based on the buildings erected at Teotihuacán. It may be that Tula was built by Teotihuacán refugees after they fled that city following its destruction by fire in AD 750. Although it is smaller than Teotihuacán, Tula is nevertheless a large and impressive city that controlled an empire that included many of the Post-Classic Mayan sites, such as Chichén Itzaá.

Probably the most important building at Tula is known simply as Pyramid B. This sizable temple pyramid was dedicated to Quetzalcoatl, the Feathered Serpent, and its substructure carries reliefs of prowling jaguars and coyotes, and of eagles eating hearts, reflecting the warrior ethos of the Toltec peoples. Immediately in front of the pyramid is a low wall surmounted by conch shell carvings depicting Quetzalcoatl in his guise of the Wind God.

According to Aztec interpretations, Tula was founded by Quetzalcoatl after the destruction of Teotihuacán, when he and his retinue of lords and priests were forced to flee. His father, the demi-god Mixcoatl, or Cloud Serpent, was probably the first to establish Toltec

dominance. It is nevertheless clear that the Toltec combined the qualities of gods and men and adopted the myths of Teotihuacán to legitimize their own rule, and that it was at Tula that the cult of Quetzalcoatl reached its peak. So important was Quetzalcoatl that the Toltec ruler, Ce Acatl Topiltzin, who was either the founder of the city or its last ruler (the chronology is unclear), was renamed Quetzalcoatl.

Burned in disgrace

In AD 1156 an Aztec attack destroyed Tula. This was apparently because it was a vulnerable frontier city, open to attack and incursion by nomad tribes from the north. To justify this act of wanton destruction, when the entire city was burned and its monuments defaced, the Aztec claimed a cosmic battle had taken place between their patron deity Tezcatlipoca (or Smoking Mirror) and Quetzalcoatl.

According to this myth, Quetzalcoatl was a divine and celibate deity. His purity was dependent on his abstention from sexual relationships and devotion to the austere duties and responsibilities of a high priest. But Tezcatlipoca contrived to get him drunk on pulque, and while in this inebriated condition introduced him to the beautiful Xochiquetzal, the Goddess of Prostitution, with whom he had intercourse. By doing so, the disgraced Quetzalcoatl made himself subject to punishment of death by fire, hence providing justification for the destruction of Tula. Quetzalcoatl's heart rose through the flames and ascended into the heavens to become Venus, the Morning Star, and he was established as the Creator God who would one day return to oust Tezcatlipoca and bring Aztec domination of Mesoamerica to an end.

Much of Tula has not been excavated; only the central monuments, the Burned Palace, Pyramid B, the Serpent Wall, and a great ball court have been fully explored. Even these were severely damaged when the site was destroyed by the Aztec. Pyramid B had most of its stucco facing removed and was cut into to make a ramp, down which the temple structures from

its summit were hurled. Surrounding this central region and extending a considerable distance are numerous overgrown mounds that have so far remained uninvestigated but which give an indication of the size of the original city.

Above: *A coatepantli, or Serpent Banner, frieze at Tula. These friezes surrounded temple enclosures and were carved with representations of the rattlesnake in honor of the Earth Mother.*

The major excavated monuments at Tula. The only other two structures that have been uncovered, Pyramid A and "El Corral," are to the east of this plan at the top.

Great Ball Court

North Square

North

Burned Palace

Serpent Wall (*coatepantli*)

Site of modern museum

Pyramid B (Temple of Quetzalcoatl)

Pyramid C

Central Altar

Central Plaza

Ball Court No.2

0   150   300 ft
0   50   100 m

GULF OF MEXICO

Tula
Lake Texcoco • Teotihuacán
• Cholula

Monte Albán •
• Mitla

PACIFIC OCEAN

QUETZALCOATL ABANDONS WAR
Myths of mercantile vs military prowess

Below: *Bas-relief depicting two Toltec warriors. Their bird headdresses indicate that they were members of a highly ranked warrior elite. The oval shape between them is a body shield.*

In one of the myths that describes when Quetzalcoatl was forced to abandon Teotihuacán and founded the city of Tula, he leaves in anger and is responsible for Teotihuacán's destruction. Although defeated in a bitter fight with Tezcatlipoca, Quetzalcoatl and his followers burned the city and vowed to return to avenge themselves. His retinue of followers is described in fantastic terms as consisting of giants, dwarfs, and strange,

deformed creatures.

But in addition to his warrior prowess, Quetzalcoatl had undergone rigorous training as a priest, and this gentler aspect of his character appeared to gain precedence when he arrived at the future site of Tula. The legends tell us he

was a great reformer, too, and when he founded Tula he abandoned his fighting ways and set about establishing a pacific regime. Among the most famous of his reforms was to stop the practice of human sacrifice. Offerings made to Quetzalcoatl at Tula are said to have consisted of fruit, flowers, and butterflies.

As part of his new peaceful program of reforms, Quetzalcoatl established trade links with neighboring groups. Toltec traders traveled widely, both influencing and borrowing from the peoples they came into contact with, to create a hybrid culture of their own that blended elements from all around them. Architectural features at Tula and other sites where the Toltec established a presence show a curious blend of styles. A cosmopolitan outlook pervaded their religious beliefs and influenced their buildings, which suggests that the Toltec were open to new ideas and willing to embrace the ideologies of their trading partners.

A boastful city
According to this scenario, Tula was built on the basis of a great trading empire that incorporated all the achievements of previous Mesoamerican cultures. Its jewel-encrusted buildings represented the seat of all learning and knowledge, and it was at Tula that poems celebrating the joys of beauty and nature were composed and the ritual calendar and writing systems were supposedly invented.

Much of this, however, was fanciful speculation on the part of the Aztec. While the Toltec undoubtedly controlled mercantile relations throughout much of Mesoamerica during the Post-Classic period, the cult of Quetzalcoatl was not their invention. They elaborated on previously existing myths and, of course, the written and calendric systems were established long before

Above: *Although equipment and dress varied little from society to society, in Toltec times a back shield was worn by warriors to protect the kidneys. This one is made up from mosaics depicting Xiuhcoatl serpents.*

the Toltec came to power. It is also apparent that much of their trading was conducted as tribute and tax, which the Aztec were to bring to perfection, and not on the mutually co-operative terms that the myths suggest. Much of Tula is dedicated to warrior cults.

The Aztec had myths to explain this, too. These say that Tezcatlipoca, fearful of Quetzalcoatl's promised revenge for the destruction of Teotihuacán, decided to conquer and kill his arch-rival before he could put his threats into action. He attacked and destroyed Tula, forcing Quetzalcoatl to flee once again.

Quetzalcoatl walked into the sea, again accompanied by his strange retinue of followers; but this time his anger was not to be contained. He vowed to rebuild his strength and to return during the dark days at the end of a *katun*, the closing period of the Aztec 52-year cycle, when all was uncertain and the world would be destroyed or renewed. Then Quetzalcoatl would bring all the powers he possessed as the Creator God and the God of Light to oppose the destructive and dark forces of Tezcatlipoca and bring about the complete and final destruction of the usurpers to his throne.

GLORIFICATION OF A WARRIOR CASTE

War and sacrifice for Quetzalcoatl in Tula

Despite the claims in myth that Tula was founded by Quetzalcoatl as a peaceful mercantile empire, investigations at both Tula and Mayan sites suggest that the reality was very different and that from its inception Tula was a warrior state.

Ce Acatl Topiltzin (Quetzalcoatl) was the son of Mixcoatl (Cloud Serpent) and his wife Chimalman (Prostrate Shield), and it is likely that Mixcoatl founded the city. The character of Mixcoatl and his later adoption as a patron by the warrior Chichimec — the precursors of the Aztec — and then incorporation as a deity into the Aztec pantheon points toward the warlike nature of Tula expansion.

Under the leadership of Mixcoatl, Toltec warriors and their mercenaries conquered all of central Mexico and virtually depopulated the Yucatán countryside, concentrating the Mayan nobility as hostages in the city of Chichén Itzá. Although a part of Chichén Itzá known as Old Chichén is Classic Mayan, much of the city was rebuilt with Mayan labor under the dominance of Mixcoatl's Toltec warlords. In fact, the only other important Mayan site of this period is Balankanche, situated in a cave close to Chichén Itzá, where there is an underground ritual chamber dedicated to Tlaloc, the Toltec rain god.

Watching over the hunt

Depictions of Mixcoatl do not show him as a beneficent father figure. His body is usually painted with red and white stripes that are associated with captive warriors destined for sacrifice. In this guise he represents death and the souls of warriors who float into the sky, where they become stars of the Milky Way.

Mixcoatl was elevated to the role of a deity in the Aztec calendar and, significantly, presided over the Aztec equivalent of the months of October and November. This time was known as "Honoring the Dead," when the Aztec undertook a great communal hunt and successful hunters were celebrated as the "captors" of the animals they had killed. The hunt was followed by the sacrifice of humans trussed as deer.

The buildings at Tula also suggest the presence of powerful war cults. There are depictions of Coyote and Jaguar Warriors who formed the elite troops of the

Toltec, and these are associated with eagles eating human hearts. If human sacrifice was banned at Tula by Quetzalcoatl, this is not indicated in such imagery. We know that the main function of the Coyote, Jaguar, and Eagle Warriors was to obtain sacrificial human victims, and they were trained to disable enemies without killing them. During the sacrifice the still-beating heart of the victim could be excised and offered to the gods.

Even the Temple of Quetzalcoatl is embellished with warrior symbols. The most impressive of these are huge basalt columns 15 feet high that supported the temple roof. Each of these depicts a Toltec warrior bearing arms and in full military dress, and each has a firebird symbol, emblem of the Tula ruling elite, on his chest. Thus, although the warriors were not rulers, their status as a highly professional army directly answerable to the leading nobility of the city is patently obvious.

Their association with Quetzalcoatl as the supporters of his temple also suggests that Quetzalcoatl was far from being the pacific deity that some Aztec myths proclaim. Support for Quetzalcoatl was shown by the provision of sacrificial human hearts, rather than offerings of fruit, flowers, and butterflies, and the figures are a focal point for the militaristic regime that seems to have flourished at Tula.

Above: *A carved jaguar frieze from the Temple of Quetzalcoatl. The jaguar, as a patron of warriors, emphasizes the fact that Tula was founded as a warrior state.*

Facing: *Monumental warrior columns from the Temple of Quetzalcoatl. These figures are dressed in the full battle regalia of the Toltec warrior elite. Note particularly the firebird symbol each has on his chest, which identified the warriors with the ruling nobility at Tula.*

TOLTEC EXPANSION
Domination of Mesoamerica by war and trade

Below: *A carving on the Temple of the Warriors at Chichén Itzá. The warrior wears a bird headdress and feathered costume, and a back shield similar to that on page 127.*

Facing: *Part of the Temple of the Warriors with its sculpted serpent columns. The reclining figure in front of the temple is a Chac Mool. Although these are often described as "sacrificial altars," their exact function is unknown.*

Within one hundred years of their invasion of the central Mexican plateau in the ninth century AD, the Toltec had extended their influence deep into the south of Mesoamerica. There is virtually no Mesoamerican city of this period that does not show some degree of Toltec influence.

Some of the buildings at the Mayan center of Chichén Itzá are almost identical to those at the Toltec capital of Tula, although recent arguments suggest that, as the buildings at Chichén Itzá are better built than those at Tula, this may represent the Toltec assimilating ideas from the Maya, rather than the reverse. Toltec presence is apparent in the Valley of Oaxaca and the highlands of Guatemala, and may have extended even further south to include contact with Andean cultures outside Mesoamerica.

Part of the reason for this rapid expansion of Toltec influence was military. The rule of the priests appears to have been superseded, at least in part, by a bureaucracy composed largely of military leaders. Indeed, at some cities there appears to have been a virtual overthrow of the existing royal lineages and their replacement by Toltec war captains. Yet warfare alone is probably insufficient to explain Toltec domination of almost the entire Mesoamerican area.

Another factor was certainly trade. Since the time of Teotihuacán, the south had always held a fascination for the north and The Toltec opened up and expanded the trade routes that had previously been used by the Teotihuacános. Feathers, cotton, and, most importantly, cacao could only be obtained from the south, and were all valuable trade items.

A monetary feast

Cacao was used to make chocolate, an expensive and luxurious drink throughout central Mexico, but the beans also served as a form of currency that could be used by noble families to purchase the feast items they needed to establish and maintain their prestigious positions. Feathers of tropical birds from the highlands of Guatemala were highly valued; those of the quetzal bird becoming a symbol of royal rank and linked the wearer with Quetzalcoatl, the Feathered Serpent. Cotton came from the Yucatán peninsula and was important for both clothing and for use in warriors' armor.

Warrior strength was, nevertheless, essential in maintaining control over the various states that the Toltec established. In addition to central Mexico, controlled from Tula, there were Toltec states in the Yucatán, Tabasco, and Guatemala. Warrior insignia is very conspicuous at all of these, and we can surmise that the Toltec found it necessary to keep armed garrisons in the territories they controlled.

There would certainly have been resistance, both active and passive, from the priests whose autonomy the Toltec attempted to overthrow, and these priests undoubtedly had recourse to peasant armies that could offer considerable resistance if provoked. In fact, most of the Toltec states show adjustments to local conditions and at least a recognition of local deities.

The history of Toltec expansion is only poorly known. This is not due to a lack of records, but rather to an abundance of mythical accounts created by the Aztec to legitimize their later claims to the areas previously under Toltec control. The Toltec come through these myths as exemplary characters, whose wisdom was such that they invented mathematics and writing. These, of course, are Aztec stories, and bear as much relation to the truth as tales of Toltec growing colored cotton so that the weavers did not have to dye it, and a land that had never known sadness or hunger.

CHICHÉN ITZÁ
Invading forces influence Mayan city's architecture

In Maya, chi means "mouth" and chen means "well," while Itzá is a tribal designation. A translation of the name Chichén Itzá would therefore be "the Mouth of the Well of the Itzá," a reference to the sacred *cenote* (natural well) that features so prominently at this site (*see pages 136–137*).

Chichén Itzá is located approximately 75 miles east of the city of Mérida, the capital of Yucatán. According to the *Chilam Balam* (one of the sacred books of the Maya, written in Maya at the time of the Spanish conquest), it was founded about AD 450; this date corresponds reasonably well with those derived from archaeological study.

All the early buildings at Chichén Itzá are completely Mayan in style and are located in the southern section of the site. These include the Red House, Nunnery, Deer House, and the Akab-Dzib, and are distinguished by numerous carvings of the Long-Nosed Rain God, or Chac.

The *Chilam Balam* tells us that the Yucatán was subject to continual invasions by outside tribes from the beginning of the tenth century, who used Chichén Itzá as a base for their incursions into the area but were finally overthrown when the Itzá returned to claim their lands. Although the return of the Itzá cannot be verified through archaeological research, it is clear that from the tenth century onward Chichén Itzá was invaded and its architectural features transformed.

During this later period the old Mayan rain god, Chac, was associated with Tlaloc, the rain god of the Valley of Mexico. Similarly, the Mayan Feathered Serpent, Kukulcan, was now depicted as Quetzalcoatl. Buildings from this period are carved with intertwined serpents and jaguars and eagles eating human hearts.

Unexplored landscape

There are columns adorned with non-Mayan warriors and skull platforms (*tzompantli, see pages 156–157*), as well as other architectural details that link Chichén Itzá with the Toltec capital of Tula. Whether the Toltec completely overran Chichén Itzá or formed some kind of Maya-Toltec alliance is unclear; the buildings in the northern part of the site nevertheless contain elements derived from both cultures.

These later buildings were mostly erected during the 11–13th centuries, the period when Chichén Itzá was the most important city in the Yucatán. Toltec Plumed Serpent columns support the lintels of the Warrior and Jaguar temples, and Toltec elements are evident too in the Hall of the Thousand Columns, El Castillo (also known as the Pyramid of Kukulcan or the Pyramid of the Serpent), and the ball court, where they appear alongside representations of the Mayan Long-Nosed Rain God.

At the height of its power Chichén Itzá

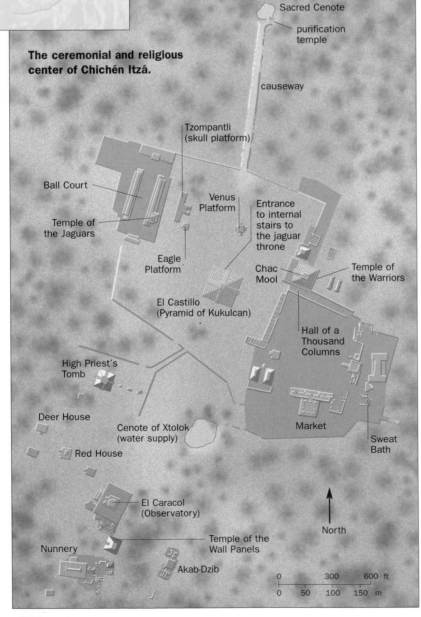

The ceremonial and religious center of Chichén Itzá.

Sacred Cenote

purification temple

causeway

Tzompantli (skull platform)

Ball Court

Venus Platform

Entrance to internal stairs to the jaguar throne

Temple of the Jaguars

Eagle Platform

Chac Mool

Temple of the Warriors

El Castillo (Pyramid of Kukulcan)

Hall of a Thousand Columns

High Priest's Tomb

Deer House

Cenote of Xtolok (water supply)

Market

Sweat Bath

Red House

El Caracol (Observatory)

North

Nunnery

Temple of the Wall Panels

Akab-Dzib

| 0 | 300 | 600 ft |
| 0 | 50 | 100 | 150 m |

covered an area of more than 1¹/₂ square miles, but this extended beyond the city for an as-yet unknown distance. Although hundreds of buildings have been investigated, ranging from mighty pyramids such as El Castillo to the remnants of post holes that supported small huts, only about 20 of these can be visited. Viewed from the top of El Castillo, the surrounding area is dotted with numerous "hills" covered in dense vegetation, and the majority of these are undoubtedly unexplored pyramids that once formed part of Chichén Itzá.

Chichén Itzá was overthrown in the middle of the 13th century and its power relinquished to that of a rival city, Mayapan. No new buildings were erected and no new carvings were made after this time. Only a small, scattered population continued to live permanently in its vicinity. It nevertheless remained as a place of pilgrimage, and offerings were still being cast into the sacred *cenote* well after the beginning of the Spanish Conquest .

ASTRONOMICAL OBSERVATIONS
Impossible alignments for an ancient culture?

Below: *This round building is El Caracol, which was used as an observatory by Mayan astronomers at Chichén Itzá. A spiral staircase inside it leads to an observation platform where small holes cut in the walls face the four cardinal directions and other significant astronomical points.*

Mayan observations of the sun and moon and the movements of the planets were used for divinatory purposes, and in this sense the Mayans were astrologers rather than astronomers. The sun, moon, planets, and stars were deities whose movements and conjunctions had a direct bearing on the lives of the people. While this does not imply that their observations were inaccurate – they were, in fact, close to modern reckoning and in advance of the astronomy of the Old World of the period – it gave the heavenly bodies a significance that was closely bound to ritual and the priests' activities.

Because the heavenly deities controlled events on Earth, it was important that the priests devised means whereby their movements could be accurately observed and their intentions divined. Part of this was incorporated within the ceremonial centers, in the alignments of major buildings and their positions relative to each other.

At Chichén Itzá the architectural features of the huge pyramid of El Castillo represent important elements in the late Mayan calendar. It has 91 steps on each of its four sides which, with the temple platform, total 365, the number of days in a solar year. Each side of the pyramid has 52 panels contained in nine terraced steps, equal to the number of years in the Mayan-Toltec calendric cycle. The nine terraced steps of the pyramid are each divided

in two by a stairway, giving 18 sections on each side, corresponding with the 18 months of the Mayan year.

Gastropod formation

Architectural details such as those of El Castillo are unlikely to have been accidental or incidental; but more direct evidence is presented at Chichén Itzá in a building known as El Caracol. El Caracol is a round tower on a rectangular platform, and within it a winding staircase leads from the second story to an observation platform. It is this stairway that gives it its name: in Spanish, "caracol" describes the winding shape of a snail's shell. We know that later buildings of this form were dedicated to the Toltec deity Quetzalcoatl in his manifestation as Ehecatl, the God of the Winds, and this is probably also true of El Caracol.

The eastern part of El Caracol is in ruins; however, enough remains for us to understand something of the significance this building had for the Mayan priests. Window-like openings in the thick walls provide sighting points for astronomical observations. Among those that remain, one points due west to the position where the sun sets at the vernal equinox;

another points to the setting of the moon at its greatest southern declination, another to its northern declination. Yet another sets El Caracol precisely on a south-north axis.

The question arises as to how the Mayans, without the benefit of modern astronomical instruments, were able to make such extremely accurate observations. This has led some scholars to suggest that these sightings and alignments are coincidental rather than planned. Their frequency and precision, however, suggest otherwise, and drawings in the codices of central Mexico provide some clues in the absence of direct evidence from the Mayan area.

In these drawings observers are depicted before two crossed sticks that are used as a sighting device for distant points on the horizon. By matching the setting or rising of a heavenly body against the position of a natural feature, its synodical cycle can be established — one simply needs to wait until it rises or sets in exactly the same position again. These known factors can be matched against other celestial movements to arrive at complex calculations, and, over a period of time, refine them to a high degree of accuracy.

Above: *Crowds visit Chichén Itzá during the autumnal and vernal exinoxes. They come to see the shadows cast by the stepped edge of the pyramid on the side of the northern staircase of El Castillo. The last wave of shadow reaches the ground to coincide wih the gape-jawed serpent's head, which can be seen to the left of center in the picture.*

THE SACRED CENOTE

Sacrifice at Chichén Itzá's life-giving well

Below: *This view of the Sacred Cenote shows the raised causeway that leads off from the top-left toward El Castillo. The Sacred Cenote was not used as a water supply (a second cenote at Chichén Itzá served domestic purposes) but was solely for sacrifices to water deities.*

Water, as a crucial element in human survival, was the focus for a great amount of ritual attention by the ancient Maya. The vast majority of ceremonial sites are located on or near water courses, and in some cases, such as Palenque, the river is an incorporated architectural feature within the site. Numerous figures of the Rain God and his assistants appear throughout Mesoamerica, and the blood of human sacrifices was frequently referred to as "living water" paid in homage to deities.

For the Maya of the Yucatán, water took on special significance. There is little or no surface water for most of the year, and much of the water needed for their agricultural pursuits was collected in reservoirs and cisterns constructed near ceremonial complexes.

The limestone escarpment of the Yucatán does, however, have a unique feature in the presence of deep, circular, natural wells, or CENOTES, that remain viable for the whole year. At Chichén Itzá the centrally located Xtoloc *cenote* provided sufficient water to satisfy the needs of the entire local populace and contributed greatly to the importance of the site during the Classic period.

A second *cenote* at Chichén Itzá, the Cenote of Sacrifice, had a different function. It is connected by a 984-foot long causeway to El Castillo, the great pyramid at the center of Chichén Itzá, and attracted pilgrims from as far south as Panama and north to the Valley of Mexico, who came to

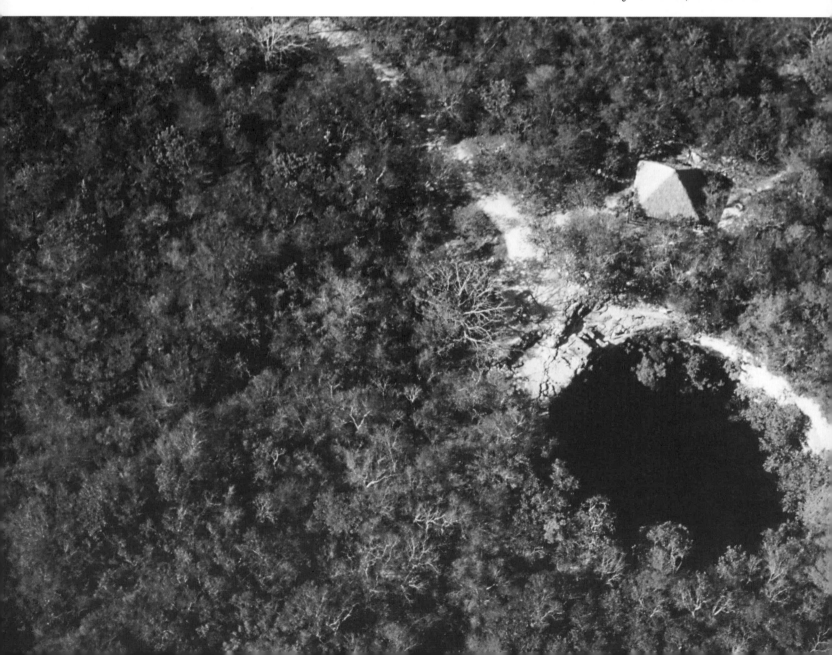

cast their offerings into its depths. Hundreds of blocks of pom (copal resin), which had been made into small cakes and painted a brilliant turquoise, have been recovered from its depths during archaeological investigations by the Peabody Museum between 1905 and 1908.

Pom burns with a fragrant odor and was placed in small pottery incense-burners decorated with images of the deities. From this we know that many of the offerings at the Cenote of Sacrifice were made to Chac, the Rain or Lightning God.

Young and precious offerings

Legend has it that the Cenote of Sacrifice was where virgin girls were cast into its depths by Mayan priests, together with their jewels and other valuable offerings. Although there is no clear archaeological evidence that virgins were especially selected as sacrificial victims, the dredging of the *cenote* uncovered a number of human bones and crania, many those of children.

Bishop Landa, one of the Spanish chroniclers, observed that on occasion children were cast into the *cenote* at daybreak; if they survived until noon a rope was lowered and they were hauled out. It was felt that during the period of their ordeal they had been in communication with the deities and were therefore able to predict events for the forthcoming year. He also noted that if they drowned, the Mayan lords fled from the *cenote* in great fear and alarm. Landa tells us that the Maya "had the custom of throwing live men into the well during the dry season as a sacrifice and although the men were never seen again it was not felt that they had died."

Many of the objects recovered from the *cenote* were items the Maya considered valuable, either because of their exquisite workmanship or because they were made from materials that had to be imported and were therefore of precious value. Among them are masks, gold jewelry, gold and copper plaques, wood and stone carvings, polished jade beads and ornaments, jade ceremonial ax heads, and carved bone and shell sacrificial knives. Some, such as a number of *atlatls* (spear-throwers), relate to hunting and warfare, as do carved human long bones that were, presumably, trophies of war.

Above: *At the point where the causeway reaches the cenote is a small temple, here partly reconstructed, that was used during purification rituals that preceded sacrifices. The Sacred Cenote averages about 40 feet deep, below which is a 10-foot layer of mud. Partial dredging revealed human bones and numerous artifacts.*

QUETZALCOATL AS KUKULCAN
Mayan leader becomes Feathered Serpent god

Above: *The gaping serpent jaws and feathered mantle of Quetzalcoatl from a Teotihuacán carving.*

In Nahuatl, the language spoken by the Toltec and Aztec, Quetzalcoatl is the name for the Feathered Serpent featured so prominently in the beliefs and rituals of the Post-Classic period. To the Maya of the Yucatán, he was known as Kukulcan, and to the highland Maya of Quiche and Cakchiquel as Gucumatz. Although of considerable importance in this later period in the Mayan areas and Mexico, the Feathered Serpent is curiously absent throughout most of the Classic period, despite the fact that the other major deities have clear antecedents during this earlier era.

Even so, the Maya of the Colonial period spoke of Kukulcan as one of the Twin Creator Gods, in a manner very similar to the way in

138

which Quetzalcoatl was considered by the Toltec and Aztec. These myths also name the place of origin as Zuyua, a name linked with the Toltec capital of Tula. The inference, of course, is that Quetzalcoatl/Kukulcan was an invention of the Toltec.

Yet at the same time we know that the Toltec freely borrowed the names of existing deities for their prominent gods, and that they were essentially a warrior society, rather than one dominated by priests. It seems highly unlikely that a theocracy intent on inventing new gods, such as is found among the Aztec, existed among the Toltec.

Mayan historical sources give a detailed account of a man calling himself Kukulcan who came to the Yucatán from the west in AD 987. In these stories Kukulcan seized control of the Yucatán peninsula and established a capital city at Chichén Itzá, the later phases of which contain Maya-Toltec buildings. He is said to have introduced idolatry, but was good and just.

The tales tell us that Kukulcan later returned to Mexico, where he was worshipped as the god Quetzalcoatl. They probably refer to the Toltec invasion of Yucatán under the leadership of Mixcoatl (Cloud Serpent), whose son, Topiltzin, later adopted the name of Quetzalcoatl as a royal title.

Topiltzin-Quetzalcoatl expelled

The suggestion is that Quetzalcoatl/Kukulcan was a real person, who was later raised to the status of a deity. This has precedents in Mesoamerican history, where the ruling lineages frequently claimed descent from the gods. The identification of Kukulcan as being good and just may reflect the fact that the Yucatán was under Mexican domination when they were recorded. The Toltec exercised considerable control in the Yucatán, where they ousted the old Mayan lineages. In the murals at Chichén Itzá, Kukulcan is shown hovering in the sky, where he awaits the gift of sacrificial hearts excised from the chests of Mayan rulers.

Other accounts, although differing in details, also credit the Toltec with introducing the cult of Quetzalcoatl. In these a division arose between the followers of Topiltzin-Quetzalcoatl and the Toltec military orders who paid homage to Tezcatlipoca (Smoking Mirror). Through trickery, Tezcatlipoca forced Topiltzin-Quetzalcoatl to leave Tula. He and his followers fled to the Gulf Coast, where they set sail on a raft of serpents to travel to Tlapallan (Red Land). It is perhaps significant that the date given for the expulsion of Topiltzin-Quetzalcoatl is again 987, thus corresponding with the presumed date of Toltec migrations into the Yucatán.

A speculative conclusion can therefore be drawn that the cult of Quetzalcoatl originated with the insignia of a ruling Toltec lineage. Forced into exile following a military coup at Tula, Topiltzin-Quetzalcoatl may have founded an independent Toltec state in the Yucatán, where he ousted the existing rulers and established himself as king. To legitimize his position he followed an ancient tradition of identifying the ruling families with the deities, and Quetzalcoatl-Kukulcan became a god. The position of Quetzalcoatl as a major deity was later confirmed by the Aztec, who claimed descent from the ruling lineages at Tula.

Above: *There is little evidence that the cult of Quetzalcoatl originated among the Maya, although Mayan myths state that a feathered serpent they named Kukulcan was one of the Twin Creator Gods. El Castillo at Chichén Itzá was dedicated to Kukulcan, but is of late Toltec-influenced construction. This tenth century fragment of a Kukulcan carving was recovered from the site at Chichén Itzá.*

MYTHS FROM THE INHERITORS
Fanciful versions of Toltec history

Below: *Detail from the Pyramid of Quetzalcoatl at the Toltec capital of Tula. The outer coating of the pyramid has worn away to reveal details of its construction. Although many Mayan buildings in the Yucatán were modeled on those at Tula, the Yucatán buildings are generally of superior workmanship.*

The history of the Toltec is almost entirely legendary. They left no dated monuments, and for years the archaeological record was both sketchy and contradictory. Their capital city of Tollan was first thought to be located at Teotihuacán, a theory that has proved to be false, and was then identified with as many as a dozen different sites. We now know it to be at Tula in the Mexican state of Hidalgo. Much of the confusion stems from the myths of the Toltec initiated by the later Aztec.

According to these stories, the Toltec came from the north and established a city in a labyrinth of caves at Culhuacán. Ce Acatl Topiltzin Quetzalcoatl built Tula with "dwellings of silver, some built of dyed and white sea shells, dwellings of turquoise and of rich feathers." His realm was a truly amazing one, with cotton, maize, and cacao growing in myriad colors and where food was so plentiful that the Toltec burned many of their maize cobs for heating baths.

Under Topiltzin Quetzalcoatl, the Toltec sacrificed only serpents, birds, and butterflies. Their offerings were of flowers, and they lived in peaceful harmony with all their neighbors. This angered the gods, who demanded human hearts, so they sent a magician who tempted Topiltzin Quetzalcoatl with a drink that was said to restore youth and vigor. While under the intoxicating effects of the magician's drink, he had intercourse with a young girl sent by the Goddess of Prostitution and Erotic Love, thus breaking his vows as a priest and opening a path through which the War God, Tezcatlipoca, could take control. A different version of this story has been used to explain Tula's destruction (*see pages 124–125*).

Condemned for desire

Topiltzin Quetzalcoatl was followed by a succession of kings, each of whom ruled for exactly 52 years (the length of the Mesoamerica calendric cycle). During their reigns Tula began to decline. There was drought; worms ate the corn; and fire rained from the heavens. The last ruler, Huemac, was also the victim of Tezcatlipoca's machinations. Huemac, who was not under the vows of abstinence

that had governed Topiltzin Quetzalcoatl's rule, had a beautiful daughter who had refused all suitors. Tezcatlipoca sent a magician, Toueyo, to the market place in Tula with the intention of undermining Huemac's rule.

Toueyo posed as a seller of green peppers, and like other peddlers from the rural districts he did not wear clothes. Huemac's daughter, now under the magician's spell, saw his penis and was overcome with desire. She retired to her rooms in the palace where she became listless, refused to eat, and her body began to swell. Her servant girls pleaded with Huemac to release her from her misery, and once he had determined its cause he called Toueyo to the palace and gave his daughter to him as a wife.

The story of Huemac was used by the Aztec to explain the collapse of Tula. Huemac had married his only daughter to a foreigner and, worse, to a mere peddler of green peppers. By marrying into the lower classes, he broke the aristocratic heritage of the Toltec kings. It also justified the Aztec invasion of Tula, which they destroyed in an attempt to revive the cult of Quetzalcoatl, from whom the Aztec rulers claimed descent.

Although much of the content of these tales is fanciful imagining on the part of the Aztec and, in part, a justification of their own rule, archaeological records tend to confirm the internal dissensions that tore Tula apart. The conflict between the cults of the priests, represented by Quetzalcoatl, and those of the military leaders, under Tezcatlipoca, formed the foundation for ideological conflicts that later arose within the Aztec capital of Tenochtitlan.

Above: *The Toltec invasion of the Yucatán in the tenth century set Toltec warriors and expansionist policies against the more conservative doctrines of Mayan priests. The basalt figure (left) is a Toltec warrior wearing a suit of padded armor. Opposition to the Toltec invasion was led primarily by the priests, such as the one shown on the right from a Mayan porcelain vase.*

141

CHAPTER SEVEN

THE AZTEC
The Mexica and Chichimec ally with Mexican cities

[handwritten annotations: "Aztec = an inhabitant of the village called Aztlan ← mythical (location unknown)"; "Mexica (better Mexihka) = an inhabitant of the city called Mexihco"]

The final phase in Mesoamerican history began with the founding of Tenochtitlan in the Valley of Mexico in 1325 by a tribal group whom we know today as the Aztec. The Aztec were the dominant group in Mesoamerica during the century leading up to the Spanish Conquest in 1519–21, and at the height of their power they ruled over most of Mexico.

Theirs was, however, a late flowering of Mesoamerican culture: By the time Tenochtitlan was established, the great city of Teotihuacán had been in ruins for more than 600 years, Mayan influence had been waning for 400 years, and the Toltec capital of Tula had been razed 100 years earlier.

The Aztec called themselves the Mexica or Tenocha, and in company with another tribal group called the Chichimec, they had only entered the Valley of Mexico during the early 13th century. Here the Mexica-Chichimec formed an alliance with the cities of Texcoco and Tlacopan, known as the Triple Alliance, and it is generally this alliance that is meant when we use the term "Aztec."

[handwritten: "He does not use it for this —"]

Aztec history is one of conquest and domination, and most histories dwell on the roles of the Eagle and Jaguar Warriors, human sacrifice, and the gruesome practice of ritual cannibalism. We are given accounts of 15,000 or more people being sacrificed each year, their hearts torn from the still-living bodies and their corpses thrown down pyramid steps to crowds waiting below. Some estimates place the number of annual human sacrifices as high as 50,000.

Yet although sacrifice was an important element in Aztec culture — it served not only to propitiate the gods but also to control the Aztec Empire through the threat of ritual destruction of leading warriors and nobles of subject states — this is only part of the story. Far from being the savage brutes that the Spanish chronicles depict, the Aztec had developed a rich mythology based on the beliefs of Teotihuacán and Tula, perfected the arts of monumental building and land reclamation, and had a love of poetry and rhetoric (*see pages 160–161*). Significantly, the highest official in Aztec society was known as the Great Speaker.

Key to numbers on main map:
(1) Cortés made landfall in April 1519. While his ships proceded north to the pre-arranged point that later became Villa Rica (2), Cortés may have traveled overland via Oceloapan (3) before joining the main force.

At Ixtacamaxtitlan (4) Cortés encountered stiff resistance from Indians who impressed the Spanish with the might and power of Moctezuma and the Aztec capital.

The inhabitants of Tlaxcala (5), resolutely independent of Tenochtitlan, eventually became allies of Cortés.

November 1519, Cortés arrived at Ayotzingo where he was greeted by Moctezuma's nephew who led the Spaniards in triumph to Tenochtitlan to meet the Aztec emperor.

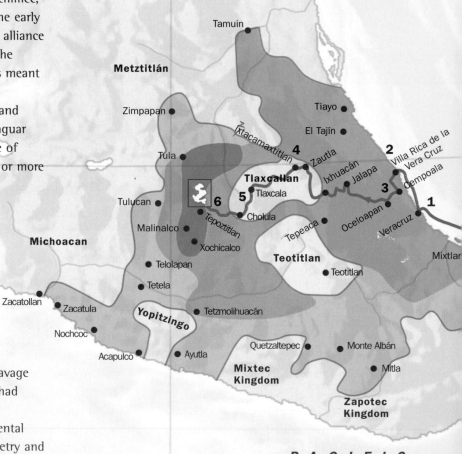

900 AD	1200	1250	1325	1345	1428–1430	1434	1440–68
The end of Classic Mayan civilization	The Mexica (Aztec) and Chichimec enter the Valley of Mexico	In Africa, the Benin kingdom is founded	Tenochtitlan is founded by the Aztec	Tenochtitlan becomes capital of the Aztec Empire	The Aztecs defeat the Tepanec, earlier settlers in the Valley of Mexico	Triple Alliance formed between Tenochtitlan, Texcoco, and Tlacopan	The Aztec Empire expands south of Tenochtitlan

War, religion, farming, crafts

Aztec society was highly complex. The Great Speaker was head of state and a high priest and was believed to hold this position through divine right. Beneath him was a war captain whose role included the conduct of Aztec secular affairs, and an array of priests who dedicated their lives in homage to one or other of the Aztec deities. This elite group was supported by a nobility from whose ranks the Eagle and Jaguar Warriors were chosen. There was no regular Aztec army; instead every boy received training in defensive warfare and in the use of the *atlatl* and obsidian-bladed sword (*see pages 162–163*).

Despite the emphasis given to warfare, the Aztec economy was an agricultural one, supported by raised fields or *chinampas* (*see pages 164–165*) in the control of local wards or *calpulli*. Each *calpulli* had its own leader and its own temple. In addition, numerous quarters within Tenochtitlan were dedicated to the manufacture of craftwork, or to occupations such as masons or goldsmiths. Although excluded from high office, women were highly respected and enjoyed virtually the same freedoms as men, and some female roles, such as that of midwife, had status equivalent to that of the temple priests in the ruling elite.

Aztec life was deeply religious. Nothing was undertaken without the sanction of the deities and each household had its own shrine to which daily offerings and prayers were made. Each day of the year and every activity had its own patron deity, and matters of major significance were settled only after the temple priests had consulted their calendars and determined an auspicious date.

Yet the Aztec were never dogmatic. Although they demanded tribute in the form of taxes from conquered peoples, they never attempted to impose their beliefs.

FLORIDA

CUBA

CARIBBEAN SEA

Legend

- Aztec empire, 1440
- Expansion under Moctezum I and Axayacatl, 1440–81
- Expansion under Ahuitzotl and Moctezuma II, 1486–1520
- Borders, c.1520
- Route of Cortés between April and November 1519

Chichén Itzá
Mayapán
Cobá
Cozumel
Yucatán
Uxmal
Tulum

GULF OF MEXICO

BAY OF CAMPECHE

Tabasco
Petén
Chiapas

Huitzlan
Mazatlan

Scale for enlarged map on the right

0 5 10 15 20 miles

0 10 20 30 kilometers

Valley of Mexico map

Tizayuacán
Citlaltepec
Coyotepec
Lake Zumpanco
Xoloc
Teoloyuacan
Xaltocan
Lake Xaltocan
Cuautitlan
ruins of Teotihuacán
VALLEY OF MEXICO
Ecatepe
Chiconaulta
Tenayuacan
Tepeyacac
Lake Texcoco
Texcoco
Azcapotzalco
Dike of Netzahualcoyotl
Tlacopan
Chapultepec
MEXICO
TENOCHTITLAN and TLATELOLCO
Culhuacan
Ixtapalucan
Coyohuacan
Zapotitlan
Lake Xochimilco
Xochimilco
Chalco
Atlapulco
Lake Chalco
Ayotzingo
Tezompa

Timeline

1470
In Peru, the rival Chimú Empire is conquered by the Incas

1493
Founding of Hispaníola, the first Spanish settlement in the Americas

1494
The Tordesillas Treaty divides new territories between Spain and Portugal

1502
Moctezuma Xocóyotzin (Moctezuma II) becomes Great Speaker of the Aztec Empire

1519
Hernán Cortés and his conquistadors arrive on the Gulf Coast

1520
Aztec warriors led by Cuauhtemoc drive the conquistadors out of Tenochtitlan

1521
With the aid of Cempoala and Tlaxcala allies, the Spanish conquer the Aztec Empire

1522
The Spanish found Mexico City on the ruins of Tenochtitlan and Tlatelolco

CHICHIMEC-MEXICA ORIGINS
Checkered history of a mercenary tribe

Aztec history does not begin until the early 13th century, when a small tribe calling themselves the Mexica entered the Valley of Mexico. Legend only tells us that the Mexica came from Axtlan in the north, which is sometimes associated with Mictlan, the Underworld; but it is clear from this that they

no!

Aztlan

were not native to the valley.

The Mexica had perhaps been nomadic hunter-gatherers or small-scale farmers who were driven south by adverse conditions. At the time the Mexica entered the Valley of Mexico, it was dominated by three rival powers: the Tepanec of Atzcapotzalco, the Toltec-inspired city of Texcoco, and the city of Culhuacán, whose leaders claimed descent from the

Tolteca-Chichimec of Tula.

The Chichimec themselves, despite their claims to a Tula ancestry, were also strangers from the north. Their presence seems to have been resented by Tepanec and Texcoco, since the name Chichimec derives from "chi-chi-chi": an unintelligible chirping instead of proper speech, designating the Chichimec as "foreigners."

NO!

The Mexica formed a small settlement called Chapultepec on the western shore of Lake Texcoco. They were small in number and unable to establish themselves as a power in the area as the Chichimec had done, so instead they were mercenary warriors employed by one of the valley's rival factions. They eventually formed a more permanent alliance with the powerful Chichimec city of Culhuacán, with whose residents they had an affinity as a result of their foreign status in the region.

Legend tells us that the Mexica, wishing to impress their Culhuacán allies, held a major festival at which the daughter of Lord Culhua was to be honored. Culhua readily agreed, anticipating that the honor would be marriage into a Mexica noble family, which would strengthen the political alliance between Culhuacán and Chapultepec. The Mexica, however, sacrificed the girl to their patron deity, Huitzilopochtli.

Exiled into legend

In retaliation, the Culhuacán warriors drove the Mexica out of Chapultepec and forced them into exile on small islands in a swampy region of Lake Texcoco. Lord Calhua expected the Mexica to perish in this hostile environment, and exiled rather than destroyed them in order to prolong their agony; but the Mexica were tenacious and survived by becoming mercenaries for Texcoco and Tepanec. By coincidence, their exile fulfilled the first part of a Mexica legend that stated they would found a great city — "the center of the

NO!

world" — on a swampy island.

After many years of great difficulty, the second part of their legend was fulfilled. This was that the foundations of the city were to be laid on an island where they found an eagle — the symbol of Tezcatlipoca in his guise as Huitzilopochtli — sitting on a prickly-pear cactus and holding a snake in its beak. This prophesy was realized in AD 1325, when the Mexica began building Tenochtitlan (Place of the Prickly-Pear Cactus).

With the establishment of this permanent base, military experience the Mexica gained through mercenary activities stood them in good stead. They were familiar with the tactics of all the neighboring war captains, and used this to their advantage to overthrow Tepanec and forge a new alliance with Texcoco.

Thcy also allied themselves with another city,

Tlacopan, to form the Triple Alliance of the Aztec, and subjugated a close neighboring city to the north to create the twin city of Tenochtitlan-Tlatelolco. The leading power within the Triple Alliance was the Mexica-Chichimec, who now legitimized their rule by claiming descent from the Toltec and Teotihuacán.

Above: *The original Aztec settlement was at Chapultepec on the western shore of Lake Texcoco. Today, the area is covered by a park in Mexico City.*

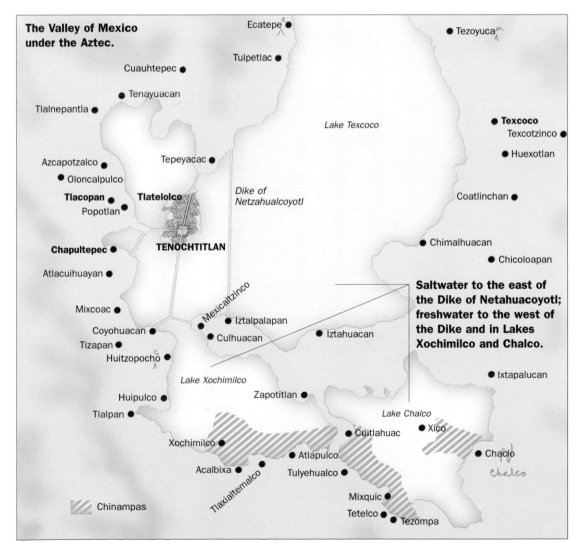

The Valley of Mexico under the Aztec.

Ecatepe

Tezoyuca

Tulpetlac

Cuauhtepec

Tenayuacan

Tlalnepantla

Lake Texcoco

Texcoco
Texcotzinco

Azcapotzalco

Oloncalpulco

Tepeyacac

Huexotlan

Tlacopan   **Tlatelolco**
Popotlan

Dike of Netzahualcoyotl

Coatlinchan

Chapultepec

TENOCHTITLAN

Chimalhuacan

Chicoloapan

Atlacuihuayan

Mixcoac

Coyohuacan

Mexicaltzinco

Iztalpalapan

Iztahuacan

Saltwater to the east of the Dike of Netahuacoyotl; freshwater to the west of the Dike and in Lakes Xochimilco and Chalco.

Tizapan

Culhuacan

Huitzopocho

Ixtapalucan

Lake Xochimilco

Huipulco

Zapotitlan

Tlalpan

Lake Chalco

Cuitlahuac

Xico

Xochimilco

Chaclo

Atlapulco

Acalbixa

Tulyehualco

Tlaxialtemalco

Mixquic

Chinampas

Tetelco

Tezompa

Facing: *According to Aztec visionaries, their capital city of Tenochtitlan was to be founded in a swamp where they found an eagle sitting atop a cactus and holding a snake in its beak. This Aztec drawing depicts the founding of the city, with the eagle and cactus at its center. Note the blue lines that divide Tenochtitlan into four parts and represent the canals on which the city was built.*

[Handwritten margin note: "The picture shows NO snake because there wasn't one"]

[Handwritten: "Chalco"]

Aztec Aesthetics
Carving the appearance of true objects

Right: *An Aztec sculpture of an eagle head. Note the anatomically correct beak and eye.*

Below: *This painted female figure gives a good impression of everyday clothing for Aztec women.*

For the Aztec, the world was imbued with beauty. They were careful observers of the minutest detail that nature offered to the eye. An Aztec carver working in stone or jade could produce these details so closely that a trained botanist looking at a carving of a fruit is able to state with certainty the species-specific fruit that is represented.

Yet it is important to remember that in the Aztec world everything was considered a gift of the deities. In some senses the "real" object, what we might call its essence, lay not in the human realm but in the other worlds that the deities occupied. This is recognized in the

Spanish records, where Aztec carvers are noted as saying that all they produce is the "appearance" of something: it is an emblem, or symbol, of something greater.

Thus the Aztec artist was always working within the sphere of sacred representation, and was accordingly granted status almost equal to that of royal scribes and leading members of the nobility. While this sacred duty of the artist is, perhaps, unremarkable in monumental carving, where the deity or glyph signs of the deity were incorporated, this thinking extended to other forms of Aztec art.

In a sense, every carving or painting was thought to contain "elemental" qualities that linked it with the first, the origin, of the species, and each of these elements linked it further with the Creator Gods, thus carrying mythological and ritual significance. A carving or painting of a butterfly was not considered to be a representation of an individual of that species, but embodied all the symbolic and mythical associations of the original butterfly. It

was, therefore, also representative of the warrior whose soul "hovered like a butterfly" in the other world after his death, and further associated with the "flowery wars" in which the warrior's skill was tested.

Hallucinogenic discourse with gods

Similarly, realistic carvings of mushrooms or the maguey cactus invoked images, respectively, of the "flesh of the gods" and the "milk of the gods." The mushrooms had hallucinogenic qualities and were consumed by priests during their divinatory rites, and it was through them that deities put words into the priests' mouths. The maguey cactus was used to make a fermented ritual drink that was mildly intoxicating, and anyone partaking of this was said to be transported to the edge of the sacred

In their monumental carvings Aztec artists had less recourse to realism in our sense of the word, yet nevertheless there were strict formulas to be followed that, to the Aztec, were as real as anything that might be observed in nature. The deities had their unchanging symbols, and although each might assume any of a number of different forms, each had very specific attributes that the carvers faithfully encompassed in their work. An Aztec looking at one of these carvings did not see a representation of the god; instead, he saw the path by which the god's presence was made real.

Aztec carvings, as those of the rest of Mesoamerica, can be admired from a distance for their aesthetic qualities. Indeed, they are avidly collected as "works of art." This was not, however, the way in which they were viewed by the Aztec themselves.

Top: *An Aztec eagle-shaped container that was used as a receptacle for the hearts of sacrificial victims.*

Left: *This small statue depicts Quetzalcoatl in his guise as Ehecatl, the God of the Wind. Ehecatl was associated with priestly knowledge and identified with the planet Venus in its aspects as both the evil Evening Star and the benign Morning Star.*

147

Tlatelolco
Activities and opinions simmer in the market center

The city of Mexihco consisted of two parts: Tenochtitlan and Tlatelolco

Below: *Night-time floodlights over Tlatelolco (now the Plaza de Tres Culturas) reveal Aztec ruins in the foreground, a colonial church and, at the back, modern apartment buildings.*

There is much discussion among scholars about the relationship between Tlatelolco and Tenochtitlan. While some claim that this was a rival city that Tenochtitlan conquered, others state that Tlatelolco was merely a suburb that had a specialized function. Alternatively, it may have been a small village on the outskirts of Tenochtitlan that was gradually absorbed as Tenochtitlan expanded.

It is nevertheless clear that Tlatelolco was always regarded by the Aztecs as separate or different in some way from the great city itself, even though it was well within the boundaries of Tenochtitlan when the Spanish arrived. The late designation of the Aztec capital as a twin city, Tenochtitlan-Tlatelolco, confirms the divide.

Tenochcas [annotation above "Aztecs"]

Tlatelolco functioned as the trade center of Tenochtitlan. It was here that the *pochteca* guild performed its function of obtaining the luxury goods and materials that were in such demand among the Aztec nobility, and it is partly this that caused the rift. The *pochteca* grew immensely wealthy through this trade, to the extent that their personal fortunes exceeded those of many nobles; yet the nobles did not have the connections to obtain the goods they required by any other means. Thus many of the nobles were little more than political puppets of the *pochteca* and the traders' views carried disproportionate weight in many of the council meetings.

The *pochteca* regarded themselves as only nominally under the control of the ruling council. Their patron god, Yacatecuhtli, the Long-Nosed God, was the most prominent deity in Tlatelolco and the wealth of the *pochteca* ensured that festivals in Yacatecuhtli's name rivaled anything that could be offered elsewhere in Tenochtitlan.

Yacatecutli or Yacatecuhtli [annotation]

In addition to the power of the *pochteca*, Tlatelolco contained all the principal public markets of the Aztecs. According to Spanish accounts, their main market could accommodate 80,000 people. Apart from Tlatelolco's control of commerce that this implies, the markets were also the forum for public comment — and criticism — on the decisions of

the Aztec council and the behavior of the ruling elite.

Sidestepping the law

Although direct criticism of the Great Speaker was punishable by death, with the execution carried out as an "object lesson" in the marketplace itself, even he could not totally ignore murmurs of discontent that reached him from market gossip. In fact, the war captains patrolled the markets regularly to test political feeling and were subject to discrete, but nevertheless disrespectful, responses from the market habitues.

Tlatelolco appears to have resented the restrictions on freedom imposed by the council in Tenochtitlan and therefore gained a reputation for its unruliness, as well as attracting resentment over the power held by the *pochteca*. The Spanish tell us the markets were also the haunts of prostitutes and drunkards. Although prostitution did not carry the same negative connotations for the Aztecs as it did for the Spanish, it is likely that it stepped beyond the Aztec sense of propriety within Tlatelolco's markets.

Drinking was an altogether different problem, since intoxication was sanctioned only during specific ceremonial activities and otherwise infringed ritual law. Yet even here the death penalty meted out to nobles in Tenochtitlan was tempered among the commoners at Tlatelolco's markets and usually amounted only to an admonishment and public disgrace; a clear indication that the courts in Tenochtitlan exercised caution in their dealings with Tlatelolco and were careful not to pass judgements that would inflame local feeling.

The mutual hostility between Tenochtitlan and Tlatelolco nevertheless came to a head when some Tenochtitlan noble youths visited the main market "for fun." Fired up by the tales they had heard of the abandonment to be found in Tlatelolco, they abducted and raped the daughters of a Tlatelolco lord. The ensuing battle between the two rival factions is significantly replete with marketplace references.

Above: *In addition to their carvings of deities, the Aztec delighted in making small painted clay models of everyday events. This one depicts the hustle and bustle of a village marketplace.*

TENOCHTITLAN
A dream-like spectacle for the conquistadors

Above: *The exact extent and layout of Tenochtitlan is difficult to determine, since much of the ancient site is now buried beneath Mexico City. Some indication of the general plan of the city can be determined from early maps, such as this one prepared by Cortés at the time of the Spanish Conquest.*

"When we saw all those cities and villages built in the water, and other great towns on dry land, and that straight and level causeway leading to Mexico, we were astounded.... These great towns and pyramids and buildings rising from the water, all made of stone, seemed like an enchanted vision from the tale of Amadis. Indeed, some of our soldiers asked whether it was not all a dream."

These words were written in 1519 by Bernal Diaz, a foot soldier with conquistador Hernán Cortés, when the Spanish first set eyes on the Aztec capital city of Tenochtitlan, the site of present-day Mexico City.

Tenochtitlan occupied a series of small islands

and reclaimed land in Lake Texcoco, which were connected by a complex series of canals and linked to the mainland by five great causeways. It covered an area of more than $4\frac{1}{2}$ square miles, with a central ceremonial center encircled by a residential zone, which in turn was encircled by *chinampas*, or raised fields, that formed fertile garden plots.

The heart of the city was a rectangular walled enclosure that contained the principal temples and ball courts, as well as skull racks that served as grim reminders of the Aztec practice of human sacrifice. This enclosure was dominated by the massive Templo Mayor, a twin pyramid dedicated to the deities Tlaloc and Huitzilopochtli and which, for the Aztec, represented Serpent Mound (or Mountain), the spiritual and temporal center of the Aztec world.

The residential area surrounding this enclosure was divided into quarters by the main causeways, with the old city of Tlatelolco forming a fifth sector. Within the residential zones were numerous secondary temples and palaces, courtyards, and great open plazas where public meetings and markets were held. There were orchards and carefully tended gardens, filled with flowers and ponds and stocked with birds and tame animals.

Cleansed in the name of a goddess

All the public areas were regularly cleaned and swept; the Spanish commented on their cleanliness. There was even a goddess,

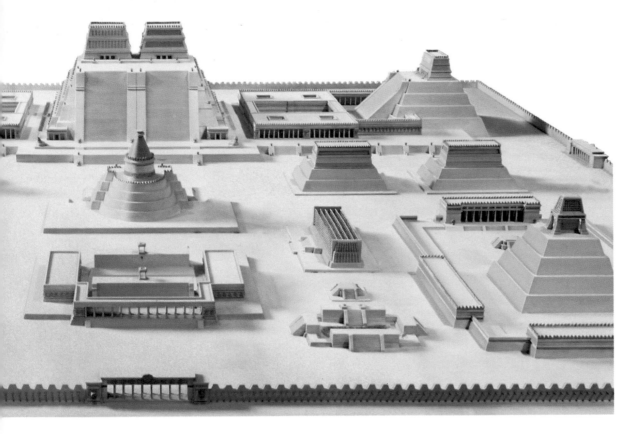

Left: *A model of the ceremonial center of Tenochtitlan. The walled enclosure sets the buildings aside as a sacred precinct. At the center back is the Great Pyramid, or Templo Mayor, surmounted by twin temples.*

Tlazolteotl (Eater of Filth), whose function was to ensure that the streets were kept clean and who presided over a major annual festival where the entire city was washed and scrubbed and all the houses swept out.

The number of canals connecting the various parts of the city was such that the conquistadors described Tenochtitlan as "another Venice," and most transportation within the city was by water. It was access to water transport that made commerce such a vital part of Tenochtitlan's economy and ensured its survival. The early Mexica had clearly turned what was previously seen as an inhospitable environment to their advantage, and through this eventually controlled an empire containing perhaps ten million people.

The population resident at Tenochtitlan is very difficult to determine, largely because much of the site lies beneath Mexico City and its full extent is not known. It was at least 150,000, although it may have been many times greater than this — Tenochtitlan's main market place alone could easily accommodate 60,000 people. It is little wonder that the Spanish were impressed, since few Old World cities of the time could match the extent and splendor they encountered here.

Despite the awe with which the Spanish first beheld the city, after its conquest in 1521 they began to destroy it. The great Templo Mayor was dismantled to provide building materials for the Metropolitan Cathedral. Its palaces and temples were turned into residences for the Spanish, its canals filled in. Today it is buried beneath Mexico City, which makes archaeological excavation impossible. It is only through incidental works, such as the construction of the Mexico City Metro transport system, that its full extent is finally being realized.

Below: *In February 1970 Aztec relics were discovered while building the subway station below the Pino Suarez pyramid.*

THE WAR OF FLOWERS
Sacrificial victims taken in glory

One of the aspects of Aztec life that most horrified the Spanish chroniclers was the widespread practice of human sacrifice. Almost every deity demanded sacrifice, usually of captive warriors but in some instances also of women and children, and the Spanish recorded rituals at which hundreds of people were destined to die by having their hearts ripped out and their bodies flung down pyramid steps. The need to obtain captives for sacrifice was so important that Aztec warriors were trained to disable and capture an enemy rather than to kill him, and the most exalted warriors were those who had taken the most captives.

At the peak of Aztec power, human sacrifices had reached unprecedented proportions. Conservative estimates place the numbers of annual sacrifices at approximately 15,000; the dedication of the Templo Mayor in Tenochtitlan in 1487 reportedly required the sacrifice of more than 20,000 prisoners. Some estimates even place the dedication sacrifices as high as 80,000, although this is probably exaggerated. Nevertheless, on this occasion the chief priest of the Aztec, Ahuitzotl, is said to have torn the hearts from his victims over a period of so many hours that he collapsed, exhausted.

The Aztec may have obtained a proportion of their victims from the War of Flowers. "Flowers" was an Aztec euphemism for blood, particularly for blood that spurts from a still-beating heart; the War of Flowers was a unique accord made with neighboring states that the Aztec had failed to conquer. Two states in particular, Tlaxcala and Huejotzingo, participated in these treaties, under which staged battles were held at certain times of the year for the specific purpose of obtaining captives for sacrifice.

Evading the horror of Mictlan

It should be emphasized that Tlaxcala and Huejotzingo people held similar views to the Aztec, and that none of these states looked upon sacrifice with the same horror as the Spanish. To them, sacrifice was an honorable act, and a captive who died bravely was esteemed. Indeed, it was not unusual for

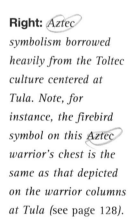

Right: *Aztec symbolism borrowed heavily from the Toltec culture centered at Tula. Note, for instance, the firebird symbol on this Aztec warrior's chest is the same as that depicted on the warrior columns at Tula (see page 128).*

Left: *This bas-relief carving shows Aztec warriors and their weapons. In battle the Aztec relied primarily on short thrusting swords studded with obsidian points that could be used to slash at an enemy's legs to disable him.*

someone to offer himself to the sacrificial knife.

To the Aztec, Mictlan, the Land of the Dead, was a place of unspeakable terror; a realm of perpetual misery where the spirits of pestilence, famine, and poverty held sway. The sacrificial victim did not, however, go to Mictlan. Instead he became a star and spent his afterlife in a glorious condition as a companion of the sun. Under such circumstances, death by sacrifice may have seemed infinitely preferable to other means and it is certain that this view was held both by the Aztec and their opponents in the War of Flowers.

Thus the War of Flowers may have offered ideal opportunities to the warriors of the Aztec and of Tlaxcala and Huejotzingo: these were the chance to become a sacrificial victim and thus to lead an exalted afterlife, and the opportunity to become a famous warrior through the capture of prisoners and thus lead an exalted life on Earth. Whether he defeated his foes or was defeated by them, the War of Flowers provided the Aztec warrior with the opportunity of earthly or heavenly success.

While the above concept was strange to the conquistadors, we should remember that the Spanish concept of a glorious death in battle was equally strange to the Aztec and offered no advantage to the warriors. Although the conquistadors were horrified by the scale of sacrifices, the numbers killed in this manner were, in fact, far fewer than those killed on the battlefield by the Spanish during their Mesoamerican campaigns against the Aztec and other nations.

BLOODLETTING AND HUMAN SACRIFICE

Appeasing the gods in return for a bountiful harvest

Below: *Detail from the Codex Magliabecchi showing an Aztec sacrifice. Victims were stretched over altars at the top of pyramids, where their hearts were cut out by priests, prior to throwing the bodies down the pyramid stairways.*

There is no doubt that the Aztec placed great value on personal bloodletting and human sacrifice as a means of appeasing their deities. The scale at which this was done – at least in the later years of the Aztec Empire – was unprecedented. Most of their gods, including even the apparently benign ones, demanded human blood.

In order to understand this phenomenon, we need to accept Aztec concepts of the relationship between humans and deities. Many of the gods' births are depicted as violent and unnatural, and it is frequently through their sacrifices that the people are able to survive and the plants and animals are nurtured. The giving of this sacred blood placed the people under an obligation known as *tequitl*, or the repayment of debt. In a sense, the food people consumed had been nourished by the blood of the gods. Since in the Aztec view blood was a non-renewable resource, the people were expected to make offerings of their own blood on which the gods could in turn be fed.

The degree of personal bloodletting in *tequitl* appears to have varied according to rank: the commoners frequently merely pricking their ears and flicking the drops of blood on the ground, while the celibate high priests were expected to lacerate the foreskin of the penis.

Parallel to these personal blood offerings were two forms of institutionalized human sacrifice. One was the performance of the *ixiptla*: male or female impersonators of the gods. The other was the mass killing of victims at the four principal festivals of the year – Tlacaxipeualiztli, Etzalqualiztli, Ochpaniztli, and Panquetzaliztli – or during the dedication of major public works.

Gods among the people

The *ixiptla* were thought to represent the deities in their earthly form, and as such were dressed sumptuously and feted wherever they went. Every desire was attended to, they lived in the most regal of the palaces, and, although carefully watched, they had virtually unlimited freedom. They might continue in this guise for an entire year, during which the god was felt as a palpable presence. By bringing the god among the people, the Aztec were expressing a sense of continuation, a reliving of the mythical past during which the deity's actions and purpose were explained.

According to Aztec logic, the *ixiptla* had to return to the spirit realm at the end of their tenure – which could only be achieved through sacrifice. The Spanish records tell us that many

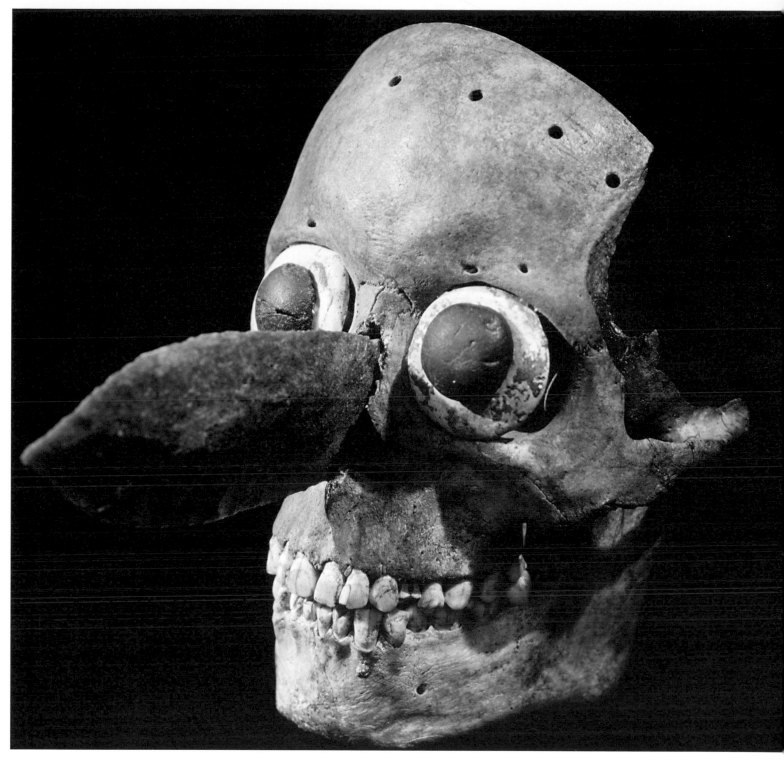

of the *ixiptla* went willingly to their deaths, confident they would be reborn in the image of the god they had represented.

The mass killings are more difficult to explain in terms of Western ideals, since they appear to show a blatant disregard for human life. We need, however, to apply Aztec logic. The greater the sacrifice made by the gods, the greater the debt incurred by people, and the four major festivals of the year corresponded with important aspects of the agricultural cycle on which the Aztec were dependent. It was therefore appropriate that the numbers of offerings should be large to reflect the original beneficence of the gods.

Another aspect of the mass killings also needs to be considered. The victims were not usually Mexica – the Aztec blood stock – but slaves and captives taken from subject tribes as a tribute or captured during the War of Flowers between Tenochtitlan and Tlaxcala. During these ritual killings, in addition to the need to appease the gods, there must have been an element of political domination and demonstrations of Aztec power. Through mass sacrifice the Aztec made the hold they had over the tribute-paying tribes abundantly clear, and through the proceeds of the ritual wars with Tlaxcala gave tangible proof of the ability of Tenochtitlan's warrior elite.

Above: *An Aztec skull mask is used to form the hand-guard of this sacrificial knife. It is not uncommon in Aztec work to find similar associations between form and function.*

TZOMPANTLI
Skulls, real and represented, displayed as tribute and totem

they were not adopted here until after Toltec influences reached the area from Tula, and it is likely they were originally brought to Tula in the Toltec migrations from Teotihuacán.

There is some inconclusive evidence to suggest that the *tzompantli* may have served a symbolic function at Teotihuacán and at the sites directly influenced by Toltec ideas. Few post hole remnants have been found on the tops of these platforms, which we would expect to find if they had a display function, like that of the Aztec structures, and the skulls are merely representational bas-relief carvings on the wall surfaces.

There can be little doubt that the *tzompantli* were originally associated with the Eagle and Jaguar Warrior cults. On the *tzompantli* at Chichén Itzá, for instance, in the northern Maya-Toltec part of the city, the carved skulls are accompanied by carvings depicting warriors, feathered serpents, and eagles eating hearts. All of these served as warrior insignia among the Toltec and may have been imported to Chichén Itzá by them.

Significance of the head

Some interpretations of these carvings suggest the carved heads are shown as if on wooden poles, which would indicate that the practice of display was already known to the Maya-Toltec. This interpretation is, however, only an impressionistic one; other interpretations could just as easily be made.

The Aztec undoubtedly took the idea of trophy head display to an extreme, and although there are only passing references to *tzompantli* in the literature, we can make some reasonable assumptions about the function they served. The Aztec believed that representations of deities gave them a tangible presence in the human world. It is logical to assume from this that the display of skulls belonging to those who had given their hearts and blood to feed the gods would create a permanent presence for them as well.

We also know that the head had especially sacred meaning. After the decapitation of a sacrificial victim the head became the property

Above: *Turquoise mosaic skull mask of Quetzalcoatl, shells inset to represent teeth. The original cedar wood base has rotted away.*

Facing, top:
A full-scale tzompantli.

Facing, bottom: *Part of a platform in the Templo Mayor complex, Tenochtitlan. The top was originally covered with real skulls on short poles.*

The Spanish conquistadors at Tenochtitlan were horrified by the *tzompantli*, low platforms walled in stone and covered with human skulls. During the Aztec period many of the skulls were those of war captives and sacrificial victims, and were placed on upright wooden stakes that covered the tops of the platforms. Spanish claims that some of the *tzompantli* — the Aztec word translates as "wall of skulls" — held thousands of skulls is, however, an exaggeration of the kind that the conquistadors were apt to make in emphasizing the barbarity of the Aztec as a means of justifying their own excesses and religious zeal.

Tzompantli did not originate among the Aztec. There is evidence of them in some lowland Mayan sites, although it appears that

of the priests who performed the sacrifice. It was presented directly to the deities on the platform at the top of the pyramid, whereas the body was thrown down the stairway to the crowds waiting below. It is likely, therefore, that the *tzompantli* functioned as a repository of this sacred power.

Psychologically, of course, the *tzompantli* served as a reminder to the Aztec that their ritual duties had been carried out through sacrifice, and the greater the number of heads displayed, the more thoroughly this could be seen to have been accomplished. For the non-Aztec it also served as reminder of the power of the Aztec and of the successes of Aztec warriors. Power invested in the *tzompantli* thus had a sacred character in its affirmation of the effectiveness of sacrifice and as a means of concentrating this within Tenochtitlan, as well as a secular function that asserted the role of the Eagle and Jaguar Warriors upholding Tenochtitlan's political supremacy over subject states.

GENDER ROLES
Sex and sexuality in Aztec communities

Below: *Statue of the Water Goddess, Chalchihuitlicue, or Jade Skirt. She was the ruler of the Fourth Sun, the era when maize was introduced, and was both sister and wife of the Rain God, Tlaloc.*

The Aztec were a warrior society, and the recorders of Aztec customs were male Spanish priests and conquistadors. It is hardly surprising, then, that the early chroniclers of Aztec life emphasized its masculine aspects, or that the Spanish priests wrote at length about the celibacy of their, also male, Aztec counterparts. The female role is given little attention, and what it does attract is usually derogatory. Likewise, sex and sexuality are absent from Spanish records.

Yet some Aztec records and myths paint a different story. The rights of women are made explicit, and the joys of sexual interplay and erotic love are emphasized. Young girls were chaperoned and expected to be virgins when they married; but the tales make it clear that access to women was forbidden to young men before they attained the status of warrior.

At marriage the care of the young man was transferred from his mother to his bride, and there is no indication that the woman ever became the "property" of her husband. During the marriage speeches, she was encouraged to explore her own sexuality while he was exhorted to satisfy her demands. She was economically independent, and although barred from the highest forms of public office, was nevertheless a powerful and influential voice in all public affairs.

The Spanish recorded that the market place in the Aztec capital of Tenochtitlan was frequented by prostitutes who wandered unashamedly between the stalls, soliciting the favors of men, and that women from state-run brothels formed part of the "reward" given to successful warriors. While prostitution and brothels undoubtedly existed, the Aztec view of these was altogether different and more positive. They portrayed "tribute girls," as the Spanish called them, as the Daughters of Joy, symbols of sexual delight, in much the same way as they extolled the virtues of the virile warrior.

Chastity of the priesthood

According to the Spanish, those who followed the teachings of Xochiquetzal, the patroness of erotic love, were afflicted with boils and pustules; yet a closer reading of the texts makes it clear that the Aztec believed she punished those who exceeded her commands. As in many other aspects of Aztec life, excess was frowned upon, since improper or inappropriate behavior would offend the gods and was therefore dangerous; but this is not a denial of eroticism and sexual pleasure.

Even the dedication of young girls to

permanent temple service was seen as an act of piety, and not forced prostitution to satisfy the needs of novitiate priests, as the Spanish claimed. While the conquistadors are on record as having violated girls who were in temple service, it is likely that both the temple girls and the Aztec priests made vows of chastity as personal sacrifices to the deities.

Many of the most powerful Aztec deities were female or encompassed both masculine and feminine attributes, or they appeared in complementary male-female pairs. Not all of these pairings were sexual ones, since they are often brother and sister — although at times, Aztec deities did marry siblings.

The emphasis throughout is on the equality of the sexes and stresses that female roles, though sometimes different from those of men, were no less important. Even the dreaded god Tezcatlipoca sometimes assumed another guise as Lord of the Here and Now, and in this aspect was patron of childbirth and children; whereas female deities such as Coatlicue or Coyolxauhqui regularly acted as warrior gods.

Above: *Circular bas-relief showing the dismembered body of Coyolxauhqui. The elder sister of Huitzilopochtli, she was killed by him after she incited the Centzonuitznaua, or Stars, to kill their mother, Coatlicue. Huitzilopochtli sprang from his mother's womb fully armed and struck Coyolxauhqui down with a single blow from his serpent torch.*

THE POWER OF RHETORIC
Lyricism of the *tlamatinime* equal to the divine fire of sacrifice

In its concentration on warfare and sacrifice, the study of the Aztec often overlooks the gentler side of their nature. This is partly due to the nature of the materials from which scholars deduce their facts and make their conclusions. Most are reports from conquistadors that emphasize the meaning of warfare and violence, or the reports of Spanish priests that overlook the spiritual significance of Aztec customs when they conflict with those of their own religious upbringing.

By contrast, from Aztec records, there is nothing to suggest that they gloried in the shedding of blood or the sacrifice of human victims. They believed these acts were motivated and understood through the spoken word.

Parallel to the priests who carried out sacrifices was a group of equal status, known as the *tlamatinime*, who underwent special training in the use of language to discover ultimate truths. They posed riddles that asked fundamental questions, constructed metaphors and proverbs, organized rhetorical speeches, and wrote poetry. At the head of the *tlamatinime* was the Aztec supreme ruler, who was also head of state and high priest, but whose formal title was *tlatoani*, Great Speaker.

Flower and song, poetry and truth
Beneath this emphasis upon language was the concept of *teyolia* (divine fire), which warriors also possessed. *Teyolia* is a kind of energy or spiritual force that has sustaining power. It is released when the heart of a captive

Right: *The wooden slit-drum (*teponatzli*) was hollowed out and carved from a pice of hardwood. The carving served a decorative purpose and also a musical one. Two tongues were slotted at the top, and the way they were carved out altered the drum's tone.*

dictated by the gods and to do otherwise would be disastrous and bring swift retribution, since the offerings of hearts and blood gave life back to the deities who safeguarded it for the people.

Although training in warfare and understanding the ritual cycle was important, Aztec education emphasized the essential qualities of obedience, diligence, humility, self-discipline, and rhetoric, and included subjects such as arithmetic, history, astronomy, and agriculture. They understood that things could be brought into being through the violent act of sacrifice, but also realized that they could be

is given as an offering to the deities, but is also released when a poet composes a particularly fine verse or when one of the *tlamatinime* makes a profound speech or statement. The connection with war is carried into the War of Flowers (*see pages 152–153*), in which flowers symbolize human hearts, since the Aztec phrase "flower and song" can also be translated as "poetry and truth."

Closely linked with the concept of poetry and

language was the use of dance and song. Many of the poems that the *tlamatinime* composed were intended to be recited to the accompaniment of a drum rhythm, and every great lord had his own retinue of poets, composers, and dancers to write and perform new compositions on the occasion of major public feasts and ceremonies.

At these times the Aztec believed *teyolia* was released from many sources, through the poems and the sacrifices, as a nebulous force that pervaded everything and inspired those who came into contact with it. Similar energies were supposed to emanate from sacred mountains and the temples on the summits of pyramids that echoed mountain shapes, and through this the *teyolia* of the poets and priests combined with that of the deities.

Perhaps it is unsurprising that the Spanish failed to recognize this deep spiritual force inherent in words and responded only to what was immediately obvious. To do so, the Spanish friars would have conceded higher motives to the Aztec priests and poets, and admit they were not barbarians to whom they could offer salvation. The Aztec did not volunteer the information, since they felt there was no need to explain to the chroniclers of their traditions what was so patently obvious to themselves.

Above: *Although wood was the favored medium for the manufacture of* teponatzli, *a few stone examples exist. They are made from stone of different densities to provide variation in tone.*

Left: *Xochipilli, the God of Flowers, was also the God of Feasting, Music, and Dance, and as such he was closely associated with the* tlamatinime. *His female counterpart, Xochiquetzal, was Goddess of Flowers and of the Obsidian Butterfly, and also patron of love-making and ladies of easy virtue.*

EAGLE AND JAGUAR WARRIORS
Noble lives of the most grand and skilled soldiers

Above: *A life-size statue of an Eagle Warrior. He wears a costume that imitates the eagle's wings and peers out through a mask that represent the bird's gaping beak.*

To the Aztec, the eagle and the jaguar were, respectively, the noblest bird and the Lord of the Animals. They earned these reputations in the distant past, at Teotihuacán, when they followed Nanahuatzin into the sacred fire when he sacrificed himself to become the sun. It is said that thereafter the eagle and jaguar bore the signs of courage in their discolored and mottled feathers and fur.

The eagle gained a reputation as a fearless and incomparable hunter, who was able to gaze into the sun. The jaguar, in contrast, became a creature of the night and a solitary, cautious, and wise hunter. It is thus a fitting tribute that the elite warriors of the Aztec were associated with these creatures.

In many respects the Eagle and Jaguar Warriors occupied a position analogous to that of European knights. Noble birth was a prerequisite, but so too were extreme bravery and a notable war record involving hand-to-hand combat and the capture of enemy prisoners in battle. In return, they acquired status little short of that accorded to the deities themselves, and were entitled to wear attire appropriate to their high rank, conferred on them at special ceremonies held exclusively for that purpose.

The appearance of the Eagle and Jaguar Warriors is known to us from paintings, carvings, and figurines. At the great Aztec capital of Tenochtitlan, for instance, the Precinct of the Eagle Warriors contains a small temple guarded by life-size carvings of warriors wearing feathered and winged cloaks, eagle helmets, and bird claws, and covered with white body-paint resembling feathers.

In addition to their military duties, the Eagle and Jaguar Warriors formed a royal guard for the Aztec king and were responsible for the training of young men in martial skills. Despite their mercenary nature, the Aztec maintained no standing army, but every young man spent part of his youth in the plazas reserved for the warrior elite, where he was educated in military exercises and the use of weapons.

Contrasting but united

The Eagle and Jaguar Warriors taught the use of the obsidian thrusting sword, spear, and *atlatl* (spear-thrower), as well as the defensive use of the shield. In times of war, these young men were called up from their respective *calpullis* (wards or districts) as part of the tribute paid to Tenochtitlan.

The Eagle Warriors, as "Soldiers of the Sun," and the Jaguar Warriors, as "Attendants of the Underworld," form a symbolic opposition between sky and earth, and between life and death, and day and night, which the Aztecs inherited from earlier Mesoamerican cultures. In fact, paintings and carvings of the Aztec figures clearly show features associated with the earlier Toltec, from whose dignitaries Aztec nobles claimed descent.

The concept of the Eagle and Jaguar Warriors, and the opposition between them, is earlier still, however. At Cacaxtla, an early Mayan site, a realistically painted *talud* (a low, sloping wall supporting a vertical panel) depicts a battle between warriors wearing jaguar costumes and others in feathered cloaks.

In battle, the Eagle and Jaguar Warriors formed the advance troops of the Aztec, but their fighting tactics were different. The Eagle Warriors attacked at dawn, sweeping out of their ranks in a body before seeking out individual enemies to attack and capture. The Jaguar Warriors adopted a more stealthy approach, waiting until the enemy ranks had been broken before suddenly rushing upon their chosen victims.

Their courage was not in doubt, since both wore elaborate costumes and headdresses of resplendent plumes while fighting, marking them as obvious targets for their opponents. The capture of an Eagle or Jaguar Warrior and the display of his war regalia was a high honor, and few enemies could resist the temptation to try.

Above: *Although dressed in military costume, the mask the Jaguar Warrior would wear in battle lies at his feet. He holds his back shield in his left hand.*

SUPPORT FOR THE CITY

Agriculture, pochteca traders, and calpixque tax collectors fund Tenochtitlan

Below: *Aztec farmers building* chinampas *in Lake Texcoco.* Chinampas *were made from mud dredged from the shallows of the lake, spread over pole frameworks to keep it above water level. Channels between the raised vegetable gardens were kept free, to allow access by canoe.*

When Lord Culhua banished the Mexica from Culhuacán to the swamplands, he had little idea that this inhospitable region would prove, under Aztec ingenuity, to be one of the most productive areas in Mesoamerica. Without a strong economic base, it is doubtful whether the Aztec would have been able to establish Tenochtitlan as anything other than a lakeland village, and they would never have been able to maintain a vast empire.

Aztec economy was built on three fronts: an agricultural system based on *chinampa* (raised field) cultivation; the merchandising of goods through the *pochteca* system; and the levying of taxes on tribute states.

Chinampas, sometimes referred to as "floating gardens," were rectangular plots of dredged silt and lakewood compost set upon rafts of branches and brushwood and floated in the shallow waters of Lake Texcoco's perimeter and the southern lakes of Chalco and Xochimilco. A complex system of dykes, aqueducts, and canals kept the water in the *chinampas* at a constant level.

A combination of moisture from the freshwater lakes, the richness of the soil and its continual replenishment by annual dredging of the canals that bisected the *chinampas*,

together with the industriousness of Aztec farmers, made these small plots incredibly productive. It has been estimated that slash-and-burn techniques in the lowland required 2,965 acres of land to feed a hundred families, while the same number could be fed on only 213 acres using the *chinampa* system.

Although their extent was not large enough to feed the entire population of Tenochtitlan and some foodstuffs had to be imported, the *chinampas* provided the agricultural mainstay for the city's occupants. Lake Texcoco has been drained to accommodate the expansion of modern Mexico City, but remnants of the once-extensive *chinampas* can still be seen at Xochimilco.

Wealth of traders and tax collectors

The second aspect of Aztec economy was a hereditary guild of long-distance merchants who traded produce from Tenochtitlan for luxury goods that were unavailable in the city. The guild of the *pochteca* traded primarily from the Tenochtitlan suburb of Tlatelelco, and was largely responsible for importing the precious materials that the ruling families required as symbols of their status. As a consequence the *pochteca* amassed wealth of their own and had considerable political influence over their noble clients.

The third part of the Aztec economy came in the form of tribute, or tax, paid by subjugated cities. Although there was no uniform system,

those cities closest to Tenochtitlan generally paid their tribute in foodstuffs, while more distant ones supplied textiles.

They were also expected to supply provisions for the Aztec armies and, in the case of a major campaign, provide armed warriors to supplement those from Tenochtitlan. They sent laborers for the construction of dams and other public works, and many of the attendants and servant girls of the nobles and most of the prostitutes working from the Houses of Joy originally came to Tenochtitlan to fulfil tribute quotas.

But the tribute system was a double-edged sword. The *calpixques* (tax collectors) had absolute authority and were greatly feared. If they felt that a tribute payment was at all deficient, they could call on the Eagle and Jaguar Warriors to enforce their demands; similarly, if they were molested in any manner, the elite Aztec warriors would exact retribution. Most of the *calpixques* were extremely wealthy and kept concubines from among the prettiest girls in the regions they controlled.

There was a system whereby a local lord could bring grievances against *calpixques* before the ruling council at Tenochtitlan, but there is no record of any such grievance ever having been successfully upheld. The excesses of the *calpixques* and the fear in which they were held created resentment, and it was largely due to this disenchantment that Hernán Cortés was able to enlist local warriors as mercenaries when he marched against Tenochtitlan.

Above: *Few of the original chinampas survive, since most were destroyed when the greater part of Lake Texcoco was drained to provide land for modern Mexico City. An exception exists at Xochimilco, where modern "floating gardens" can be seen in this aerial photograph, with clusters of flower boats.*

XIPE TOTEC – FLAYED GOD
Elaborate sacrifice and combat mirror the maize life cycle

The majority of Aztec rituals were closely linked with events of the agricultural year, but were nevertheless tied to concepts involving sacrifice and warlike activity. Among the most important of these was Tlacaxipeualiztli, the festival of early spring, which was held during a period corresponding to March 5–24. This, the second month of the Aztec calendar, was dedicated to Xipe Totec, the Flayed God, a deity who first appeared in the tropical lowlands and was venerated at Teotihuacán.

In many ways, Tlacaxipeualiztli was a celebration of the new skin that the earth acquires in spring and the revival of vegetation. According to the Aztec, new life demanded death and burial, just as the seed needs to be harvested and planted so that it may regenerate itself.

This symbolism was carried to extremes during the rituals involving Xipe Totec. The skin was flayed from the body of a sacrificial victim and the human *ixiptla* (god representation) of Xipe Totec was sewn into it. The bloodied side of the skin was left outermost, since Xipe Totec, like all the maize deities, was a red god. As the skin dried, it tightened about the man inside, whose living body thus became one with the dead spirit of the sacrificed man.

The symbolic association with maize is a very specific one. The *ixiptla* is enclosed in the skin of the victim, just as maize is enclosed in its husk. As the maize germinates, the husk slowly lessens its grip, just as the flayed skin gradually decomposes and becomes weaker. Finally, the maize breaks free from its bonds — echoed by the weakened bindings of the skin bursting apart. To conclude the ritual, the flayed skin is buried, as the maize is planted, so that new life can begin.

Feathered club vs obsidian swords
The sanctity of the Xipe Totec *ixiptla* was emphasized by the costume he wore: a skirt of quetzal feathers to signify his regal and divine status, a headdress of red spoonbill feathers, and gold earplugs and nose crescent. He carried a gold disc shield and his red sandals were adorned with quail feathers, both symbols of the new sun.

A number of associated rituals clarify the sacred functions of Tlacaxipeualiztli and Xipe

Totec and their link with the warrior ethos of the Aztec. The victim from whom the skin was flayed was no ordinary mortal; he was selected from the captives because of the valor and bravery he showed during his capture. He was given a chance to save himself by engaging in gladiatorial combat with his captors, although he was armed only with a wooden club set with feathers — against the obsidian bladed swords of four Eagle and Jaguar Warriors. In the unlikely event that he won, he would become a captain in the Aztec army but would not be expected to fight his kinsfolk.

The mock combat celebrated the role of the warrior and brought this into close connection with the sustaining life forces, and to this end token morsels of the flesh of the victim were consumed by his captor and the captor's family. His life forces were thus ingested by the Aztec to give courage, just as maize is eaten to provide strength.

The political power of the Aztec Triple Alliance was made evident during Tlacaxipeualiztli. This was the first major public ceremony of the year, and the leaders of the allied groups appeared before the people to offer their blessings and dance together in a show of solidarity. In this way, Tlacaxipeualiztli brought all the important elements of Aztec culture together: It celebrated the arrival of spring and the start of the agricultural season; honored the warriors and emphasized the significant link between secular and sacred activity; and made the political unity of the Triple Alliance manifest and renewed this for the forthcoming year.

Top right: *Back of the head of an Aztec figure of Xipe Totec. The symbol is that of Tezcatlipoca, of whom Xipe Totec was an aspect.*

Left: *The Aztec borrowed the symbolism of Xipe Totec from elsewhere. The statue shown here is from Teotihuacán.*

Facing: *Statuette of Xipe Totec, the Flayed Lord, wearing the skin of a sacrificial victim.*

TRIBUTARY STATES
Physical and psychological threats ensure loyalty

Below: *Tlaxcala maintained its independence from Tenochtitlan, although the Aztec chronicles claim this was only because they were a source of victims for the War of Flowers. Tlaxcala nevertheless resented Tenochtitlan's apparent interference in its affairs and provided mercenaries to assist Cortés in his conquest. The ruins of a pyramid at Tlaxcala are shown in this photograph.*

At the height of its power the Aztec Empire controlled the entire Valley of Mexico and exacted tribute from its subject states. The administrative authority for tax collection lay with the *calpixque* (tax collectors) who, although under the nominal control of the council at Tenochtitlan, were able to do much as they liked within the provinces they administered.

Emphasis is often placed on the fact that Tenochtitlan was never self-sufficient; imported products were essential to the survival of the city. While this was true of foodstuffs, since the *chinampas* (raised fields) were not extensive enough to support the expanding population, many tribute payments were in the form of non-essential goods and served an entirely different function.

The ruling elite of the Aztec, the Mexica, were relatively few and alone could never have exercised authority over such a vast area. Their right to do so was justified by an invented history that claimed divine ancestry (*see pages 180–181*), and their ability to militarily support such claims was achieved through strategic political marriages into the influential families of neighboring tribes. In emergencies, these families provided warriors to fight alongside the professional Eagle and Jaguar Warriors of the Mexica.

More distant nations did not always willingly accept Aztec dominance and ancestry, however, and may have doubted their ancestral claims. In

such cases, the tribute system was used to exert psychological pressure and force recalcitrant tribes to conform to Aztec ideals.

Within this system the *calpixques* were the dominant figures. They resided within the territories they governed, thus providing permanent Aztec presence in even the most distant parts of the empire, and each had a small garrison of warriors sufficient to put down any minor disputes that might arise. More serious issues were seen as a threat to Aztec hegemony and an insult to the Great Speaker, and in such cases the *calpixques* could ask the Council of Four at Tenochtitlan to send military support.

Tributes of vermin

Such perceived insults were put down with ruthless brutality, and following military punishment the tribute demands were doubled. Since tax demands were already high, few provinces were willing to take the risk of incurring additional burden by defying the Aztec, unless they were assured of support from other disaffected nations. By careful juggling of threats of swift retribution and the conferring of "favored nation" status on more compliant subjects — with a consequent lessening of tribute — the Aztec usually kept their empire in balance.

When this failed, as it did when Cuetlaxtla rose against the Aztec after being promised help from Tlaxcala, subsequent tribute demands for non-essential goods were intended to demoralize the offenders. Cuetlaxtla's revolt against Moctezuma the Elder was swiftly put down when Tlaxcala reneged on its promise of assistance, and among the increased tribute demands was one for a considerable number of live snakes to be delivered twice yearly to Tenochtitlan. To meet this demand, most of the able-bodied male population was forced to spend a large part of the year in snake-infested caves. Other instances include tribes being forced to send basketloads of centipedes, spiders, or scorpions, in addition to valuable tribute goods they had previously supplied.

Through the tribute system, the Aztec demonstrated physical and psychological dominance; the latter element was probably the most significant. It is certain that a large proportion of the tribute goods paid a minor role in the Aztec economy. The Spanish record that the Aztec were continually constructing large storehouses to hold surplus, and excavations of the Templo Mayor at Tenochtitlan revealed numerous caches of tribute goods placed there to symbolize Aztec imperial power.

COATLICUE – SNAKE SKIRT
Multiple identities of the blood-fed mother goddess

Coatlicue (Snake Skirt or Serpent Skirt) is the mother of Huitzilopochtli, the Aztec patron deity. The legends that surround her do much to explain the Aztec insistence on sacrifice and the violence that was endemic in their rituals. Huitzilopochtli was born in a violent manner after Coatlicue became pregnant from swallowing a ball of feathers (the insignia of a warrior). His outraged sister, Coyolxauhqui (She of the Belled Cheeks) led the Uncounted Stars against Coatlicue, intending to kill the unborn child in her womb, but Hutzilopochtli leapt forth fully armed, carrying the Fire Serpent, and routed them. He dismembered Coyolxauhqui's body and threw her down to Earth (*see picture on page 159*). In the battle Coatlicue was also killed; her head was severed and great fountains of blood gushed from her neck.

Here we already have the origin for sacrifices carried out at the Templo Mayor in Tenochtitlan. The great pyramid was a representation of Coatepec (Serpent Mountain or Mound), which is an aspect of Coatlicue, and was dedicated to Huitzilopochtli. The decapitation and dismemberment of sacrificial victims, followed by casting the bodies down the pyramid steps, is a re-enactment of the fate that befell Coyolxauhqui.

Coatlicue, however, is a more complex character. Near Huitzilopochtli's temple on the Templo Mayor is the shrine of Cihuacoatl (Place of Blackness) which, again, is another name for Coatlicue. This shrine represents the womb of the earth, and the figure of Coatlicue is seen wreathed in symbols of fertility and agricultural abundance.

Yet she is far from being a benign mother goddess. Twin jets of blood spurt from her severed neck, her necklace is composed of human hearts and hands, and there are fanged faces and claws at her knees and elbows. She

has aged and withered breasts, and it is clear that the fertility and abundance she offers is not nurtured by a mother's milk. Her shrine is, significantly, at the center of the site reserved for the elite Eagle and Jaguar Warriors.

God/Goddess of Duality

The symbolism at the shrine is consistently of blood and sacrifice. Coatlicue's gaping mouth, which is so characteristic of carvings that depict her, reveals her voracious appetite for the blood and hearts of human victims.

In another legend, the twin gods Quetzalcoatl and Tezcatlipoca seized Coatlicue as she lay basking in primeval waters, prior to the creation of the world. They tore her body in two: one part forming the sky, the other the earth. Because of this story, she is also the androgynous God/Goddess of Duality, and is sometimes depicted in masculine form as Tlacatecuhtli (Lord of the Earth).

They made herbs and trees from her hair, grass and flowers from her skin, wells and springs from her eyes, and mountains from her shoulders. But all these things were dead and Coatlicue refused to breathe life into them until she was fed — and she could only be satiated with blood and human hearts.

Through the legends of Coatlicue, the earth is given a human form and composed of human parts, and it is made explicit that this form can only be sustained through sacrificial offerings. If these are withheld, she crippled by striking at people's ankles, knees, and elbows; techniques that were used by the Eagle and Jaguar Warriors to disable their victims without killing them so that they might be offered in sacrifice. At her beck and call were the feared Ilhuica~Cihuapipitlin (Celestial Princesses), the spirits of women who returned to Earth with their hair flowing wildly and their breasts bared, carrying anger, aggression, and death with them.

Above: *Coyolxauhqui, Lady of the Belled Cheeks, is the daughter of Coatlicue and half-sister of Huitzilpochtli, She lived with her mother at Coatepec, Serpent Mountain.*

Facing: *Coatlicue, mother of Huitzilopochtli, was killed during fighting instigated by Coyolxauhqui. Although a benevolent Earth Goddess, Coatlicue has an appetite for human hearts to atone for the suffering she underwent.*

THE AZTEC YEAR
Purposes and dedications of their 18 months

The Aztec year, Xiuitl, was divided into 18 months of 20 days each, followed by a five-day period called Nemontemi. During these "Barren Days," the old fires were extinguished and new ones kindled. Nemontemi was a period when evil forces were abroad and unconstrained by ritual, and was therefore a time of anxiety and fear.

The year began with Atl Cauala (Ceasing of Water), which was dedicated to Tlaloc and Chalchihuitlicue – the God of Rain and his consort. This was followed by Tlacaxipeualiztli (Flaying of Men), dedicated to the fearsome Xipe Totec (*see pages 166–167*), during which there were pyramid sacrifices and feasts on the victims' flesh. Planting rituals were carried out during Tococtontli (Little Vigil), again dedicated to Tlaloc, and in the following month the growing maize stalks were brought into the city centers during Uey Tococtli (Great Vigil) to be blessed by Aztec maidens.

The growing crops were under threat during the next month, which corresponded roughly to the period May 4–23, when rains were

Below: *A granite carving of a serpent with 13 segments in its tail, one for each year of its life, since a new rattle is formed annually when the serpent sheds its skin. The number 13 has symbolic significance in the ordering of time, since it recalls the 13 levels in the Aztec celestial world.*

infrequent. This was dedicated to Toxcatl (Dryness) and marked by the dances of the Aztec women. Following Toxcatl, Tlaloc and Chalchihuitlicue were again invoked during Etzalqualiztli (Eating of Maize-Bean Porridge), during which the last of the by-now depleted food reserves were freely shared.

The next two months were Tecuilhuitontli (Little Feast Day of the Lords) and Uey Tecuilhuitl (Great Feast Day of the Lords). These celebrated the growing young maize and earthly pleasures. During Tecuilhuitontli, salt farmers were under obligation to drink large quantities of pulque (fermented maize), although intoxication during any other festival was punishable by death. At Uey Tecuilhuitl "pleasure girls" performed erotic dances and enticed the young warriors. This, however, was a test for the warriors, since they would be punished if the enticement led to "joking" — an Aztec euphemism for sexual intercourse.

The Aztec honored their ancestors in the next two months — Tlaxochimaca (Little Feast Day of the Dead) and Xocotlhuetzi (Great Feast Day of the Dead). During these months they made offerings of field flowers to the sacred ancestral images and, in Xocotlhuetzi, a greased pole was raised and xocotl (a kind of fruit) was placed at its summit. Young men were challenged to demonstrate their skills by climbing the pole and "capturing" Xocotl, which ensured a successful harvest and for which they were rewarded and acclaimed.

Ritual harassment of women

The harvesting of the maize took place during Ochpaniztli (Sweeping of the Roads), which was dedicated to Centeotl, the Young Lord Maize Cob. This was also the period when the Aztec war season was inaugurated and the honored young men received their war costumes and insignia.

Until now the gods had been invoked "in absentia," but in Teotleco (The Gods Arrive)

they were thought to be present in the cities in great numbers. Teotleco was therefore dedicated to all gods and was celebrated by feasting and merrymaking.

The female and male principles were celebrated during the next two months. Tepeilhuitl (Feast of the Mountains) was dedicated to Xochiquetzal, Precious Flower Feather, the Goddess of Dance and Pleasure and the patron of weavers and craftworkers; Quecholli (Roseate Spoonbill) was dedicated to Mixcoatl, the God of Hunting, and a communal hunt was undertaken.

Panquetzalitli (The Raising of Banners) saw the culmination of the hunt, which was synonymous with war, and the large-scale sacrifice of captured warriors. This month was dedicated to Tezcatlipoca, the Aztec's patron deity, in his guise as Huitzilopochtli, or Hummingbird on the Left, the God of War. The rituals honored established warriors, those who had proven themselves by bringing in captives to be offered during sacrificial rites. Unproven warriors, young men who were still in training, were honored during Atemoztli (Descent of Water).

The Aztec year began to draw to a close with Tititl (The Stretching). There was a sacrifice of the llama Tecutli Ixiptla, the "reverse" image of the leading Aztec priest, and the ritual harassment of women during Casting of the Bags. The women's roles, which until now had been honored ones, were also thrown into reverse order. The final month of the year was Izcalli (Growth), when recently weaned children were presented at the temples for the priests' blessings.

Above: *This illustration of an Aztec relief carving depicts Quetzalcoatl, the Feathered Serpent, descending between two year glyphs. The left-hand date refers to the year of the rebuilding of the great temple at Tenochtitlan.*

THE AZTEC PANTHEON

Forms and functions of the manifold deities

The Aztec pantheon is peopled by a bewildering array of deities. Every activity had its own patron god or goddess, each day had its god, and each month was presided over by yet another. Every force in the world was controlled through the activities of the deities, and each of them might assume any one of a number of guises.

The most important god was undoubtedly Tezcatlipoca (Smoking Mirror). He was the patron of sorcerers and the master of human destiny, and was associated with Tepeyollotl (Heart of the Mountain) and the Jaguar God of the earth's interior. In his guise as Huitzilopochtli he was both the God of War and the Sun God, and thus the patron deity of the entire Aztec nation.

In opposition to Tezcatlipoca was

This page: *The snow-capped peak of the volcano, Popocatepetl. It was believed to be home to many of the major gods; the shape of pyramids at major centers were said to echo its form.*

Quetzalcoatl (Feathered Serpent), an old Mesoamerican god. The Aztec priests and nobles legitimized their claims to power through lineages that were traced back to the priests of Quetzalcoatl at the earlier sites of Tula and Teotihuacan. Quetzalcoatl's opposition to Tezcatlipoca reflects a basic dualism between good and evil that pervades Aztec thought; Quetzalcoatl appears as the evil Evening Star or the benign Morning Star. He also appears as the God of the Winds in the form of Ehecatl.

Below these dual gods were other important deities, such as Tlaloc, the Rain God and master of agricultural fertility. He is sometimes referred to as He Who Lives on Earth, and was assisted by the Tlaloque or Tepictoton. These dwarfish creatures lived in the mountains, where they made the rain and clouds under Tlaloc's direction. Tlaloc was married to Chalchihuitlicue (Jade Skirt), who was also his sister, renowned as the Goddess of Fresh Waters.

Opposing and allied gods

Although many of the important Aztec deities were associated with agriculture, they nevertheless demanded human sacrifice. The Aztec felt that everything worked in cycles that were based on opposition and that it was only through death that life could be sustained. Coatlicue (Snake Skirt) embodies this principle and was the Mother of the Gods. She was both Earth Mother and Mother of the Sun, Moon, and Stars, and in her aspect as Cihuacoatl (Woman Snake), she demanded war and sacrificial victims. She is sometimes identified as Teteo Innan Toci, Our Grandmother.

An identification with war is evident too in the form of Coyolxauhqui (She with the Belled Cheeks), who was Huitzilopochtli's malevolent warrior sister and who led her brothers, the stars, against him when he was an infant. She was defeated and her body torn to pieces by Huitzilopochtli, but her blood stained the sacred mountain called Coatepec (Serpent Mountain) at Tula and could only be avenged by casting sacrificial victims down the Aztec pyramids.

Centeotl (Young Lord Maize Cob) and Xilonen (Goddess of the Young Corn) were again paired

deities. They presided over the growth of Aztec crops and the ripening of maize, and as such were often in alliance with Tlaloc and Chalchihuitlicue. But they were also associated with Xipe Totec (Flayed God), who demanded sacrifice and whose priests wore the flayed skins of their victims.

Among other important deities are: Mayahuel (She with Four Hundred Breasts), the female personification of pulque, and her associate Ometochtli (Two Rabbit), the God of Pulque; Cihuateto (Celestial Princess) and her assistants the Five Cihuapipitlin (Women Warriors), who are the spirits of women who died in childbirth; Yacatecuhtli (Long-Nosed God), the patron of merchants; and Mictlantecuhtli, the Lord of Mictlan, which is the Aztec equivalent of the Mayan's Xibalba, the Land of the Dead.

The oldest god is Xiuhtecuhtli (Turquoise Lord or Fire God), who is identified with Huehueteotl (Old, Old God), who connects the household with the heavens, via the Fire Drill Stars, and the very deepest layers of the earth.

Above:

Mictlantecihuatl was consort to Mictlantecuhtli, the Lord of the Dead. Between them they ruled Mictlan, the Land of the Dead, where they decided the fate of human souls. Like other Aztec deities, it is probable that Mictlantecuhtli and Mictlantecihuatl were originally worshipped at Teotihuacán and later "borrowed" by the Aztec.

QUETZALCOATL VERSUS HUITZILOPOCHTLI

Old and new gods signify Aztec tradition and innovation

In the beginning, the Creator Gods gave birth to four sons: Red Tezcatlipoca, Black Tezcatlipoca, Quetzalcoatl, and Huitzilopochtli. Between them, the brothers created the heaven

world, created by Tezcatlipoca, was destroyed when Quetzalcoatl threw him into the sea; the second, Quetzalcoatl's world, was thrown down by Tezcatlipoca. When Quetzalcoatl and Tezcatlipoca became allies in the creation of the fifth world, Huitzilopochtli, the cult deity of the Aztecs, was introduced as Quetzalcoatl's arch-enemy.

Although Huitzilopochtli has attributes of Tezcatlipoca, as well as of Mixcoatl (Star God) and Xiuhtecuhtli (Fire God), he is a purely Aztec deity and was not worshipped beyond the sphere of Aztec influence in the Valley of Mexico. In this respect he is unlike Quetzalcoatl, whose origin lies far back in the depths of Mesoamerican antiquity. The opposition between Quetzalcoatl and Huitzilopochtli is an opposition between the old and the new, and this is fundamental to understanding Aztec beliefs and culture.

For the Aztec priests, an illustrious past, even an invented one, was a matter of major significance. They used the past to legitimize their own positions, thus they turned to Quetzalcoatl as evidence of their ancient ancestral links. In this way, the Aztec placed themselves firmly within the continuum of Mesoamerican cultures and associated themselves with the great empires of the past.

But in order to establish themselves as a new force in the

Above: *A carving of Quetzalcoatl in the city of Xochicalco, regional outpost of Teotihuacán, and linked with Tula.*

and the earth, made fire, sea, and the underworld, and brought the first human couple and the sacred calendar into being.

From the start there was tension between Black Tezcatlipoca and Quetzalcoatl: the first

area and exert their supremacy over the old ruling families of the Toltec, who continued to have influence, the Aztec also had to proclaim their independence. They did this through Huitzilopochtli.

The realization of Huitzilopochtli

Huitzilopochtli was the warrior aspect of Tezcatlipoca, whose role was to throw down established order and set Aztec hegemony in its place. It is, therefore, appropriate that this deity, or at least this aspect of a recognized deity, should be an Aztec invention. The city of Tenochtitlan and all its splendors was, first and foremost, tangible evidence of the power of Huitzilopochtli. Thus Tenochtitlan celebrated the present power of the Aztec gained through warfare; whereas Tula and Teotihuacán, both of which now lay in ruins, represented the ancestral, sacred power of Quetzalcoatl.

The opposition between Huitzilopochtli and Quetzalcoatl was further emphasized and given cogent form through the festivals dedicated to them. Huitzilopochtli's festival of Panquetzaliztli (Raising of Banners) was marked by its frantic activity. This was no tranquil glorification of the deity, but a headlong rush through the crowds by the priests and relays of warriors, often to the extreme of exertion where they collapsed breathless at the pyramid steps. From this the people were made aware of the ferocious and unrelenting Huitzilopochtli, who would descend and rush upon his enemies in the same manner.

In contrast, the festivals dedicated to Quetzalcoatl were marked by their subtlety. In these the image of a serpent or snake gradually breaks into plumage and then transforms into the face and split tongue of Quetzalcoatl. Slowly the body adopts an upright posture, when it can be seen that the whirling mass of brilliantly colored feathers envelopes a face with human features. Quetzalcoatl's approach is methodical and studied, while Huitzilopochtli's is heedless and rash.

The opposition between Huitzilopochtli and Quetzalcoatl therefore expresses a sense of duality that was basic to the Aztec view; a view that embraced the old but which was also the harbinger of change. For the Aztec, these oppositions were always in a state of tension rather than repose.

Above: *The skull of the Smoking Mirror, Tezcatlipoca. The base for the mask is a human skull, covered with turquoise and lignite mosaic. The back of the skull is cut away and lined with leather, and leather straps allow the jaw to hinge. The turquoise was sent to the Aztec capital, Tenochtitlan, as tribute from several states, such as Veracruz and Oaxaca.*

THE FESTIVAL OF TOXCATL

A flawless warrior becomes Tezcatlipoca for a precious year

One of the most important Aztec ceremonies was the festival of Toxcatl, dedicated to their patron deity, Tezcatlipoca, in the fifth month of the ritual year. The Spanish considered this to be the most significant festival of the year.

Preparations for each Toxcatl festival began a year in advance, at the close of the previous Toxcatl, when a young captive warrior was chosen to represent Tezcatlipoca for the forthcoming year. The Spanish records tell us that the chosen one was renowned for his beauty and deportment; his body and his manner were considered flawless, he was "neither too tall nor too short; firm of flesh, the skin smooth and without break or blemish." The honor of being chosen was marked by the captive being presented with the richest garments and jewels that the empire had to offer by the Aztec king; in the Spanish period by Moctezuma.

For the entire year the warrior was feted as Tezcatlipoca. Wherever he went, people came out from their homes to call his praises and offer him flowers. He wore flowers in his long hair, had golden bells around his ankles, and wore ocelot skin sandals. He played the "most beautiful melodies" on the flutes he carried as

Right: *The Festival of Toxcatl ended with the voluntary sacrifice of the Tezcatlipoca impersonator. This Aztec drawing shows the final moments of his year-long reign, when he was sacrificed at a small temple on an otherwise deserted island. Note the broken flutes that have been thrown down the temple steps.*

his entourage paraded themselves through the streets of Tenochtitlan. The adoration shown by the people, and especially the longing glances and loving comments of the young girls and the homage paid to him by seasoned warriors, must surely have had a powerful impact on an impressionable young man.

Twenty days before Toxcatl his long hair was cut, the symbol of an experienced warrior, and he was presented with four young women – presumably trained tribute slaves – who represented the Goddesses of Young Maize, of Flowers and Erotic Love, of Salt, and of Fresh Water.

A better afterlife

During this period the Aztec king withdrew from the city and his palaces were opened for the Tezcatlipoca impersonator. In effect he was king during this period; his every wish was granted, except, of course, a wish for freedom. Then on the fifth day he and his entourage left the city and went to an island, where there was a small temple dedicated to Tezcatlipoca.

At a moment of his own choosing, "Tezcatlipoca" climbed the temple steps to the platform, where the priests waited with sacrificial knives. At the moment when the priests excised his heart, the flutes of the new

Tezcatlipoca could be heard sounding in the streets of Tenochtitlan.

According to all the records, the young Tezcatlipoca impersonator went willingly to his death, something that has long been a puzzle to students of Aztec culture. Why should a young man, in the prime of life, willingly offer himself up as a sacrifice?

Psychologically, he had spent a year in ritual preparation for the moment of his death. Throughout this period he had been feted as the ideal warrior, first as a youth and then at maturity with the offering of four goddess impersonators. Warriors were expected to meet death bravely and without fear, so it is likely that he was acting out the ultimate fate of the warrior as he climbed the pyramid steps. His death was inevitable, and warrior pride may have been sufficient to persuade him to choose it honorably, rather than face the afterlife as a coward.

As Tezcatlipoca he was assured the most pleasant of existences in the other world, a world that the Aztec conceived as full of pleasure, where warrior souls hovered "like butterflies." We are reminded of the splendid murals at Teotihuacán showing the other world as full of beautiful pastures and flowering fruits, which the Aztec used as their model; an ideal they could aspire to reach.

REWRITING HISTORY
Creating links with Teotihuacán and Quetzalcoatl

Both pages: *The 15-foot long strip of fig-bark paper known as the* Codex Boturini *records the holy beginnings of the Aztec people. The page above depicts the simple life of Aztec forebears on an island in a lake – probably Aztlan. The migration begins by paddling across the lake to visit Huitzilopochtli, sitting in his leafy arbor on Culhuacán ("curved mountain").*

The Aztec first entered the Valley of Mexico as a small band of roaming hunter-gatherers. They shared none of the glorious past that had been passed onto other occupants of the valley from Teotihuacán and Tula, who considered the Aztec to be barbarians from the north.

The arrival of the Aztec coincided with a period of disruption in the valley. All the old empires had gone and Teotihuacán lay in ruins. There was bitter rivalry between those cities that remained viable. By clever political alliances and intrigues, the Aztec established themselves as the dominant force in the area, but to do this they needed a history that would justify their position.

They began inventing this past through an alliance with the Chichimec, who were themselves relatively recent arrivals in the valley. The Chichimec had married their daughters into noble families of the Toltec, then resident at Tula, who in turn claimed an original homeland at Teotihuacán. The Chichimec-Toltec-Teotihuacán connection was enough for the Aztec to begin claiming that they too originated from Teotihuacán, which they thought of as "the Place the Gods Came From."

As pressure to consolidate their position increased, the Aztec sought even more illustrious grounds for their claims to supremacy and began to exploit the link between Teotihuacán and the ancient deities. Their own patron, Huitzilopochtli, was a god of war and conquest who until now had suited the Aztec character and sustained their plans for expansion; but another power was needed for the Aztec to be able to claim divine inspiration, rather than only military might. Teotihuacán provided this in the form of the Feathered Serpent, Quetzalcoatl.

Dynamic tension

Quetzalcoatl had been established throughout Mesoamerica since the time of the early Maya and was deified at both Tula and Teotihuacán, where there were legends that credited him with extraordinary creative power. By re-inventing Quetzalcoatl as the twin brother of Hutzilopochtli, the Aztec combined the creative and destructive forces. In this new mythos, the earth was brought into being when Quetzalcoatl and Huitzilopochtli attacked and dismembered the Earth Mother and fertilized the soil with her blood.

Quetzalcoatl was seen as ruling over priestly functions, whereas Huitzilopochtli continued in his old role as the patron of warriors, and a dynamic tension was introduced in the form of sibling rivalry between the two gods, as well as between the secular and the sacred. This duality, and the possibility of role reversals, became dominant in Aztec thinking: When

women died they went to the sky as stars and became Warrior Maidens; warriors, however, came to Earth at death in the form of harmless butterflies. In a sense, Quetzalcoatl and Huitzilopochtli depend on this duality and neither can be considered as complete by himself; both require the balancing power of their opposite to be effective.

The new functions of these deities did, of course, rely on previous incarnations of the gods, particularly those from Tula, and this was used by the Aztec to explain their wanderings prior to becoming the dominant power in the Valley of Mexico. Thus their ignominious past was turned to an advantage as a kind of spiritual migration, rather than a forced exile from Culhuacán. In later years they increasingly relied on these migrations as a means of justifying their sudden arrival in the area and subsequent rise to power.

*Having been instructed by Huitzilopochtli to continue on their way, the migrants set off in the company of eight other tribes (on a section between the two pictured pages). They are led by four god bearers, **above**, who carry effigies of the gods on their backs. The codex follows their journey all the way to the shores of Lake Texcoco, where the Aztec settle at Chapultepec.*

THE CALENDAR STONE

Aztec creation myth inscribed on 18th-century discovery

Although much of what we know about Aztec life comes from the records made by Spanish chroniclers, and therefore reaches us in a somewhat biased form, new advances in the decipherment of Aztec texts are beginning to help us read the history from the Aztec point of view.

Unfortunately, many of the texts were destroyed in the 16th century by the Spanish,

who considered them to be satanic inscriptions and an impediment to the conversion of the Aztec. Juan de Zumarraga, the Bishop of New Spain, proudly declared in 1531 that he had destroyed 20,000 heathen idols. Yet despite this wholesale destruction, many texts remain. Spanish dominance had broken the material power of the Aztec, but their beliefs remained unshaken, and many carvings were secretly carried to the mountain tops or hidden in caves.

By 1790, when the remarkable discovery of the Calendar Stone and a statue of Coatlicue was made beneath the foundations of colonial Mexico City, attitudes had changed and the newly discovered sculptures were treated as objects of learning and study, rather than idolatrous examples of Aztec belief. They stand today as testimony to the greatness of the Aztec as the main attractions in the Museo Nacional de Antropologia in Mexico City.

The Calendar Stone is of particular interest, since it refers explicitly to Aztec ideas concerning the creation of the world and of their place within it. At the center of the stone is inscribed the date Nahui Ollin, that is it refers to the present (the time when the stone was carved) in relation to the creation of motion as established at Teotihuacán.

It makes specific reference to the movement of the sun at that time, thereby defining the stone as a solar calendar. Aztec legend makes it clear that "the gods gathered themselves together and took counsel among themselves there at Teotihuacán," and that Nanahuatzin leapt into a sacrificial fire there to emerge as Tonatiuh, the Sun.

Destroying to create

Within the flanges of the Nahui Ollin sign are the calendar names for the four previous creations. These worlds were linked with the four elements of earth, wind, fire, and water. The symbolism associated with them speaks not only of the creation and of the qualities inherent in these worlds, but also of their destruction.

The Black Tezcatlipoca ruled over the first world, Quetzalcoatl over the second, Tlaloc over the third, and Tlaloc's wife, Chalchihuitlicue, over the fourth world. Each worlds was destroyed in succession through conflicts between Tezcatlipoca and Quetzalcoatl, and although the earth is transformed through the cosmic battles that take place between them, it is a disharmonious world unable to support human life.

It is only in the fifth world, the present world of the Aztec, that Tezcatlipoca and Quetzalcoatl act in consort as allies rather than adversaries. In one version of the myth that explains the fifth world, Tezcatlipoca and Quetzalcoatl are described as two gigantic trees that support the heavens. The tree of Tezcatlipoca is hung with brilliant obsidian mirrors, while that of Quetzalcoatl is adorned with the iridescent emerald feathers of the quetzal bird.

The reading of the Calendar Stone thus far reinforces a mythology that was already ancient when the Aztec entered the Valley of Mexico, but this is overlaid with other representations that are purely Aztec but which they attributed to Tula. Among the deities referred to here are Huitzilopochtli, his mother Coatlicue, and his half-sister Coyolxauhqui. Both Coatlicue and Coyolxauhqui are slain and dismembered during the birth of Huitzilopochtli (*see picture, page 158*), and the statue of Coatlicue discovered with the Calendar Stone shows her with blood spouting from her wounds.

Above: *Much of Aztec history has been lost through the ruthless desecration of cities around the time of the Spanish Conquest. The Spanish religious orders, under the leadership of men such as Juan de Zumarraga, considered the carvings they found to be pagan idols and ordered their destruction.*

Facing: *The face peering from the center of the Aztec Calendar Stone is a representation of Nahui Ollin and refers to the date on which the carving was made. Analysis of the carvings suggests that it is a solar calendar originally derived from Teotihuacán and uses different criteria from the calendars employed by the Maya.*

MOCTEZUMA'S VISIONS
The Great Speaker foresees the empire's destruction

Below: *The unknown Spanish artist of this 16th-century painting probably used the gifts Moctezuma II presented to Cortés as reference, since there is no record that the Aztec ruler ever posed for a portrait.*

The last Great Speaker of an independent Aztec empire was Moctezuma Xocoyotzin, or Moctezuma II, who ascended to the throne in 1502. He was the fifth ruler of Tenochtitlan, and by 1508 had achieved his aim of consolidating the power base established by his predecessors. Under Moctezuma, all of Anahuac (ancient Mexico) was under Aztec control, and this control was exercised not by decree but through claiming divine rights from the ancient deities of the Toltecs.

As the Great Speaker of the Aztec, Moctezuma's patron deity was Huitzilopochtli, the terrifying God of War aspect of Tezcatlipoca. Under Huitzilopochtli's protection, the Eagle and Jaguar Warriors, at the head of armies numbering as many as 16,000 combatants, had crushed any resistance and brought the rulers and war captains of the subdued nations back to Tenochtitlan as sacrificial victims.

Yet Moctezuma's divine authority came not from Huitzilopochtli but from a Toltec lineage dedicated to the Feathered Serpent, Quetzalcoatl, who was Huitzilopochtli's arch rival. Moctezuma's allegiance to the Feathered Serpent was further emphasized by the fact that he had been born in a year dedicated to Quetzalcoatl.

Moctezuma was fully aware of the apparent contradiction and conflict between his asserted ancestry and the patron deity of the Aztec. In his dual role as Great Speaker and High Priest, he had been trained in the esoteric laws of the Aztec and the concept of duality, and knew it was necessary to maintain a balance between these opposing forces to ensure the stability of the Aztec state.

He was also familiar with the divinatory calendars used by the priests and competent in reading the signs and omens they contained; but his incarnation as Quetzalcoatl made his own position both unique and dangerous. Moctezuma II would need to rely on his visionary experiences to enable him to foretell, and perhaps influence, future events.

Casting thunderbolts

Moctezuma must have been deeply troubled in the years immediately preceding the arrival of the Spanish. Although the Aztec Empire seemed secure, they were close to the year Ce Acatl (One Reed) and the end of the ritual 52-year calendric cycle. At this time the Aztec world would either be renewed or destroyed, and Moctezuma had visions that Ce Acatl would see a test between the powers of Huitzilopochtli and Quetzalcoatl. His worries were compounded

by the visions of his aunt, Princess Butterfly, who told him of her dreams in which shining white men had walked across the water into Aztec domains and killed many people.

Aztec legend stated that when Tezcatlipoca defeated Quetzalcoatl and forced him out of Tula, Quetzalcoatl sailed to sea with his retinue of followers and vowed to return to avenge himself. Moctezuma's visions and those of his aunt must therefore have been uppermost in his mind when Aztec runners returned from distant parts to report that strange white men had arrived from across the sea and thrown thunderbolts against the occupants of villages under Aztec control. This was in 1519, the same year as Ce Acatl, and it was inevitable that Moctezuma would identify these disturbing reports with the legends and conclude that they signaled the return of Quetzalcoatl and the beginning of the confrontation between Tezcatlipoca/Huitzilopochtli and himself.

Unsure of his position, Moctezuma failed to take any decisive action against these intruders. He dispatched emissaries with gifts and devised ruses by which he might better understand who they were and whether, indeed, this was the returning Quetzalcoatl. But his emissaries returned with disturbing and at times conflicting reports of white men clad in shining coats, who killed at a distance, and who possessed terrifying animals that were taller and braver than any mortal. They were reporting the arrival of the conquistadors under Hernán Cortés.

THE ARRIVAL OF CORTÉS
Conquistador leader capitalizes on Moctezuma's confusion

Hernán Cortés and 600 Spanish conquistadors arrived on the Gulf Coast of Mesoamerica in April 1519, making landfall close to what later became La Villa Rica de la Vera Cruz. Their arrival had been seen in the visions of Moctezuma II, and within days, emissaries from the Aztec Great Speaker were in contact with Cortés' forces.

The Spanish chronicles of the conquest of Mexico that was to follow make much of Spanish valor and superiority of arms, and they stress Moctezuma's apparent indecision. It is important, however, to consider this from the Aztec point of view. Moctezuma was certainly

Spanish ignored the feathers, despite the fact that these were the symbol of divine kingship. Moctezuma had sent the gifts as an indication of his supremacy and wealth, but the Spanish regarded them as a kind of bribe – a gesture of submission.

Even more peculiar was the fact that Cortés had a woman with him, Malintzin (known to the Spanish as Dona Marina), who spoke Nahuatl, the language of the Aztec, and acted as his spokesperson. The Aztec found it unthinkable that a woman might fulfil the role of Speaker in this way.

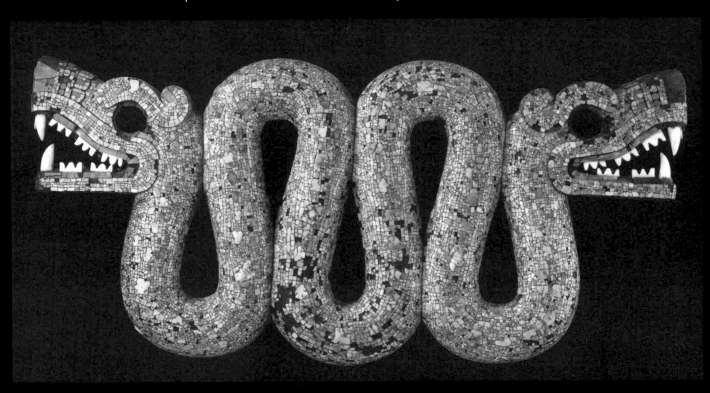

Above: *In his attempts to understand Spanish intentions, Moctezuma sent numerous emissaries to Cortés with lavish gifts. Among them were splendid ornaments, like this turquoise mosaic double-headed serpent.*

worried: the Spanish arrival coincided with Ce Acatl, the time of troubles, and the armor-clad conquistadors' appearance seemed close to that which Quetzalcoatl would assume when he returned from exile to engage in battle with Huitzilopochtli.

Moctezuma's first contacts with the Spanish were therefore tentative ones: He was trying to find out what threat the Spanish posed and whether they were mortals or deities. The behavior of the Spanish did little to allay his fears. When Moctezuma sent Cortés lavish gifts of gold and precious quetzal feathers, the

Allies of Eagle and Jaguar
During three months of negotiations on the beach at Vera Cruz, Moctezuma received constant reports of the peculiarities of these bearded strangers' war customs. In battles with some of the local tribes, they had killed warriors from a distance, rather than engaging in honorable hand-to-hand combat and taking them alive. They had attacked villages at night and slaughtered women and children. Instead of leaving their bodies exposed in battle, they covered themselves in sheets of iron. Most despicable, however, was that they showed no

bravery – if pressed, they fled the battlefield without shame.

Cortés was well aware of the confusion in Moctezuma's mind, since this was explained to him by Malintzin, and he adopted a deliberate policy of using it as a means of destabilizing Moctezuma's authority. Moctezuma's indecision was taken as a sign of weakness and he was presented as a feeble ruler, hardly worth the status given to one who claimed descent from Quetzalcoatl and ruled under the patronage of Huitzilopochtli.

Cortés gradually gained the allegiance of local tribes, many of whom already resented the tax burdens imposed on them by the Aztec and were happy to accept Cortés as their war leader against their overlords. When Cortés finally marched against the capital city of Tenochtitlan he was accompanied by warriors from these tribes and, shortly before laying siege to the city, was joined by over a thousand elite Eagle and Jaguar Warriors from Tlaxcala.

Cortés' arrival in Mexico and his subsequent conquest of the Aztec has to be seen in the context of Mesoamerican politics. He was well aware of the power held by Moctezuma, even while denigrating this, and saw himself as the future *tlatoani*, or Great Speaker, of a Mesoamerica that had been brought under Spanish control. At the same time, he was conscious of European political intrigues that presented him as an ambitious adventurer, and in his letters to Charles V (1516–56) sought to reassure the Spanish king of his loyalty.

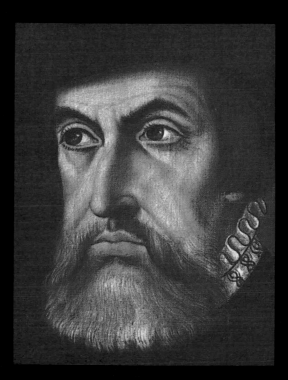

Above: *After defeating the Aztec, Cortés traveled among other tribes to ensure them of his goodwill. His Indian allies at Vera Cruz, who had largely been subdued by force, were particularly troublesome. This photograph shows the ruins of a modest villa in the forest near Vera Cruz that Cortés built about 1524.*

Left: *Hernán Cortés from a 16th-century portrait.*

SPANISH DOMINANCE
Superior weaponry and inferior ethics defeat the Aztec

When Hernán Cortés and his conquistadors arrived at the great Aztec city of Tenochtitlan on November 8, 1519, Moctezuma II was expecting them. In a show of diplomacy he invited them into the city as his guests,

Above: *The Spanish and their Indian allies from Tlaxcala attack Aztec warriors on the outskirts of Tenochtitlan. The drawing is taken from a 16th-century Mexican codex.*

where he expected them to be overwhelmed by the glory of the pyramids, temples, and palaces.

The Spanish enjoyed a few uneasy months of peace, but in April 1520 Cortés received news that Diego Velásquez, Governor of Cuba, had sent a force to arrest him on charges of treason. Cortés left Tenochtitlan to confront and defeat Velásquez' army, but during his absence his deputy, Pedro de Alvarado, ordered the massacre of a number of Aztec warriors. Cortés found Tenochtitlan in open revolt and the conquistadors barricaded in a royal palace.

In an attempt to reach a peaceful solution, Cortés captured Moctezuma, but the Aztec warriors stoned and killed their leader, and in a bloody revolt drove out the Spanish on June 30, 1520. Under the leadership of war captain Cuauhtemoc (Swooping Eagle), the Aztec killed more than half the Spanish and destroyed all

their cannons.

Cortés rebuilt his army and, supported by Indian allies from Cempoala and Tlaxcala who were disenchanted at Aztec interference, laid siege to Tenochtitlan in May 1521. The Spanish gradually claimed the city until a final confrontation within the ceremonial center on August 13, when the "New Venice" Cortés had promised Charles V was reduced to rubble.

The Aztec continued to resist: in their eyes, nothing in Spanish behavior warranted the description "warriors," therefore no negotiation was possible. Aztec chronicles record the daring of Quetzal Owl, a Mexica ruler, who leapt into the midst of the Spanish forces armed only with flint-tipped darts. Not only was the battle fought with an imbalance of weaponry — mounted Spanish lancers against Aztec foot soldiers; muskets and crossbows against obsidian-tipped swords — it was also fought on ideologically imbalanced ground. The Eagle and Jaguar Warriors sought to capture rather than kill; the conquistadors killed indiscriminately. But the Aztec only capitulated when Cuauhtemoc was captured.

Defeated but unbroken

As the Aztec left the ruins of their destroyed city, the Spaniards seized the girls and young boys and branded their faces to indicate possession. The men were sent back to recover materials that could be used to build the Spanish colonial center of Mexico City over the ruins of Tenochtitlan. The priesthood, whom the Spanish still regarded as a threat, were torn apart by dogs. Cuauhtemoc, who had been promised leniency as a term of surrender, and the other leaders of the Triple Alliance — Tetlepanquetzatzin (Tlacopan) and

Cohuanacochtzin (Texcoco) — were carried off to Honduras and charged with conspiracy, tortured, and hanged.

With the fall of Tenochtitlan, all the Aztec territories in Mexico came under Spanish control; yet Aztec spirit remained unbroken. They had taken symbols of the old deities from Tenochtitlan before its destruction and hidden them; and the living memory of the people could not be erased. They recalled the old stories of the exiled Mexica and the mighty empire they built from the swamplands. The destruction of Tenochtitlan was tragic, but was not the end of Aztec belief.

Domination of these territories was, therefore, not immediate. The Spanish were too few to resist the demands of their native allies, and in turn the allies were reluctant to have a variant of the Aztec system imposed upon them.

Cortés was subjected to political pressure and intrigue from Spain. He was granted the title of Governor of New Spain on October 15, 1522, effectively giving him control over the Mexican realm, but in 1526 Ponce de León arrived to investigate claims against him. Cortés was stripped of his title. In an attempt to consolidate his position, he returned to Spain and an interview with the Emperor, where Cortés was given the lesser title of Marques del Valle de Oaxaca. His ambitions were finally thwarted when Don Antonio de Mendoza was appointed Viceroy in 1535. Thereafter, Cortés had no official position in Mexico and died in poverty in Spain in 1547.

Spanish dominance of Mexico was assured at the same time as Cortés' death, however, when a smallpox epidemic killed 95 percent of the indigenous population. By the end of the 16th century, Mesoamerica faced a new reality, based on Hispanic beliefs and territorial possessions.

Below: *Conquistadors fighting in the streets of Tenochtitlan, from a contemporary painting by an unknown Spanish artist.*

INDEX